RIDING NORTH ONE SUMMER

By the same author

Riding the Mountains Down
Riding to Jerusalem
Riding the Desert Trail
The Fragile Islands

Riding North
One Summer

BETTINA SELBY

Chatto & Windus
LONDON

Published in 1990 by
Chatto & Windus Ltd
20 Vauxhall Bridge Road
London SW1V 2SA

A CIP catalogue record for this book is available
from the British Library.

IBSN 0 7011 3416 X

Map by John Flower

Typeset by Opus, Oxford

Printed in Great Britain by
Mackays of Chatham,
Chatham, Kent

Contents

1 *Consuetudo Peregrinandi* 1
2 Setting Out Along the Ridgeway 7
3 Through the Cotswolds 15
4 The Coloured Counties 23
5 Shropshire and the Midland Plains 32
6 A Small Town in Derbyshire 42
7 Mill Towns of Yorkshire 52
8 The Lancashire Moors 62
9 The Southern Lakes 73
10 A Forest in Lakeland 84
11 Storming the Passes 94
12 A Wilderness under Siege 103
13 North to the Borders 114
14 Wall Country 125
15 The Frontiers of Empire 139
16 The Kingdom in the North 150
17 Northern Castles 161
18 Midsummer on Holy Island 171
19 Making Tracks South 182
20 A Vision on a Hill Top 190
21 Fish and Chips and Synods 199
  Equipment for the Journey 210

*This book is dedicated to all those
who are concerned with
preserving the green places of England*

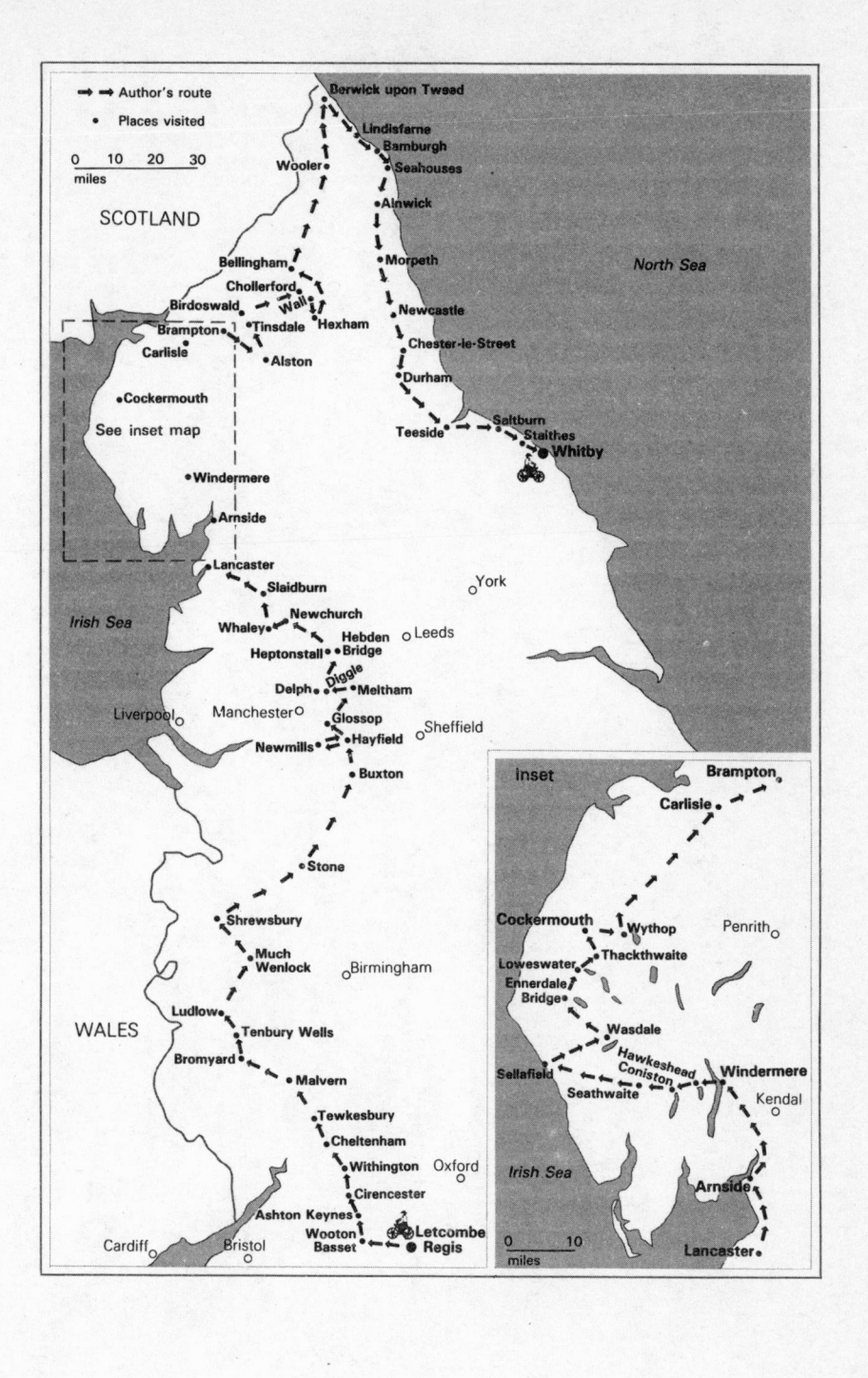

→ → Author's route
• Places visited

0 10 20 30
miles

SCOTLAND

North Sea

Berwick upon Tweed
Lindisfarne
Bamburgh
Wooler
Seahouses
Alnwick
Morpeth
Bellingham
Chollerford
Birdoswald
Brampton
Wall
Tinsdale
Hexham
Newcastle
Carlisle
Alston
Chester-le-Street
Durham
Cockermouth

See inset map

Saltburn
Staithes
Teeside
Whitby
Windermere
Arnside
Lancaster
Slaidburn
York
Newchurch
Whaley
Leeds
Hebden Bridge
Heptonstall
Delph
Diggle
Meltham
Dalton
Glossop
Liverpool
Manchester
Sheffield
Newmills
Hayfield
Buxton

Irish Sea

Stone

Shrewsbury
Much Wenlock
Birmingham
Ludlow
Tenbury Wells
Bromyard
Malvern
Tewkesbury
Cheltenham
Withington
Oxford
Cirencester
Ashton Keynes
Wooton Basset
Letcombe Regis
Cardiff
Bristol

WALES

Inset

Brampton
Carlisle
Cockermouth
Wythop
Penrith
Loweswater
Thackthwaite
Ennerdale Bridge
Wasdale
Sellafield
Hawkeshead
Coniston
Windermere
Seathwaite
Kendal
Arnside
Lancaster

Irish Sea

0 10
miles

CHAPTER ONE

Consuetudo Peregrinandi

It was a rare golden afternoon in February that gave rise to the idea of spending a few summer months bicycling around England. February 'fill-dyke' is a cold dank time of year that has often in the past proved the starting point for a trek to some hot exotic land, far removed from this small northern island locked in the dead grip of winter. On this February day, however, the unexpected sunshine flooding in through the windows brought with it a stream of recollections of places closer to home; scenes I had forgotten in the years of foreign travelling. Memories of lakes and hills, moorland and meadows, hedgerows, seashores and rivers, all lit by this same soft gilded light, filled me with a sudden longing to see my own country again. In the instant the idea took root. There and then I decided that I would spend the coming summer renewing my acquaintance with the English countryside, and set about the delightful business of planning the journey.

Although I spent a good deal of time in the following weeks poring over maps, I did not wish to tie myself down to any predetermined route or schedule, but simply to take each day as it came. The idea was to travel in as free and as easy a manner as possible, and to let circumstance dictate where I would get to before my time ran out.

It was the northern counties of England that drew me most: knowing them less well, they possessed the attraction of new ground to be explored. Also, because I did not expect the face of rural England to have totally escaped the sweeping social and economic changes of the last decade, I thought that if there was anything left of the countryside as I remembered it, it was most likely to be found in the less populous north. But most of all, it was because as a child, I learnt a song which went:

> 'O it's home, dear home;
> It's home I want to be.
> Home far away in the North Country.

Where the oak and the ash,
And the bonny el-um tree,
All are growing green in the North Country.'

I used to sing this song as a sort of talisman in the sour little
coal-mining village to which I was evacuated in the war, and I think
it did a lot towards keeping alive my hard-pressed belief in a green
and pleasant country that I would one day find. The North has ever
since possessed an almost mystical attraction for me, such as the
ancients must have felt seeing their lodestone swing always in that
direction.

I would set off, then, in a northerly direction, but I would also be
only too happy to tack to and fro along the way, eastward and
westward, in order to have the wind at my back, or to follow some
sudden fancy. There were one or two friends and one or two places
that I specially wanted to visit; these would be my fixed points, and
between them I would steer as erratic a course as inclination and
circumstances dictated. I also saw no necessity to limit my freedom
by planning a circular tour; when eventually I ran out of time, I
would simply put the bike on a train and come home.

There was never any question of how I would travel. It was on the
incomparable narrow lanes of England that I first began to discover
the joys of bicycling, and many years and many journeys later, I still
consider this strange and excellent machine to be the perfect means
of exploring places and meeting people.

Being addicted to bicycles I have acquired several of them over the
years, and like 'horses for courses' each serves a slightly different
function – one is for riding over rough terrain, another is especially
good for climbing steep hills, one conveniently folds, and so forth.
The bicycle I chose to ride to the north of England was Evans, which
had been specially built for a journey to Jerusalem. It is a classic 'go
anywhere' touring bicycle, which became known as Evans because
that was the name of the maker inscribed upon its frame, and I
thought the plain, no-nonsense sound of it suited it very well; also it
seemed friendlier than calling it 'the bike' all the time. Actually,
Evans is not as plain as its black paintwork might lead one to
suppose, and real cycle *aficionados* exclaim with pleasure over its sleek
lines and fine details. It is made from strong lightweight tubing
(Reynolds double-butted 531, for those who understand these
things) and has a crossbar because so-called 'ladies' frames are not

nearly so strong and rigid. The wheels were hand-built by the best wheel builder in London and have proved their worth over and over again, never breaking a spoke or going out of 'true'. For the rest, it is fitted with drop handlebars, good lightweight components, and lots of low gears for coping with the mountainous country I like to ride through.

Since its 5,000-mile odyssey to the Holy Land (during which it suffered not a single puncture) Evans had been resprayed and fitted with more powerful, cantilever brakes, and now has eighteen instead of only twelve gears. It also has a small palm cross around its head tube to commemorate having journeyed to the Holy City. Medieval pilgrims returning from Jerusalem carried branches of palm to let everyone know they had acquired the utmost merit. Jet travel seems to have put an end to 'palmers', it now being reckoned no great accomplishment to have been so far and to have faced nothing worse than airport delays and in-flight meals. Moslems returning from a *hadj* to Mecca, however, still exercise their right to dye their beards red, so I do not see why Evans should not wear his palm with pride.

The ultimate freedom of bicycle travel is to combine it with camping so as to be totally independent, and able to bed down overnight more or less wherever the fancy takes one. This I determined to do on my journey through England. In a small tent with the flaps tied back and the night sky visible overhead, a traveller is far closer to the natural world than under a roof. It is also considerably cheaper than paying for hotel accommodation.

Assembling the right equipment for a cycle/camping journey, however, is no simple matter, as every extra pound pedalled over anything but the flattest terrain is a serious burden, and gentle though the English countryside is, it is seldom flat. Evans, unlike R. L. Stevenson's donkey, is admirably suited to bearing loads, having strong front and back carriers and a set of four large pannier bags, faded now by desert suns to a soft pinkish-red. It was the limitations of the not-so-young rider that had to be considered. If every turn of the pedals was not to be an heroic effort, the equipment I took had to be extremely lightweight. At the same time it had to supply enough comfort to refresh me for the following day's ride. I was not planning an endurance test – I wanted to enjoy the journey.

I started making lists, and set aside a corner of my study to assemble the gear. Many things I had already, but not a suitable tent.

There are nylon tents available that weigh no more than three pounds, but they all have one serious disadvantage for prolonged use – there is not enough headroom to sit upright in them. This does not matter overmuch if they are to be used only occasionally, or only to sleep in, but in the temperamental English climate a tent often has to serve as kitchen, dining-room and dressing-room as well as sleeping quarters, and to have to cook lying full-length on one's stomach, or to wriggle out of a sleeping-bag and into clothing while lying prone with barely an inch or two to spare on either side, becomes increasingly irksome as the years pass and suppleness declines. I finally settled for a single-skin Goretex tent – Goretex is a material that 'breathes', allowing condensation to escape, while preventing rain from coming in. At four pounds it was light enough; I could sit upright in it, and it was very easy to erect, having a single flexible hooped pole that fitted into an outside sleeve, so that even if it was pitched in pouring rain, it would be dry inside. With the flaps open and looped back it gave me a good field of vision, and I could see a large arc of sky when lying down. The firm who manufactured the tent generously made one specially for me in a drab shade of green, as I thought the standard brown and yellow model would be altogether too conspicuous if I wanted to do any 'wild' camping. I practised putting up this tent in my sitting-room and was delighted with the spacious feel of it, and with the cheerful buttercup-yellow of the interior.

Quite as important as what went over me was what I would lie upon. When I was younger, I quickly got used to sleeping with nothing at all to cushion the ground. No longer, alas, and finding a suitable mattress was a problem, which, until solved, seriously curtailed my enthusiasm for camping. I tried the very lightweight extruded polystyrene mats, but although these act well enough as insulation, they offer too little in the way of cushioning for tired bones. A lilo is fine, but canvas ones are impossibly heavy and plastic ones puncture almost at first use. Eventually, at no small cost, I purchased a luxurious self-inflating mattress. This was made of a two inch-thick sheet of special lightweight foam in an airtight nylon cover fitted with a valve. Rolled up, with the air squeezed out of it, it occupied little space; arriving at the camping place, I simply opened the valve, and while the tent was being erected the mattress slowly unrolled itself with strange writhings and contortions as the foam expanded to its full thickness. Apart from its entertainment value, it was very comfortable.

I chose a stove that used methylated spirits, because meths, unlike paraffin and petrol, doesn't spoil anything if it leaks in the pannier, and a meths burner is simplicity itself, needing no priming or pumping. This particular stove worked efficiently even in a gale of wind, and it had the sort of design features dear to the hearts of people who set up temporary homes in the wilderness – two nicely shaped pans, an attractive little red kettle and a frying plate, all fitting one inside the other. It was rather heavier than I would have liked, but not too bulky, and I could see I would enjoy using it.

A plastic mug and plate, a knife fork and spoon set, a wooden spoon for cooking, a plastic bottle for water, containers for meths, coffee, tea and honey, a small plastic pill bottle for washing up liquid, a third of a nylon scouring-pad and a J-cloth completed the kitchen equipment. Food I would buy on a daily basis.

My clothes did not weigh much. I would ride in chamois-lined cycling shorts, which are very comfortable for long days in the saddle, though rather too anatomical for strolling about in. A long cotton shirt worn over them somewhat modifies their lines, and on all but the hottest days they would be concealed entirely under a lightweight cotton suit that had trousers with velcro fastenings at the ankle, which converted them into 'plus fours', and a cagoule top with a hood. I packed one spare riding shirt – my method when touring is to wear one set of clothing, and to have the other washed and drying on the panniers as I ride along. I made a cotton inner for my sleeping bag that could be taken out and washed, thus doing away with the need for night clothes. For smart occasions, I took a separate poly/cotton shirt, trousers and socks, and for rainy days I had a Goretex jacket and trousers, which could also be worn over everything else if it became unseasonably cold. Instead of a sweater, I decided to take a padded waistcoat, which could also serve as a pillow. I would have no spare shoes, since they are such heavy items, but would rely on a pair of nylon pedal muffs to keep my only pair reasonably clean and dry.

Useful oddments I included were a candle for lighting and heating (dangerous in a small tent, but a great comfort), a small torch, safety-pins for securing the washing to the panniers, sun glasses, insect repellent, a small compass, and a penknife with a lot of blades that could do anything from opening a tin to skinning game. In wilder parts of the world, where it is not customary for women to travel alone, and where men can be particularly chauvinistic, I have sometimes waved this knife around in a vaguely threatening manner in order to drive off the more importunate of them. I didn't think I would need to use it for that purpose in England; and indeed, the only aggression I met throughout my English wanderings (with one exception) came from those drivers who consider that bicyclists have no right to a share of the road, and against them I doubt that my Swiss army penknife would have been much help.

Luxury items were one slim paperback (to be replaced as read), a tiny radio with earphones, and some good malt whisky, which tasted none the worse for being kept in a plastic flask. Actually I am not sure that the last item can be strictly thought of as a luxury, since whisky has long been considered a universal catholicon for all manner of ailments, particularly those liable to afflict a traveller in a damp climate, and I thought of it in that capacity, and carried no other medications. A small tot before turning in, I reasoned, would ward off cold and rheumatics.

What spare time I had in the months before I set out, I spent reading up on the origins of Britain and its subsequent history, and one thing I came across early on was that when man was still in the mesolithic stage of his slow evolving, he too was thought to have wandered around England, carrying tents made of animal skins. As I do not like being laden down with burdens on my back, I am very glad that I was born after the invention of the wheel, so that I can load up the bicycle instead. But it was with a sense of great delight that I contemplated this atavistic link back through the ages, thinking that perhaps my love of travel had come down to me through all the millennia as a bequest of this early carefree ancestor.

CHAPTER TWO

Setting Out Along the Ridgeway

My route lay westward out of London, through the Thames Valley towards the Wessex Downs, along the top of which runs a broad green track known as the Ridgeway, one of the oldest highways in the northern hemisphere. The Ridgeway is thought to have been in use long before 8,000 BC, when Britain was still joined to the Continent, before the seas finally wore a way through the chalk to form what is now the English Channel. These chalk lands run through southern England in two great sweeps, one coming down from the coast of Norfolk, the other running westward from Dover. They join in the Thames Valley and continue over the Wessex Downs into Dorset, to end abruptly in fossil-rich white seacliffs.

When the land bridge was still in place, and when the North Sea was still just a shallow fordable marsh, our ancestor, mesolithic man, crossed into Britain in search of food. The chalk uplands became his highways, for they were well-drained and clear of the marshy and densely wooded river valleys of his day.

In the neolithic age, when his descendants had begun to keep flocks, and to practise the rudiments of agriculture, it was the slopes of these chalk Downs that pastured his animals, and where the first furrows were scratched, with the antlers of deer providing rudimentary ploughs. Soon the highways were marked by causewayed camps and tumuli, and the Ridgeway became the route to the great stone circles of Avebury and Stonehenge – the most extensive of all such neolithic and Bronze Age sites. Apart from the fact that I find the Ridgeway a delight, it also seemed a most appropriate place in which to begin an English journey.

We came up to the Ridgeway just above Letcombe Regis, a pretty village tucked tightly into the footing of the Downs on the spring line. The 'Regis' is said to go back to King Alfred, whose manor it was. Later, King John had a hunting lodge there, and the court rolls of Letcombe Regis are believed to be the oldest in Britain. Being close enough to Reading and Swindon for easy commuting, its old cottages have been snapped up and expensively restored in recent times, so that the village now wears a markedly prosperous and well cared-for air.

Above the village, the Downs rear up to the 800-foot mark where there are sudden enormous airy views over several counties, and where, until recently, there was an old quarry used as a rubbish dump, an eyesore for miles around. A local doctor who loves this high downland area, and who, surprisingly in these unphilanthropic times, feels that it should be made more available to everyone, had recently concluded an imaginative project here. Gone was the horrid tip, and in its place were four fine old barns rescued from demolition and transported and reassembled there to serve as a youth hostel and a centre for exploring the Downs. This is where I was to spend my first night, for by paying half the overnight fee I was welcome to pitch my tent in an adjacent clump of beech trees and make use of the hostel's amenities.

As my husband turned the car back towards London, I set about clearing a small patch of ground of all the small twigs and stones that can damage the thin ground sheet of a lightweight tent. The dumpy little half-igloo was up in minutes, an insignificant hummock in a majestic setting. The sense of being in a vast natural cathedral is specific to mature beech woods; it has to do with the quality of the light, and with the uniformity of the immense smooth trunks rising straight and serene like pillars to great heights, before the branches spread out to form an elaborate fan tracery. It was more intricate and delicate than any cathedral vaulting, particularly so at this elevation, with the evening light filtering through the high canopy of young green foliage in ever varying intensities of colour, turning individual leaves translucent and ethereal.

I had little to prepare or to unpack in this first easy camp, only the valve to open on the self-inflating mattress and the sleeping-bag to shake, so that the compressed down could fluff up cosily. Later I would go into the hostel to wash and to cook my supper, but now, as the day slid very slowly into evening, I was able to sit without distractions watching the light fade. Apart from the far drone of an aeroplane, there was no sound but a muted chittering of birds. The wood ended abruptly a few yards beyond the tent, where corn fields dropped away into the trough of the Vale of the White Horse, before rising again towards the Cotswolds in the north west. A grouse started up from the corn and I heard the small commotion before I saw the compact little body whirring away low over the field. Seeing it flying off northwards I thought suddenly that I had only to stand up and walk a few feet to see the huge ugly cooling towers of the Didcot power station and the Harwell Atomic Research Centre, and although these establishments were invisible from where I was sitting, the thought of them broke my mood of being in another time. The evening seemed grey now and chilly; it was gone nine o'clock and the last of the light was going fast. I was glad to zip up the tent doors and to go into the buildings, where there was warmth and company.

The four barns had been built around a courtyard, and organised in a way that made the most of their spaciousness and their massive wooden beams. The conversion had not been done cheaply, but imagination was as evident in the result as money. Sleeping places had been cunningly contrived in lofts and in odd corners at different levels, providing interest and a lack of uniformity, and leaving a large high central area that could serve different functions. Some walls were sheets of uncurtained glass that dramatically revealed the world outside. Now, with the lights of the towns and the villages below beginning to flicker out of the gathering darkness, the place appeared more remote and at a greater height than it was. It was not unlike being afloat in an ocean liner, or suspended in a vast airship – a self-contained separate world.

The hostel could sleep about sixty, and tonight it was full of young people from church groups round about, ending a day's conference – rather suitably considering the ambience – with a barn dance. The music was supplied by the young people themselves on accordion, fiddle, drums and guitar, with a middle-aged lady calling the movements – a person could earn a lot of money doing this, she told me, barn-dancing was very popular thereabouts. The handful of other hostellers, including myself, were politely drawn into a set, and we all stumped about, swung our partners and do-ze-doed as instructed, until it was time to stop and to seek out our various beds.

It had been the sort of evening to restore one's faith in youth hostels, which over the last few years have been engaged in a frenetic exercise to increase membership and make hostels more appealing to the young by installing electronic games, Coke-dispensing machines, and the sort of plastic entertainment most of them could probably find on their own doorsteps. Without employing any such gimmicks, this place was apparently a huge success and nearly always full. It also seemed to be more in keeping with the original spirit of the youth hostel movement, in that it saw its unequivocal purpose as being to enable more people to see more of the natural world.

Crunching back to the tent over last year's beech mast my way was lit by a moon just coming into its last quarter. It was a very clear night and rather cold, and the stars were now far brighter than the orange sodium lights trembling far down on the plain. The hostel buildings ceased to exist a few yards away so well did they blend into the surroundings. As I unzipped the tent door an owl called and I paused, not sure if I had heard it or whether it had been the noise of the zip. Then it came again, and I imagined I could also hear the scurrying of small creatures too terrified by the cry of their hunter to remain still.

I heard the owl at intervals throughout the night, together with the patter of tiny particles of twig and bark falling on the tent from high up in the canopy. I seemed to be sleeping just below the level of total wakefulness, so lightly that I knew what was happening all the time. But at some point I must have gone down to another level because it was suddenly light, a hazy morning with a spider climbing down a thread in the open doorway.

It was still misty when I set off, rather later than I would have done had I not been held up by my young dance partners of the previous evening wanting to have a look at Evans and to have his various features explained.

'You wouldn't catch my mum riding a bike,' said one of the girls.

'You wouldn't catch me, let alone my mum; too much like hard work,' said another.

It was not really Evans that interested them; they were trying to understand values they had not come up against before. They were looking forward to owning their first cars, and it was hard for them to accept that someone could prefer cycling to motoring, and would choose to ride a bicycle around England not for charity, or for a publicity stunt, but simply for enjoyment. I had felt much the same about owning a car at their age, but about the countryside we would never have been in sympathy. In spite of living so close to these glorious Berkshire Downs, they said they never came to walk there. It made me feel quite sorry for them.

A strong following wind – the best of all gifts to a cyclist – dispersed the mist and helped me along over the awkward rough ground, for, lovely as it is, the Ridgeway is not easy for bicycling. As the famous springy turf of the Downs has been increasingly brought under the plough, heavy farm machinery has used the track, carving deep ruts in the chalk; and horses and the occasional car and motor cycle break up the surface still further. Where the track descends to the layers of greensand and the heavy clays, water can lie in deep pools right across the track, from hedge to hedge.

It had been dry for a while, so I had only the rutted ground with which to contend today. The wide open views, and the choruses of larks and meadow pipits, present in large numbers, made it difficult for me to concentrate sufficiently upon the riding, and twice I slipped down the edge of a deep rut, a pedal scraping painfully down an ankle.

The hedgerows were everywhere white with cow parsley, the earliest flowering of the umbellifers – a vast and notoriously confusing family of plants, some of which are highly toxic. To generations of children, they served the important function of fairy wands and royal sceptres; my own favourite was the much larger hogweed, which bursts into flower in early June, producing an enormous umbrella-headed staff fit for Oberon himself. Because of the hogweed I have always felt an affection for the ritual use of umbrellas in the Ethiopian and Coptic churches' processions, where they seem to serve so similar a function.

Where the Ridgeway is intersected by roads, a few cars were parked, with sometimes someone selling fruit or ice-cream, but it was a remote landscape nonetheless, and I met only a handful of walkers all morning in spite of it being such a fine Sunday. I stopped to make an early lunch of coffee and bread and cheese at Whitehorse Hill, and afterwards I had the urge to go down the hill to see the Horse from a more suitable distance. The White Horse is a product of the Iron Age, carved into the hillside at a time when waves of Celts were pushing northwards into southern Britain, where the earlier settlers were hurriedly building forts to protect themselves and their flocks. This is the most memorable part of the Ridgeway and from below it looks impressively high and very strange. Great

earthwork forts occur all over England, but nowhere more
obviously than along the Ridgeway. I passed four of them on that
day's ride, and of them all I think the one by the White Horse,
known as Uffington Castle, is the most impressive with its extensive
views and commanding position. It stands at the head of a
steep-sided little valley that makes a deep dent in the hillside known
as the Manger. A narrow road plunges down the Manger, passing a
curious unnatural-looking flat-topped mound called Dragon Hill –
yet another site where St George is thought to have triumphed over
evil. The coombe is charged with a sense of ancient ritual and belief,
and dominating it all from above is the highly stylised dismembered
horse, striding out across the Downs, a symbol perhaps of man's
long hope of eternity.

Within a mile of Uffington Castle is a site 3,000 years older – the
neolithic long barrow known as Wayland's Smithy, a monument left
by the first true settlers of the Ridgeway. When this barrow was
properly excavated in 1919 it was found to contain three burial
chambers arranged in the form of a cross, in which were the remains
of eight skeletons. It stands now inconspicuously in a grove of trees,
a mound 185 feet long and about 20 feet wide. There is no clue as to
the identity of those who were buried there, but the immense work
of erecting such a structure before even bronze had made its
appearance suggests that the bones must have belonged to individ-
uals who were of great importance to their community. Perhaps, like
the mummified pharaohs of ancient Egyptians, they were thought to
be able to perpetuate the life of the tribe beyond death. I was
reminded of the stories of King Arthur asleep in a cave somewhere in
Britain until, in some dreadful age, his country will again have need
of him. Perhaps the noble dead of Wayland's Smithy were also
guardian warriors.

Although this ancient barrow has a decided aura about it, I didn't
have the sense of it being a cult centre, as I did at Uffington. At
Wayland's Smithy, with the cultivated fields all around, I was
prompted to speculate more about what life was like here 5,000 years
ago. We have tantalising glimpses in the artifacts this long-headed
race left behind them, in the fine flint tools and weapons, the
decorated pottery, and these large enduring chambered cairns that
have survived the ploughs of later civilisations. That they were
conscious of beauty shows in these works. Like us, they lived in a

time of change and innovation as new skills came in, disseminated along the route of the Ridgeway – weaving, bronze-smelting, new types of crops, and new methods of husbandry. Perhaps they were not able to adapt quickly enough to a changing world, for within a few hundred years of raising this barrow they had disappeared, and their place had been taken by a new race of round-headed people.

Another mile and I was out of Berkshire and into Wiltshire. The day had become progressively hotter, though this was only really noticeable in sheltered places because the wind still blew strongly from the south-east. I sat down for a rest under a thorn tree. The sun was so fierce that I shut my eyes, and no sooner had I done so than I realised I could open them again only with a great effort, so tired was I suddenly. I soon gave up the struggle and drifted off into sleep, awaking a good hour later to an early evening grown grey and chilly. It was high time to think about finding a camping place. No friendly hostel would make life easy tonight – I would have to rely on myself entirely. I had decided that Hackpen Hill on Marlborough Down would be a suitably remote spot, and I made haste to get there and seek out a well-concealed place. I didn't want to be visible from the track, as there had been written warnings at each intersection about thieves operating in the area.

Two strange-looking round clumps of trees in the adjacent fields looked promising, but when I inspected them more closely they looked less inviting. They were gloomy and overgrown, and one of them especially seemed like the site of an ancient barrow. Between them ran a narrow overgrown footpath, and going down this for about fifty yards I found a wicket gate, on the other side of which was a small, sheltered, roughly level space tucked into the corner of a sloping field. It was very bumpy ground, and closely packed with flints, but there was just space enough for my small tent. Nettles and cow parsley grew thickly against the fences, and since I could not get the tent pegs into the ground, I tied the guy ropes to the barbed wire, getting liberally stung in the process. Apart from these trivial disadvantages it was a good camping site, with extensive open views in front of me across to the Cotswolds. One of the tree circles, less threatening at this distance, lay beyond a field of young rape-seed of the softest yellow, while the other was in a newly cut hayfield, in which a little later I saw a beautiful brown hare sitting up and watching me.

The economy of movement possible when camping in so small a tent can be very satisfying, but it takes time to learn. I was not yet sure where every item was stowed in the panniers, and wasted time and effort searching for things, so that dinner took longer than it should to prepare. Not that it mattered, for there was so much to look at while I waited.

When camping the order of things sometimes works better in reverse – like washing after eating, rather than before. The nearest water would be down on the spring line far below, and knowing this I had carried a supply with me. With supper over, and the pots wiped clean, I reckoned I could spare a half a pint of water for cleanliness. The second saucepan became a washbasin, and soon all necessary parts had been flannelled clean of grime, sweat and stickiness, and the blood and oil had been scrubbed from my bicycle-savaged leg. Then, because it was so cold, I dressed in my respectable clothes ready for bed, and over them I put on my waterproofs to keep off the fierce wind.

I tried to write up all I had seen that day in the last of the light, as the sun set redly over the Cotswolds, but I kept nodding off and gave up long before I had finished. I fell asleep listening to the enormous din of the wind in the two ancient spinneys and to the night chorus of birdsong, one soloist sounding as though its song came bubbling up through water.

The same song woke me hours later when I opened my eyes to a grey, faintly drizzly morning. Without getting out of the sleeping-bag I found I could lean over and start the stove at the tent's entrance, and I sat there pleased as Punch, cooking bacon and making coffee, everything coming nicely to hand as though I had been doing it for weeks. I had slept well, and felt fit and rested in spite of the uneven bumpy ground. The sense of achievement and satisfaction that all these small triumphs gave me seemed a touch absurd – but that only increased the pleasure.

Striking camp in the fresh breeze was less gratifying, with everything light trying to blow away as I repacked the panniers. The tent itself streamed out horizontally on the wind like a deflated hot air balloon as soon as I untied the guys from amongst the burgeoning nettles. Several times I had to drop it, half-rolled, in order to chase after the nylon bags into which it had to be stowed, which were bowling down the hillside. But even stung and winded, when all was safely packed up, I felt a reluctance to leave the high open Downland for the more sheltered plains below.

CHAPTER THREE

Through the Cotswolds

Sometimes, though very rarely, I have a most wonderful dream in which I am flying. I am not in an aeroplane, or flapping my arms up and down in a parody of bird flight, but simply gliding through the air, soaring without apparent volition or effort over roofs and treetops as though I had recaptured a forgotten skill, as natural to me as walking. The nearest I ever consciously approach the exhilaration and joy of this dream is when I am bicycling down the smooth winding tarmac of a steep hill, with the wind streaming through my hair. The thrill of the speed is not important – it is the lovely sensation of the air flowing like silk over my skin, and the beautiful economy of movement, that delight. Leaning in to the bend of the road with barely perceptible shifts of weight, the slightest pressure of hands on brake levers – all second nature now, and as involuntary as the dream flight – body and machine one entity swing through the corners with hardly a check, in a graceful fluid rhythm. The descent from Hackpen Hill onto the Broad Hinton plain had me singing a 'Jubilate' in spite of the continuing drizzle and the Monday morning commuter traffic.

A maze of little lanes soon took me away from the motorists who were hurrying to join the broad tumult of the M4. I rode between hedgerows bordering wide prosperous fields and through tiny hamlets almost hidden by large farm buildings. All was rural peace except for a brief tangle with traffic on the edge of Wooton Basset.

North of the M4, along lanes plunging ever deeper into the heart of England, the scene was on a more intimate scale – smaller fields edged with raised banks and carefully pollarded trees, and a fine old manor house every few miles, all mellowed brick and carefully tended gardens. I came upon the River Thames close to its source, where it passes through Ashton Keynes, a pretty village whose three ancient market crosses show the former commercial importance of this crossing point of the young river. Now, together with the neighbouring villages of Somerford Keynes and Poole Keynes, it floats among scudding sails and water birds on the newly-created lakes of the Cotswold Water Park, where once were ancient water meadows. I rode through this drowned land on a raised twisting lane that followed the old flood ditches. The road turned a corner every few yards, presenting a kaleidoscope of images briefly glimpsed – spires, a mill, grey willows, stone slate roofs, blue water and a pale blue sky with the morning's mist curling away in thin tendrils.

All roads in this part of England lead to Cirencester, even these narrow winding ways. My back route debouched me into the maelstrom where three key Roman roads meet. Although Cirencester has long lost its strategic importance, the Foss Way, Akeman Street and Ermin Way still converge on what was the second most important Roman settlement in Britain. In Elizabethan times the town grew rich once more on the Cotswold wool trade. But for today's roaring juggernauts hurtling along the narrow roads, bumper to bumper, Cirencester is merely a bottleneck. Only travellers who manage to penetrate the modern defences of the ring road can find themselves, as I did, tossed up like some piece of flotsam before Lord Bathurst's inordinately high yew hedge.

'Thirty-seven feet and still growing. Highest yew hedge in the world is this,' said my informant, a kindly gentleman who had stopped me to point out that I was proceeding the wrong way along a one-way street. In my anxiety to escape from the horrors of the ring road I had not noticed the sign.

'They don't cut it no more with the ladders,' he continued. 'They have machines that do it now. 'Tis a sight, I'm telling you.'

These freely offered facts conveyed little of the wonder of the towering expanse of faultlessly sculptured foliage. Densely green and faintly aromatic, it followed the delicate curve of the wide Georgian street, and could only be seen in anything approaching its true glory from the opposite pavement. On this side a unifying eighteenth-century façade disguised buildings that had once housed the humbler offices of the Bathurst estate, all of which had now been converted into desirable residences or shops. In the window of the former farrier, Thomas Hudson was arranging his Georgian and Victorian wares. Nearly all his stock had the distinction of being at once exquisite and totally impractical. Expensive trinkets like polished walnut shells fitted out with silver sewing sets and tiny mother-of-pearl measures, made it seem a shop for Beatrix Potter's mice. Small and genial, Mr Hudson, with a little dog so like himself that I swear it smiled, could have walked straight from the pages of *The Tailor of Gloucester*. He told me about the Georgian veneer that overlay much of Elizabethan Cirencester. It was, he said, the work of a Lord Bathurst, who, with advice from Alexander Pope, had laid out his park in 1714, during the great age of British landscaping. The conversion of the mansion, which was almost in the centre of the town, had not been considered as successful as the park; hence the colossal hedge to disguise its deficiencies.

The glimpse I had of the park made me eager to see it in greater detail. It stretches westward for more than two miles, with mature plantations and long rides framing distant views, and with the tall tower of Cirencester's ornate church providing a perfect focus at the end of one avenue. It promised all the delights that can be created out of raw nature, with the aid of an impeccable eye for the lie of the land, allied to a bottomless purse. It also suggested the only safe cycle route out of Cirencester. But, alas, the present Lord Bathurst does not care for bicycles. While walkers and horse riders are generously granted access to the broad vistas, bicyclists are lumped together with drivers of motor vehicles, and excluded. I had no choice but to screw up my courage and leave the town in close company with the thundering juggernauts banging horribly through the pot-holes of the arrow-straight Roman road.

I got out of this death trap as soon as I was able, climbing a precipitous hill onto high Cotswold ground between two river valleys. At once a blissful silence descended. It was lunchtime, and I stopped by the side of the road to boil up a kettle and sat there eating the last of the bread and cheese I had brought from London. Not a soul passed. I plugged the tiny speakers of the radio into my ears and tuned in to a Schubert song cycle. Perfect though the music was for the day, I was suddenly so tired that my eyes kept closing, and I fell asleep, waking again only some forty minutes later when the music had been replaced by someone talking. I could only hope that it had worked its magic subliminally.

It seemed a fine and carefree existence to be able to sleep by the side of a road without fear of molestation – not something that can be done just anywhere. But this southern end of the Cotswolds is still relatively remote and unaffected by the huge numbers of tourists who pour through the better-known villages. Cotswold country is naturally attractive, and also instantly recognisable because of the oolitic limestone that underpins it all. This type of limestone is full of fossils and easily quarried, but grows harder with exposure to the atmosphere. The stone also splits naturally into flat slabs with clean sharp edges, and it is used all over the Cotswolds to roof houses and to build drystone walls around fields and gardens. The traditional buildings of the area are therefore all of a piece, with walls and roofs in shades of mellowed grey and gold.

The many small rivers that have cut a way through the limestone mass have created a varied landscape, open and secret by turn. All afternoon I plummeted from open ridge-top views down into steep-sided little valleys and wooded coombes, only to climb out again to a wider world on the other side. There were many scattered houses and small hamlets, some with streams trickling across the road, and all as pretty as could be. Yet although it was clearly a settled, prosperous part, and very well cared for, I had still not seen anyone about.

I stopped to visit Withington's fine wool church, and inside was a tombstone with the following inscription: 'Here lyeth the body of one Honest Jhon [sic] Stockwell who dyed of the plague and was buried on the 25th day of September Anno Domini 1665.' I came out of the porch wondering whether a twentieth-century calamity akin to the Black Death could account for the lack of people everywhere today. But beyond the churchyard hedge was the village school, and the piping of young voices at play dispelled thoughts of rows of corpses blackening behind leaded mullioned windows. The deserted streets betokened nothing more sinister than that the villages had become dormitories for people who daily commuted to town.

Long before nightfall I was down from the high wolds and installed in Cheltenham, in the house of friends who live in an elegant Georgian terrace there. At least, it seemed elegant to me, but according to my friends, Cheltenham is really all a sham – jerry-built Georgian of the worst kind. Where Bath sits primly and securely behind its splendid terraces of solid Bath stone, Cheltenham, my friends inform me, is a façade thrown up by unscrupulous speculators. Underneath a thin skin of stone facings or, more usually, of stucco painted to look like stone, everything is shoddily laid brick, the whole structure cobbled together anyhow. Even the pillars supporting the porticos are brick disguised as stone. These defects have remained invisible until recently – like wrinkles under heavy make-up. But now, everywhere, the veneer is cracking in a series of huge grimaces. All over Cheltenham I was shown walls where the facings had fallen or been stripped away, leaving exposed brickwork courses gaping open like huge wounds. The work of restoring it all is difficult and very costly. It also offers a splendid moral lesson on the sins of the fathers being visited upon the children unto the seventh generation.

Cheltenham was built in a tremendous hurry, a boom town in competition with Bath. Both towns possessed valuable mineral springs, whose waters were believed to have curative properties. But whereas the waters at Bath had been developed by the Romans, it was only in the eighteenth century that Cheltenham's spring was discovered. In 1788, George III, the least stable of the Hanoverian kings, though an ardent believer in the efficacy of spa waters, fell out with Bath, and took his family off to spend a month at Cheltenham instead. At that time Cheltenham was still just a village, difficult of access and a full three days' journey by fast stage coach from London. The royal seal of approval began the town's rapid growth.

As a fashionable spa Cheltenham never achieved the status and popularity of Bath. William Cobbett, visiting the town in 1821, spoke very ill of it in his *Rural Rides*, describing it as 'a nasty-looking place'. He also objected to the clientele, claiming that all of them, male and female alike, were drunkards, gluttons and debauchees, seeking cures for bodily ailments brought upon themselves by their own excesses. Gout was certainly one of the chief afflictions of a class that could combine almost total indolence with a large consumption of port; but whether this betokened the depths of depravity Cobbett suggests seems to me somewhat doubtful. If it was so, the moral climate changed very rapidly, for in an age of expanding empire, Cheltenham came to epitomise that greatest of all English middle-class virtues – respectability. Generations of army officers and administrators retired there with their memsahibs, to end their days where decent values could be relied upon and maintained. There was said to be more Benares brassware in Cheltenham at that period than in all other British towns put together. It also came to have no fewer than eight railway stations by 1930, though why it should need quite so many is not clear; its public transport service now, in company with much of England, has reverted almost to the backwater status of its village days.

Beneath Cheltenham's façade of unswerving respectability and conformity are anomalies in plenty, quite apart from the gaping brickwork. None, however, seems more curious than the founding there in 1853 of Cheltenham Ladies' College, an act which flew directly in the face of public opinion at a time when Victorian notions of womanly propriety were more straight-laced than the whalebone corsetry that constrained their bodies, and when the term 'blue-stocking' was one of derision. Doctors of the day were moved to publish warnings that formal learning could permanently impair the fragile balance of the female brain, and have serious consequences upon the health, wealth and morals of succeeding generations. As the home of the first school in Britain to offer girls the educational opportunities considered suitable only for boys, Cheltenham struck a blow for female emancipation which is still reverberating.

I would honour Cheltenham for that reason alone, but I liked it anyway. I liked the 'onion and dragon' wrought-iron lamp standards in the courtyard of the parish church. I liked the touch of individuality with which the builder of the rose window in the church had set it off centre, to make it appear as though the wheel of St Catherine's martyrdom, which it represents, was really in motion. But I also liked the deceptively solid Georgian mansions, and the Ionic capitals on top of their fake columns. The imperfections, the ragged edges somehow allowed for a greater awareness of the Cotswold hills which curve around the town in a lovely backdrop. There is something quintessentially rural about Cheltenham that is absent from the urban elegance of Bath, and I wondered if it was this sense of *rus in urbe* that had so appealed to the hearts of Englishmen far from home, so that returning from their exiles they chose to settle here.

I cannot be totally sure that my appreciation of Cheltenham's charms was not heightened by the roseate glow in which I wandered around while there, a glow induced by the sort of bibulous over-indulgence so deprecated by Cobbett in the *Rides*. My friends, who are fine examples of energy and industry at a time of life when many people are thinking of retiring, had recently turned their hand to making wine from a kit, producing large quantities of both white and red. I was not immediately sure that I liked the taste of either, but after several glasses this ceased to matter. On the second evening, ever ready to experiment, my host placed the red in the microwave oven, and lightly chilled the white in the freezer, which seemed to improve the flavour of both.

If the wine did enhance my general impression of Cheltenham, I am sure it could have added nothing to the pleasure with which I discovered Kit Williams's clock, sited appropriately within a few yards of where the first British jet aircraft was built: I would have found it far and away the best thing in the town, whatever my condition. The variety and inventiveness of Kit Williams's work is tremendous, and this clock is the best example of it that I had come across.

It hangs against the end wall of a long, high vaulted arcade, in the new shopping precincts, in front of a blue background studded with stars. At the very top, suspended just below the roof, is an immense white goose smiling broadly as she endlessly lays her large round golden eggs. These descend on a conveyor belt and lodge in slots along the outer rim of an enormous water wheel rotating around a shaft. Beneath this is the clock itself, a great solid cube with an octagonal face decorated with the nursery rhyme characters from the Cat and the Fiddle.

At minute intervals a golden egg drops into the clock and a mouse pops its head out of one of several little doors around the clock face and rattles its long metallic whiskers. When a mouse emerges from the topmost door, a virulent green cloth snake uncoils to make a grab for it, but always just misses. Below the clock hangs a huge and wonderful fish – a symbol of happiness, emphasised by the widely smiling mouth and benevolent expression. The sinuous curves and the cunningly jointed tail of this monster fish, made from multiple moulded strips of exotic woods, is clearly the work of a master craftsman, and impeccably finished.

On the hour the clock springs into glorious motion. Hurdy- gurdy music begins to play, the clock face begins to spin, faster and faster, and out of every little door pops a mouse with furiously rattling whiskers. This is the moment for which a crowd of small children have waited with growing excitement, the moment when the great fish shakes himself and awakens, clapping his tremendous tail from side to side, while from the generous mouth issues a great stream of multi-coloured bubbles, which the children run to catch.

Like the Ladies' College, it seemed to me one more surprising treasure to find in a rather unlikely place – clever Cheltenham.

CHAPTER FOUR

The Coloured Counties

Leaving Cheltenham through its north-western suburbs is to plunge almost immediately from nineteenth-century gentility into ancient fields of battle. The gentle Vale of Gloucester, through which the River Severn winds in leisurely convolutions to join the Avon at Tewksbury, is Shakespeare country, and by extension England at its most English. I was riding through the closing scenes of the drama of *Henry VI*, Part Three, where on 4 May 1471 the forces of the House of Lancaster were routed by the usurper Edward IV and his Yorkist kinsmen. Crossing first the railway and then the M5, and hearing the roar and clatter of the traffic shrouded in the morning mist, it was not difficult to imagine the clash of steel against armour, the shrieks and groans of men, and the thunder of horses' hooves.

I was accompanied as far as the railway crossing by Bill, a veteran cyclist of seventy-nine, riding a sturdy antique roadster. He had noticed me casting about for a quiet route out of town and had offered to come along to show me the way. He was glad of 'a bit of company' he said, adding that it was a rare sight to see someone else on a bike. 'There's not many as has much use for their legs nowadays,' he observed, running an approving eye over the laden Evans. 'It's not like when we were young; they'll get the car out now just to pop down to the corner shop. It's all hurry and worry nowadays, and if it don't cost money it's not worth having.'

I was keen to know how much the area had changed from his young days, especially from a cyclist's viewpoint. 'You wouldn't recognise it then,' was his immediate response, and he hesitated, at a loss it seemed to know where to begin; there had been far too many changes for Bill. The roads, he recalled, had been mostly gravelled, slower than tarmac, but with hardly a car on them. Bill and his cycling companions had reckoned to do a hundred or so miles a day, 'and dance all night afterwards'. Farmhouses provided refreshment on their rides, at 'fourpence for as much as you could eat and as much tea as you could drink'.

'They say they were hard times,' said Bill, recalling his first job
building bikes at nearby Dursley, which brought in a mere 'twelve
bob a week, but we had enough to eat and you didn't need to spend
money in them days to be happy.' He mourned for the woods and
meadows that had been swallowed up by the motorway - 'You
wouldn't credit the acres of prime land which vanished overnight for
that! Not that any of it is like it was; not the flowers and birds there
used to be around these parts. That all changed when they grubbed
the hedgerows out. Same with the fish; rivers hereabouts are all
empty now, no cover left along the banks; fish have to have shade,
stands to reason. We used to have plenty of hedgehogs - you'd see
families of 'em shuffling along by the side of the road, when it were
getting near dusk. You'd hear the frogs then an' all, setting up such a
din you couldn't hear yourself speak. Otters there were in plenty,
and stoats, and all manner of small creatures. You only see 'em on
that danged box now.'

Comparing the Vale of Gloucester with more obviously spoilt
areas I found it, on the whole, a very pleasant place: but to Bill, who
had known it so intimately, it was a ruined paradise. Yet it was clear
that the recalling of these vanished scenes also gave him great
pleasure, and he had grown quite animated by the time we parted
company. I was glad he had his memories, for the countryside of
Bill's youth, if it existed at all, was tucked away in high remote
corners of the wolds, and Bill had 'not the breath for the hills no
more'.

Tewkesbury would have sorely tried my patience had I been
trying to park a car, for there was a solid jam on all three roads, but I
had no trouble threading a way through to the glorious Norman
Abbey rising serenely above the fret and bustle. It was from this
church, on another day in May, that those Lancastrians who had
sought sanctuary there after the bloody battle of 1471 had been
dragged out to execution in the market place; among them, Edmund
Beaufort, Duke of Somerset. Shakespeare has Edward VI boast of it:

> What valiant foemen, like to autumn's corn
> Have we mow'd down, in tops of all their pride!

Tewkesbury Abbey enshrines the Wars of the Roses as no other
church does, for it survived the Dissolution intact, when the
townspeople bought it for £453. Among the noble bones that rest

within its walls are those of the son and heir of mad Henry VI – the young Prince of Wales, slain in the Tewksbury battle. In another spot are those of his enemy, sad Clarence, who survived the fight only to become embroiled in the muddy politics of the day, and to end his life in the Tower of London, drowned in a butt of malmsey.

The horrid aspects of that brutal and cynical period are all too easily forgotten inside this glorious abbey. Chivalry is its keynote, and it seems a far more fitting setting for Mallory's high-principled company of Morte D'Arthur, or for Chaucer's 'verray parfit, gentil knyght' keeping his vigil in front of the altar before departing for the Holy Land. One of the largest parish churches in England, the nave is powerfully and majestically Norman, its massive pillars the perfect foil for the blaze of medieval reds, blues and gold of the fourteenth-century choir vaulting, and for the lovely expanse of medieval glass donated by Eleanor De Clare in 1394. These windows feature an extensive portrait gallery of armour-clad, De Clare crusader ancestors, charmingly though incongruously set among the Virgin and saints. Another great array of medieval nobility is commemorated in life-size gilded effigies and in a circlet of delicately carved chantries round the high altar. Amid all this high pageantry is a grim reminder of man's mortality: on top of a tomb, the stone cadaver of a cleric lies well advanced in the process of corruption, being slowly devoured by worm, spider, toad and beetle . . . Remember O man! Dust thou art . . .

I found all of Teweksbury notable. There are at least two dozen ancient inns with preservation orders on them; one of them, The Bear, dates back to 1308, and several of them were pilgrim hostels. Whether Shakespeare's own company performed in any of them is not known, but Dickens had Mr Pickwick and friends come through the town on their pub crawl, and stop off at The Royal Hop Pole. I took my coffee at the slightly less venerable Bible Bookshop, where it was neither cheap nor particularly good, but I had come across it in a quiet Georgian backwater when I had grown very tired of trying to see the historic glories of Tewksbury through the unending streams of intrusive traffic.

From Tewkesbury I followed the Severn towards Upton, under solid grey skies. The morning's mist was soon whole-hearted rain and I rode in waterproofs. The dim grey shapes of Bredon Hill and the Malverns seemed to be swimming along in the distance to right and left of me, like attendant whales. All the houses I passed, large and small, were of the black and white half-timbered type, many of them Tudor, and most of them very old. The cows in the fields were also black and white, and where they could they sheltered from the rain under spreading oak trees. The flat diffused light over the vivid green level fields, and the sharply etched black and white lines of both houses and cows, made the scene as two-dimensional as a primitive painting. It seemed as though it would be possible to roll it up and carry it away. It was not nearly so pretty when the rain stopped and the mist lifted. Then I could see that my mysterious whales had rows of villas halfway up to their summit ridges.

When the mist lifted again, I found I had taken a wrong turning and was lost among the lower streets of Malvern. The person from whom I sought clarification said he wasn't surprised I was lost – 'When they was putting new signposts up round here they got 'em all pointing wrong, and when we told 'em, they said it was in accordance with the EEC regulations.'

With another abrupt change of scenery I was soon riding through a string of small hamlets to the north-west of Great Malvern, in the sort of countryside that is neither hill country nor plains, but something in between. It was an out-of-the-way area of small irregular-shaped fields and rough little orchards, with sudden dips and rises, and very little flat ground anywhere. The narrow winding lanes were sunken by centuries of use, so that the banks on either side were often high above my head. Between gaps in the hedges horses poked their heads inquisitively over five-barred gates.

It was the sort of landscape I could have ridden through without retaining any clearer impression than of a peaceful, utterly rural scene. On closer acquaintance I came to realise that it was not quite such an ordinary part of the English countryside as I had supposed. This sort of broken terrain is unsuitable for modern farming methods, and as a result it has suffered less reorganisation than many areas. Much of it was still worked as small holdings, in roughly the same parcels of land as it had been for centuries.

Friends of mine had recently bought one of these small holdings – seven acres with a pretty seventeenth-century half-timbered house on it, of the sort that are two a penny in these parts. Actually it was my friend's son Colin who had bought it, having dreamed of owning a farm ever since I had known him as a young boy. He had kept the dream alive all through his schooldays and through a half-hearted attempt at an engineering course. Even when he had settled into a successful career in computers, he still yearned for a farming life, and the wife he married shared the dream. Eventually they had enough saved to set about looking for a small country living, and had settled upon this place, near the small market town of Bromyard.

I had visited them soon after they had moved in. Already they had installed a few sheep, and some ducks and hens, and were harvesting their first crop of organically-grown carrots – huge great things with a splendid flavour. Their few acres were proving to be good soil; the fruit trees looked promising, and the little stream that ran through the property was constant and of good quality. They had also been promised a substantial grant to do up the historic little house which leaned over picturesquely to one side, and which had all three bedrooms leading companionably through one another. With true self-sufficiency they were going to do all the building work themselves, and any problems with ready cash would be solved by Colin doing small building jobs for neighbours. Watching Colin turning over his soil with a borrowed rotovator, I thought I had never seen him look so contented with life.

But things had not worked out as planned. Not very long afterwards I heard that Colin had returned to fulltime computer work, and was living all week in London in a tiny flat, putting on weight and spending his evenings in front of the television. However, the improvements to the house were finished, and I had been invited to come and see them on my way north, so doubtless I should find out what had changed their plans. I almost rode past the place, so altered was its appearance. The house looked crisply new – more like a reproduction than a three-hundred-year-old building. Gone was the rambling overgrown garden and in its stead were smooth sculptured lawns, raw new brick paths and a few neat flowerbeds. From the road at least, it had taken on the guise of a desirable upper-income-bracket property in one of the more desirable suburbs; not the sort of place one naturally associated with a life of rural self-sufficiency.

It had been that splendid crop of organically-grown carrots, I learnt, that had first made Colin and his wife aware of the gulf between their dream and reality. In an area where anyone could grow vegetables of similar quality at the same time of year, they couldn't sell the crop for the cost of lifting it, and what they couldn't eat themselves or give away was left to rot in the ground. Had they been really determined, they could perhaps have organised a local co-operative to supply more lucrative markets, but as it was, growing things did not seem to them to be such a good proposition after all.

The alterations to the house had also presented problems. Colin and his wife had very high standards. They were both products of a materially conscious age. Everything had to be of the very best quality and finish, both inside and out. The entire structure was taken right down to its foundations and then reconstructed with the original timbers and materials, but without the idiosyncrasies. Although both of them were skilled and meticulous workers, they were much slower than professional tradesmen. They were living in a caravan while the rebuilding work was slowly proceeding, and there had come a point when it seemed essential to get things moving a little faster. Also their grant was dependent upon certain stages being completed within a specified time. Far from being able to hire out Colin's labour, they were themselves forced to employ a firm of builders, and as a temporary measure Colin returned to computer work, where he could command a salary high enough to pay the bills. At first he commuted between home and work, but as the best-paid contracts are in the large towns like London, he began to return to his country paradise only at weekends.

What I had not understood was why Colin hadn't given up his uncongenial employment now that the house was completed, and started to live the life he had wanted for so long. They were now both approaching forty, and with no children to educate and no expensive outgoings, they didn't seem to need Colin's large income. During my visit I learnt how their expectations had altered, or at least become clearer to them. They still wanted the country life, but they wanted it combined with all the trappings that they considered essential to enjoy it fully. They still grew vegetables, and produced eggs, but only sufficient for their own use. In their fields were a few sheep and two or three young bullocks – enough to supply them with meat, and with a little over to sell, but certainly not enough for the upkeep of the Landrover and the BMW. Colin now planned to work on lucrative computer contracts until he was fifty, mortgaging the years to pay for an early retirement. He still had his dream; but now he spoke of it not as farming, but as 'pottering about in the country'. In the meantime they were living frugally, shopping for clothes at Oxfam, and spending most weekends refurbishing the barns and sheds which will house all the equipment that they feel is necessary for this particular style of country living. Watching him hard at work on a barn roof, I thought he seemed contented enough, but the glow there had been about him as he turned over his soil that first summer was not there any longer.

From Bromyard my way lay up and over a rough common, with the wind at my back and a warm sun overhead. It was largely cattle country, with dung on the roads and the air heavy with the sweet smell of cows, especially when passing the small farmsteads, whose milking parlours opened straight onto the narrow lanes. The hedgerows were a mass of pink, yellow, white, gold, purple and blue. Black and white timber-frame houses and cottages were dotted about in no particular pattern and between them, long vistas drew the eye out over the painted counties towards the blue distances of Wales. Great mature oaks and horse chestnuts towered up into the pale blue vastnesses of sky, their branches so densely hung with leaves that the wind hardly stirred them. Every time I passed under one and gazed up into it from close to the tremendous bole, it seemed that I had forgotten how huge trees can become, seeming far larger than any building, and so teeming with life as to make the senses reel. It was a great pity not to have arrived towards evening on this plateau, for it would have been a splendid place to camp, under such trees and looking out over half of England. But as I still had the day before me, and needed to buy supplies, I tore myself away from the lovely prospect – one which has inspired many people, including A. E. Housman and Elgar – and rolled effortlessly and delightfully down to Tenbury Wells, at the crossing of the River Teme.

Tenbury is almost on the Shropshire border, and has been the market town of the valley for centuries. It had a reputation for the extraordinary longevity of its citizens, a possible reason for which was revealed in 1839, when a saline spring was discovered there. Its discovery was too late for Tenbury to achieve the popularity of Malvern or Cheltenham, so apart from a ripple or two, it simply continued as the bustling shopping centre of the district. This

Saturday morning the open market was packed with people; but the
majority of stalls were run by Pakistanis selling cheap bright clothing,
while groceries and the like were bought from the supermarkets.

Having acquired a ravenous appetite from the morning's ride, I was
attracted to a venerable-looking inn on the High Street advertising
'Roast Dinner £2'. Although it was only just midday, every seat but
one was taken, and I was told by a harassed-looking waitress that I was
fortunate to have got there early. It proved to be a most substantial
meal – lamb, potatoes, peas, carrots and gravy, all heaped up in a great
mound, enough to keep a bicyclist going for several hours. Not for the
first time I blessed a means of travel that allowed me occasionally to eat
such meals without paying the penalty of putting on weight. This is
not vanity, just experience of the effort needed to drag every extra
pound up hills. All around me families were tucking in with silent
gusto. Replete after this huge meat course, I watched with fascination
as plates piled high with fruit pie and custard followed the same paths
as the dinners. It was easy to see why figures in this part of England
tended towards the corpulent.

It was a feature of Tenbury Wells Saturday shopping, for families to
gather on the bridge and feed the ducks that frequented the pretty
River Teme. I joined them while I waited for my lunch to settle itself a
little, and then rode on, still feeling rather thoughtful. The pretty
countryside, teeming with livestock, flowed on pleasantly beside me
for the next hour or so, as did the river, and all the hundred and one
little movements that keep a bicycle going forward in a straight line
were carried on without much conscious help from me. I was in sight
of Ludlow before I surfaced properly, and the River Teme, in
company now with the Corve, was an altogether more majestic flow,
winding around the feet of the first properly planned town in
England, where it sat upon a commanding hill capped by a hoary
castle and a soaring Perpendicular church.

After the impressive approach to Ludlow across the bridge, the
steep slope of Broad Street, with its massive gateway had me off
Evans and walking, not because my gears were not low enough, but
because every inch of the way was so tremendously attractive that I
had to take it all in slowly. Nowhere had I come across such a rich
variety of charming houses and inns. Each one was entirely
individual, and yet the result was a pleasing harmony, helped no
doubt by the famous grid system of the layout of the streets. Black and

white gabled and orieled Jacobean buildings were everywhere, each one seeming to have achieved the ultimate in flamboyant decoration. But at the top of the town, in the market place known as the Bull Ring, was the Feathers Hotel, which outshone them all.

Narrow winding alleyways linked the splendid streets, each one an English version of an Eastern bazaar, each abounding in antique shops and cosy cafés. It was such fun just to wander about in Ludlow that I didn't get to the castle – not that I minded very much, as I have developed a rather 'seen one, seen them all' approach to castles. While I admire them in the landscape, especially so when they perch upon a crag as this one did, I usually find their interiors oppressive. Perhaps too many horrid deeds linger on in their cold clammy halls, too many murders cry out for vengeance from noisesome dungeons; or perhaps quite simply, the centuries of living behind such massive fortifications produce a melancholy blight that has permeated the stonework like an invisible fungus. Whatever it is, I usually prefer to muse upon the prospect of these ancient piles from a distance.

Ludlow Castle dates back to the earliest days of Norman castle-building, a symbol of oppression to the natives of Duke William's newly acquired realm. It was built in 1085 as one of a line of fortresses to contain the marauding Welsh – a troubled border castle destroyed, rebuilt and embellished by Normans, Plantagenets and Tudors. Edward IV's two young sons were taken from there by Richard III for 'safe-keeping' in London, where they soon ended their days as the tragic 'Princes in the Tower'. Henry VIII spent his boyhood there, in what was then a safe and peaceful place after his father, the son of a Welsh noble, had won the crown from Richard III on Bosworth Field in 1485. Milton's masque, *Comus*, was performed in the great hall of the castle in 1634, a century and more after its greatest days were over. All this long march of history I found very pleasant to mull over from a romantic viewpoint on the banks of the River Teme.

The lovely fifteenth-century church of St Lawrence had also closed its doors by the time I found my way to its odd unique hexagonal porch. There were all sorts of treasures inside which I was sad to miss, the misericords especially, among which was said to be one of a fox dressed up as a bishop preaching to geese: but it is no bad thing to have something left to lure one back again. I was, however, able to visit A. E. Housman's grave in the churchyard; not perhaps as remote a spot as he might have chosen for himself, but nonetheless a fine high resting place for a Shropshire poet.

CHAPTER FIVE

Shropshire and the Midland Plains

It was a morning bright with promise as I rode away from Ludlow; the sort of morning that confirms the rightness of bicycle travel and makes me sorry for anyone who has not yet discovered its delights. A brisk wind, still at my back, furrowed a mackerel sky as though with a rake, pulling the dappled patterning out ever more thinly against the high blue vault. Heavy rain, which had forced me to seek Ludlow's historic though overcrowded little youth hostel on the river bank the previous evening, was forecast to continue, but at present the sun shone, the clear air was full of bird song, and the damp earth smelled wonderful.

I followed a narrow road around a contour of the Clee Hills which rose on my right hand, tree-clad and full of secluded hollows. The ground sloped gently away on my left, down to the valley bottom, where the River Corve twisted on its erratic winding course through the heavy grass of gold-speckled water meadows. Beyond the river, the long airy ridge of Wenlock Edge sheltered the rich farm land from westerly winds. In the parks of fifteenth- and sixteenth-century manor houses, mighty sycamores made areas of dense shade under which cattle ruminated, gently swishing their tails at the early flies. Corve Dale was as lovely and as unfrequented a place as one could wish for on this radiant Sunday morning, and I stopped frequently in order to enjoy it more fully.

On one of these halts, a young man clad in nylon running gear, the first person I had encountered since leaving Ludlow, came jogging out of a cottage, and seeing me studying my map stopped to ask if I needed any assistance. When I told him I was simply riding for pleasure through the lanes of England, he urged me to visit an old chapel which he said he often ran past. It was very special, but little known about, he told me, being high up on the Brown Clee Hill, quite out of the way.

Inspired by his enthusiasm, I pushed the laden Evans with some difficulty up a very long one in four incline (marvelling that anyone could run up it). Half an hour later, having fetched the heavy iron key on its forged ring from a nearby farmhouse, I was sitting alone in one of five roughly carpentered eighteenth-century box pews, reading through the office of Prime. The church was indeed special, a rare Norman antiquity of unassuming simplicity. No longer in use, it stood quite alone, a squat venerable lop-sided little gem, in the centre of a cattle-trampled field. Inside, it was all rough rafters and beams and irregular little windows, with old lathe and plaster showing through the holes in the disintegrating roof lining. Traces of medieval fresco gleamed through the flaking whitewash of the walls. A roughly carved large baptismal font, like a stone bathtub, faced the simple altar squarely from the other end of the short nave, the two essential elements of eight hundred years of uninterrupted Christian worship.

The place seemed reluctant to let go its accumulated heritage, as though it didn't believe in its sentence of 'redundant church'. I felt it was holding its breath, waiting for the play to resume. Not long ago, everyone from the scattered dwellings in the area who was not sick, and not a non-conformist, would have met together here on a Sunday morning for a common purpose. Now the handful of the faithful who can make the effort, climb into their separate cars and drive to whichever of four or five distant churches is taking its turn at hosting the week's worship. The social dimension of an interdependent community coming together regularly has been entirely lost. As the woman at the farm told me when I returned the key, 'We don't know who our neighbours are any more.'

Steep lanes led me on over a shoulder of the Brown Clee Hill, and the need to concentrate on maintaining a pedalling cadence when my muscles were not so keen on complying stopped me from dwelling on the sadness of this breakdown of community ties. In fact, the effort proved so hard that I decided to stop at the top, at the edge of a field of barley, to boil a kettle for coffee and to make an early lunch with the good wholemeal bread and blue Shropshire cheese I was carrying. No sooner had I taken the edge off my appetite and drunk the first cup of coffee than the sudden darkening of the day warned me that some drama was about to unfold. Glancing back the way I had come, I saw that the whole of the southern sky was now the colour of a blue sword blade. At the same moment a few heavy drops of rain plopped into the dust at my feet. I reached hurriedly for

my waterproofs, but before I could scramble into them the storm
was beating down on my bowed head, and the lane was already
turning into a swift-flowing river. There was no shelter to run to,
so cramming everything back hurriedly into the panniers, I got on
the bicycle and turned my back to the almost horizontal rain. It was
all I could do to keep Evans upright on the quantities of gravel that
the flood was washing down the slopes, besides being unable to see
anything through the blinding downpour.

In twenty minutes it was all over, and soon I was riding on roads
from which the steam was rising in clouds under hot clear skies, as
though in an African jungle. This was the pattern for the rest of the
day, violent precipitation followed by equally violent evaporation –
up and down constantly like a yoyo, dramatic but tiring. I had
endlessly to stop in order to put on or take off rain gear, for it was
so hot in the dry spells that if I attempted to leave my waterproofs
on it was like riding along in a sauna.

As a result of the weather, I viewed the romantic roofless ruins of
Wenlock Abbey only briefly, fleeing for shelter to the less
interesting but drier parish church adjacent. Much Wenlock is a
very pretty little town with many fine old buildings, among them a
half-timbered gaol house of 1577. It is all so immaculately kept,
with manicured lawns and not a trace of litter anywhere, that it
seems a trifle unreal, like an open-air museum. The houses of Much
Wenlock and the farms of the surrounding area owe much of their
beauty to the ravaged Abbey, for after the Dissolution, when the
monks had been expelled, and the lead had been stripped from the
roof, people filched huge quantities of the fine mellowed stone to
use as building material, so everything looks very planned and
unified.

Because it was the Sunday of a bank holiday weekend, the place
was full of tourists – like many ancient ruins, the abbey attracts
more visitors now, in the days of the car, than it did when it was
whole and a famous place of pilgrimage. Some of these latter-day
pilgrims had also sought shelter in the church, and were huddled as
near as possible to the fine Norman doorway, as though they feared
that their purpose in being there would be misconstrued, and some
cleric would come and buttonhole them. I whiled away the time
waiting for the shower to pass by reading the outcome of an official
visitation to Wenlock Abbey in 1321. It appeared that the auditors

found a very lax regime in force, and urged immediate reform, as is suggested by these exhortations and injunctions, which I copied down:

> Monks must not hunt, and their dogs must be expelled from cloister, dormitory, and indeed from the monastery.
> Gambling on games of cards, marbles and chess is forbidden.
> The prior should not indulge in luxurious and extravagant living with a large household.
> Monks must not take boys to the dormitory.
> Monks must not indulge in late drinking.
> Standard dress of black serge, not worsted, and the regulation tonsure are obligatory.

Notwithstanding this invocation to the virtues of a hard and simple life, I decided that pitching a tent on so temperamental a day was altogether too unattractive a prospect, and headed instead for the comparative comforts of the youth hostel at Shrewsbury. I strolled through the deserted Sunday evening town later, passing more superlative churches and historic black and white buildings than it seemed possible to cram into so small a compass.

By now it was clear that a change had come over the face of England. It was still a green and pleasant land and one that, on the route I had taken, appeared to be almost entirely rural. But as with crossing the equator or the tropics, some subtle differences were immediately discernible, though it was not easy to pinpoint what they were. The rather sombre dark-red sandstone used extensively in the larger buildings was the most obvious novelty. Houses generally appeared to have grown a shade smaller, and the landscape seemed to have become a little sterner, a little less lush. Perhaps it was only imagination that smelt a hint of coal dust in the air, or thought that the mortar between the bricks was rimed with soot. But there was no mistaking people's greater readiness to initiate conversation, nor could I miss the flatter vowel sounds of their speech. The invisible line I had ridden over had brought me into another zone. The South was now firmly behind me, and I had reached the north Midlands.

Some judicious changes of direction were needed now, if I was not to run up against the major industrial complexes. Riding through the flat plain of northern Shropshire had given me a sudden longing for higher ground and wider vistas, and I decided that I would head over

to the east and follow the line of the Pennines, the high rocky spine
of England that divides the country, east-west down the middle.

It was almost June, and summer seemed to have vanished as
completely as the Augustinian canons, whose gaunt grey ruined
abbey at Haughmondon I passed without stopping. The landscape
too was now reduced to a small range of grey tones, like an early
black and white film. Only small events, like rooks riding the light
winds in a flurry of ragged feathers above the waving tops of tall
trees, or lapwings calling plaintively from the misty fields, broke the
muted stillness of it all. I wasn't finding the riding unpleasant, as
long as my rainwear continued to function adequately, but my
thoughts began increasingly to centre on creature comforts. The
notion of a pub lunch spurred me on – to sit in an over-heated
convivial atmosphere, and get away from nature altogether for a
while, seemed very desirable. In the event, the first open pub I came
to was anything but cosy, being all brown linoleum, dark brown
varnish, hard wooden chairs and settles, and a cold smell of stale
tobacco. The food on offer was equally unattractive – an
anonymous-looking meat pie that tasted as I imagined asbestos
might, with grey potatoes and watery cabbage. The only other
customers were two old men playing a silent game of cribbage,
marking their score with matchsticks on a little board with small
holes arranged in patterns of tens.

I rode on towards Stone through narrow muddy little lanes, with
the rain now bucketing down. I was growing very tired and thinking
how nice it would be to stop bicycling and to relax for a long time in
a hot bath. Even to lie in the tent reading a book or listening to the
radio would seem a luxury after the endless grey sameness of the
rain.

At a tiny village called High Offley, just over the Staffordshire
border, a church porch offered the chance of a little respite and the
opportunity to consult the water-logged map. From the slightly
elevated viewpoint a dreary scene presented itself, one of mud and
gravel and spreading pools of rain water. The problem of the night's
shelter loomed large. Camping would seem to present insurmountable difficulties, but as there appeared to be neither B & Bs nor
hostels, nor even hotels in the area, there was nothing for it but to try
and find a patch of ground above the rising water level and test my
tent's true capabilities. But putting this into effect was not easy. No

one was about on this inclement bank holiday, and I felt shy about knocking on doors to ask if I could pitch my tent in a corner of someone's field, partly because I thought that people would probably think such a request little short of madness considering the weather. Eventually I decided to make myself stop at the next farmhouse I came to, which turned out to be in a hamlet so small that I couldn't find it on the map. Having knocked on the door of an unassuming red brick cottage, I was promptly invited into a crowded untidy interior full of people tucking into beans on toast. A mug of hot milky tea was thrust into my hand, and a seat was found for me near the fire.

Between showers I pitched my tent on the only piece of the property that wasn't under water – a patch of lawn about seven foot square, between two low apple trees in the tiny front garden, a well-drained oasis in the watery wilderness. A few feet away was a henhouse, from which issued a continuous contented clucking. A little further off, just behind the small farmhouse, was the yard, with the cow sheds knee-deep in manure from a mixed herd of forty-eight milking Friesian-Charolet-Hereford crosses – which, I was told, had once numbered fifty-four before the new EEC milk quotas had come into force. A picture of six redundant cows trailing disconsolately away from the farm, nose to tail, immediately came to mind, and not for the first time I wished I could draw.

The rain continued to thunder down throughout the late afternoon. I was urged to stay by the fire and keep dry, and so had ample opportunity to get to know the family. They were gracious enough to say that my turning up on a wet bank holiday was a godsend, not just for the pleasure of seeing a new face, but for the girls to have something to talk about when they returned to work the following day. There were three daughters and a son. The eldest daughter was just visiting, as she was married now and living in Stafford, where she and her husband were nurses. They had two small children and, not owning a washing machine, she had brought her weekly wash with her to do at her mother's. I would not have considered her life a sinecure, working fulltime and looking after two young children, but she thought it was an infinitely easier lot than her mother's. She would not be prepared to work like that, she said; she relished the freedom of city life, and would never return to the country.

The youngest daughter worked in a factory twenty miles away, and the other served in a grocery where she said the customers used her as a service for relaying news, so she felt she had the best of country and town life and never felt cut off. Both the younger girls said they enjoyed helping their father about the farm and would like to be farmers' wives themselves one day. The farm was too small a living to support more than one fulltime worker, so the son, whose heart was also in farming, did contract work for other farmers while he waited to take over when his parents retired. As both parents were only just into their fifties, he anticipated a long wait.

So far the strip of England I had ridden through had appeared affluent – surprisingly so in the light of recent reports of rural poverty. Houses had looked well kept up, with replacement windows much in evidence, as well as an unfortunate rash of pseudo-Queen Anne front doors, which seem set fair to becoming the DIY success story of the age, appearing everywhere, and on the most incongruous of properties. There had also been an abundance of garden centres, dealing in expensive decorative additions to the good life; gnomery was rife. This family didn't fit into the generally prosperous image at all; perhaps there were many others like them behind seemingly comfortable façades. Not only did they have beans on toast for their main meal of a holiday, but their house seemed to be singularly lacking in many of the material comforts that are taken for granted these days. Yet in spite of this, and of the fact that they worked tremendously long hours for 365 days a year, and never went away on holiday, they seemed an unusually happy and united family. The inevitable comparison arose with Colin's desirable residence in Worcestershire: he would appear to have so very much more, and yet there was no question in my mind as to who had the richer life.

The mother, bundled up in a shapeless apron with large gumboots protruding beneath, was constantly on the go. She seemed quite oblivious of the chaotic state of her house, and indeed it really didn't seem to matter, because she created an aura of calm and contentment all around her that rendered the chaos totally unimportant. Good humour radiated from her, and she gave the impression of wanting nothing more from life than the pleasure of waiting upon her family – as well as upon any stranger who happened to come along. She was one of those very rare people who, in a prosaic and ordinary way, manage somehow to personify goodness – a goodness which is really nothing more, and certainly nothing less, than a breathtaking degree of unselfishness. You simply could not imagine her saying, or even thinking, anything uncharitable about anyone. Just being around her made the world seem a better place.

As she bustled to and fro between parlour and kitchen she imparted snippets of information. I learnt that she and her husband had lived in the area all their lives, and that each had been born into a large family of farm workers. After their marriage they had worked and saved for years to buy a little place of their own, and now counted themselves fortunate to be where they were. All around them, they told me, properties were changing hands for ever-increasing sums, and incomers who worked in the cities were moving in, transforming the area into a suburb. Their small hamlet had so far been spared – they still had a carpenter, a plumber and an electrician living there, and people continued to help one another on a neighbourly basis.

I slept well that night without any anxieties, as though some of my hostess's contentment had rubbed off on me. Sudden flurries of rain drumming on the roof of the tent only made me feel the more snug now that I knew that none of it was finding a way inside. It was broad daylight when I was awoken by the crowing of a cock and the clucking of hens. I lazily prepared breakfast without shifting from my warm nest, and the price I paid for this piece of idleness was to sleepily pour cooking oil instead of honey over my last piece of bread.

As I finally crawled out of the tent my hostess appeared with a steaming mug of tea and stayed to talk while I drank it, the pair of us standing together in the shiny wet morning on the tiny neat patch of lawn among the general chaos of mud. I struck camp, watched by an audience of a robin, head on one side, feet wide apart on the henhouse roof, and some house martins taking a brief rest on the telegraph wires overhead, in company with a single swallow.

As I loaded the last pannier my hostess came out again, this time with a steaming mug of milky coffee, determined to fortify me for the journey – she would have cooked me breakfast had I not refused. Busy as she was, she was also reluctant to let me go; we were much the same age yet living such different lives, that each was fascinated by the other's; we could have exchanged information all day without exhausting the store. Contented as she was with life, the sight of the loaded Evans clearly aroused some dormant sense of adventure in her, and she ran her eye and a hand admiringly over it. Her attention was caught by the map fixed in its place on the handlebars, and she suddenly saw names familiar to her since childhood. She traced the lanes where she had driven cattle to and from the fields – treks as long as five miles, she said, by the time she was nine years old, often with a small brother in tow, to whom she would give a pic-a-back when he got tired. Here was the town where she had visited relatives in the war and had seen barrage balloons – the incident still vivid after all those years. The map had released a spate of memories. There was the single time she had ventured as far as London, standing in the train all the way there. She had gone to a farming exhibition at Earls Court, but that had impressed her far less than London itself – she could see it still, 'the width of the pavements, the awful smell and the poisoned atmosphere'. She had found it tremendously exciting, and quite awful at the same time, and had not in the least minded standing all the way back in the train again, because she had been so glad to be going home.

Having at last torn myself away, I was plunged immediately into a world of magic. The lanes I rode through were so minor and unfrequented that they had strips of grass running down the middle of them, and so narrow that the plants and wild flowers growing at the sides brushed against the panniers, while the tallest of them met just above my head, so that I was riding through a diaphanous fragrant tunnel. Every blade and stalk was bent over under the weight of rows of water droplets that glittered and trembled. Plants passing just inches before my face, revealed small details of their anatomy magnified by the crystal drops each one of which mirrored the deep fathomless blue of the sky. Yesterday's grey waterlogged scene was totally transformed, and in the meadows young calves skipped around their steadily grazing mothers as if they too were rejoicing. Not for the first time I reflected that whatever the weather in England is like, there are tremendous compensations. Without the particular conditions of the previous day, there could not have been this marvellous morning.

Once I had left this hidden world, that seemed to know nothing of the twentieth century, my way began to grow progressively steeper. Plain little hamlets, no more than a single short terrace of nineteenth-century workers' cottages, appeared at regular intervals, and the road was edged with dark stone walls. I stopped near one of these hamlets to perform the familiar task of donning or removing rainwear, for after the morning's brief lucent hour the pattern of precipitation and evaporation had reasserted itself; a pattern infinitely preferable to the overall grey downpour, but nevertheless a sore trial to a cyclist. This time I had stopped to shed the extra layer, rolling it up under a rubber bungee on the rack to keep it handy. After I had remounted and started to regain some momentum on the slope, a villainous-looking coal delivery man, with a sack folded like a hood on his head and the legs of his trousers tied with string, called out something to me in a strange accent. I couldn't catch what he said, but I assumed it was the sort of remark best ignored, and rode on. Ten minutes later a coal lorry drew alongside, forcing me to stop. The protest died on my lips as from the cab the coalman handed out my waterproofs which he had seen falling off the rack – having failed to get me to stop, he had picked them up and driven after me with them. 'See how we look after you up here?' he said grinning, his red lips and the white of his eyes shocking against his coal-blackened face, making him look like a Black and White Minstrel. I was lost for any suitable reply other than an embarrassed 'Thank you'.

CHAPTER SIX

A Small Town in Derbyshire

Two days and quite a number of showers later I was camped in an enchanting spot, halfway up a steep overgrown meadow liberally sprinkled with tall golden buttercups and pink clover. Some adventurous brown hens with deep red nodding combs and wattles were stalking the tent from a safe distance, peering out from between the long grass stems, torn between caution and curiosity. These hens, I was soon to discover, laid eggs which had deep orange yolks and a taste remembered from the days before debeaked birds confined in wire cages produced their joyless anaemic offerings. Fortunate, freedom-loving hens, they roamed widely, flying with triumphant squawks over walls and fences when I met them, sometimes miles away. They were always prudent enough to drift home again by dusk, however, and were waiting to be shut into their stout A-shaped little house before ever the fox judged it safe to be abroad. Not so the profligate ducks, who were given to moonlight wanderings, and paid the penalty exacted for such romantic fancies. All these independent-minded birds belonged to a farmer called Nan, who owned the meadow. She too was camping, but in a diminutive cow stall cunningly converted into temporary living quarters for herself and her three grown children, while a splendid stone barn nearby was being turned into their future home.

Nan had moved up here to Derbyshire from the South because of her husband's job. When he had unexpectedly died just a few years after the move, Nan had stayed on because she liked it so much more than the Home Counties. She had drifted into farming by accident when her daughter became keen on riding and needed a field for her pony. Now Nan had forty acres on which she ran a viable flock of sheep, a few store cattle, a couple of horses, and the free-ranging birds. She was well-known in the neighbourhood, and it was one of the park rangers who had suggested she might be able to find a spot for my tent on her land.

The meadow was on the outskirts of a large village, or small town (it had not yet decided which it was) called, appropriately, Hayfield. I fell in love with it immediately, not for anything special it possessed, but because of a host of small circumstances that made it seem a very good place to live. I could well understand why Nan had stayed on there. It was nicely positioned in a fold of the Peak District, just below the slopes of Kinder Scout, almost at the start of the Pennine Ridge. Its greatest blessing has probably been the rerouting of the through Roman road from Buxton to Glossop, which means that Hayfield has quiet streets where people can hear themselves speak, and don't have to spend their time leaping for the safety of pavements, as is the case in so many traffic-plagued villages. Two of every essential type of shop makes for a wide variety of goods and for sufficient competition, so that there is no pressing need to drive to supermarkets in the neighbouring towns. As a result there are always people of all ages about in the streets, calling out greetings or stopping to talk to one another as they do their daily shopping. Six pubs and a café cater for leisure hours. Beyond its own intrinsic charms, Hayfield also attracted me because it seemed to possess what I was beginning to fear had disappeared from English country life.

The pretty River Sett flows through the centre of the village, and a modest-sized cricket field creates a stretch of open green beside the bridge. There are no grand buildings, just some pretty eighteenth-century three-storey weavers' cottages and a late Georgian church with a wonderfully pretentious clock, one of whose four vast illuminated faces lighted my way to the tent each evening, like a huge yellow harvest moon hanging low in the sky, and whose unmelodious chimes punctuated the long watches of the night at quarter-hourly intervals. This clock had been presented to Hayfield in 1884 by a prosperous mill-owner named Albert Slack, and the church tower had had to be raised to accommodate it. It had clearly been modelled upon Big Ben, and on the occasions when I lay awake listening to the stentorian tones of the clock's midnight chimes, I used to imagine Mr Slack making his generous offer to the Parish Council. 'Money's no object,' he would say. 'We'll have the best. We'll get chap up from London who did the grand job on Houses o' Parliament.'

The story of Hayfield was that of the Industrial Revolution in miniature, though not the usual unhappy episode it had often proved for less fortunate villages. Scraping a living from the thin soil, the small farming community of Hayfield, had seized the opportunity to improve its lot when the demand for cloth suddenly increased in the early eighteenth century. Because of the relative closeness of the developing new towns of Stockport and Manchester, Hayfield folk were able to set up looms in their own homes and sell finished woollen cloth to agents who toured the area. The distinctive three-storey weavers' houses were built on the proceeds of the trade, the top floor being given over to the looms, while a hoisting beam set above the new windows took the goods up and down the outside of the building, and so avoided disturbing the household living on the lower floors. Later, when cotton was king, the River Sett, tumbling down from the heights of Kinder, supplied the power for the spinning mills, and Hayfield reached the zenith of its prosperity.

By 1850 the newly-developed steam power was concentrating industry in the large towns, and the boom time for small mills was over. Thanks to a few businessmen like Albert Slack, however, Hayfield survived where similar villages became ghost towns, and its one successful cotton mill continued to function into the 1920s. There is still a single chimney pouring out smoke among the many cold brick fingers pointing mutely skywards in the Hayfield Valley, though the one remaining mill manufactures paper, not cloth.

Where the Industrial Revolution failed, modern economics have succeeded, and nearly all of Hayfield's working population now earn their living in the towns. But though this makes it in some sense a dormitory village, it had nothing in common with the silent shut-up places I had passed through further south. Although well-kept, there was no self-consciously over-preserved feeling about Hayfield either. According to my informant – the local historian and newsagent – this was because of the judicious mix of natives and incomers, the one not swamping the other. The kind of people who came to settle in Hayfield had known the place over a period, often because of spending walking holidays in the area. The new folk were energetic settlers who valued the village for what it was and didn't want to change it. A real community spirit existed, he claimed, with new ideas being welcomed. For instance, a yearly jazz festival took place here, with thousands of visitors flocking in, and the whole village gave their support to the function, even if it was only an hour or two taking money on the gate – and that was the pattern for any event, right down to the smallest Brownie cake sale.

I spent my first day at Hayfield satisfying my longing for a wide view. It was clear sunny weather as I ambled up through the Sett Valley towards the summit of Kinder. The River Sett, tamed now by a reservoir and waterworks, bumbled along merrily. Black and white dippers bobbed their tails over the small pools and a few sheep peered at me over the rough hummocks, but I saw no one until I came to the wide swathe of broken black peat hags on the Pennine Way, the longest long-distance footpath in Britain, and so popular that walkers' feet are eroding the land faster than it can be repaired. From the top of Kinder I watched party after party picking their way round the worst of the newly created quagmires, adding their mite to the destructive process, while all around the moors stretched empty and open, east and west, into the far distances.

A semi-circle of black-faced sheep gathered round me while I ate my sandwich, seeming to imitate my munching as they ruminated. They were waiting hopefully for a handout, a thing I had never seen in all my years of wandering about the hills of Britain. Long-distance paths, it seems, modify animal behaviour here, just as they do in America – though there they do so on a rather more spectacular scale, with the bears in the national parks ripping the doors off cars to get at the chocolate bars and the sliced bread inside. So far I am told, no sheep has yet attacked anyone in order to get at their lunch.

It wasn't all that long ago since ordinary citizens had fought for the freedom to roam over these moors. In the car park at the bottom of the path a plaque commemorates the events of 24 April 1932, when several hundred militant ramblers staged a mass trespass onto Kinder Scout, in what turned out to be a successful campaign to challenge the right of landowners to exclude them from walking on the open moorland. It seems very fitting that the site of this 'reasonable act of defiance' is now surrounded by the 540 square miles of the Peak District National Park, the first national park to be created in Britain.

The plaque was pointed out to me by Pam and Arthur Gee, a couple who had settled near the spot and who invited me in for a cup of tea. Arthur had first come to the area as a poor Manchester boy of eight to spend a charity holiday in what were called 'the mission fields', just below his present house. There and then, he said, he had determined that one day he would return and live there. He became a teacher, married, and had brought his family for holidays to a rented seventeenth-century farmhouse. When the National Trust acquired

Kinder, he was able to buy this rented property for a song. It was as perfectly placed a little house as I have ever seen, and Pam and Arthur had lavished attention on it over the years, so that it had been perfectly restored without being spoilt. It faced south towards a loop of the river, above wooded terraced slopes rich in bird life, and had magnificent moorland views. The rambling interior was all thick walls, odd nooks and corners and exposed beams, set off with old oak furniture collected over the years at country sales. It was a house I could happily have moved into without wanting to change a thing.

Just beyond the stone wall at the top of the meadow in which I was camping, the long succulent grass gave way abruptly to the close-cropped wind-scoured grey-green bents of the moors, a sudden transition from the sown to the wilderness. I liked to walk here as dusk was falling, and one night I heard a cuckoo calling loudly from an ancient oak tree growing just outside the wall. Looking up, I saw for the first time in my life a cuckoo in plain view, standing on a blighted limb of the tree only yards away. Its neck was stretched out almost parallel to the branch, its mouth gaping wide as it called 'cuckoo, cuckoo' urgently and continuously. It looked exactly like the bird William Morris had drawn for one of his fabric prints – a strangely predatory figure, oddly at variance with the background of quiet flowers. As had been the case when I first saw the fabric, as I looked at the bird I was suddenly very conscious of its menace – a creature of terror to all the little birds upon whom it might attempt to play its monstrous trick. Nature has cast the cuckoo in the role of arch-villain among birds, a positively *grand guignol* character, that plants an interloper in someone else's nursery where it will kill off the hosts' nestlings and force the tiny bereaved parents to work themselves practically to death to rear the huge alien, which will in its turn prey upon their species, perhaps upon their future offspring. This cuckoo appeared quite oblivious of my presence. Every pulsating inch of it seemed to be straining towards the fulfilling of its function with an almost terrifying singleness of purpose, and I supposed its pressing need to find a mate at this late date had overcome its usual secrecy and subterfuge. Already June, it was still calling out its May notes.

> In April come she will.
> In May she sings all day.

In June she'll change her tune.
In July away she'll fly.
In August go she must.

It was not the cuckoo, however, but the swallow that was to be the enduring bird of this summer, and it was at Hayfield that I first began to be aware of it as a constant feature in the landscape. Sitting over breakfast in the golden meadow, my delicious eggs grew cold as, entranced, I watched the swift darting shapes twisting and swooping, wing-tips brushing wing-tips in miracles of split-second avoidance. They were in constant movement, black long-tailed cut-outs against the sky, with sudden flashes of pale buff and blue iridescence, as they banked away dizzily at head height. A constant twittering song rose and fell with their flight. Where the cuckoo personifies brute survival allied to low cunning, the swallow seems all joy and quicksilver exuberance.

There was so much to see and do in the area that my overnight stop in Nan's meadow turned into a four-day sojourn – and I could have stayed there just as long simply sitting by my tent enjoying the view. One day I retraced my steps to Buxton, starting early in an attempt to avoid the horrors of the narrow A624 and A62T. These roads follow the route of the old Roman way from Buxton to Glossop, and both carry the usual complement of huge articulated vehicles bearing the enormous quantities of goods that once went by rail and canal. In addition, Derbyshire grits, the best road-making material in Britain, are quarried close by and rushed away in enormous high-sided lorries, whose drivers, I suspect, are paid piecework rates to judge from their impetuous progress. There is no alternative route for a bicyclist, since the roads here are so few. Ironically, it is the abandoned railways and canal banks that will eventually provide a quiet pleasant alternative for non-motorised traffic. Slowly – all too slowly, alas – stretches of these once discreet industrial arteries are being converted to leisure use: a few miles here, a few there. The idea is that one day they will all join up into a nationwide network, so that bicyclists, walkers and horse riders will be able to travel all over this island without ever having to breathe exhaust fumes or have their lives endangered by roaring juggernauts. In the meantime, one can only hope to survive such horrors as the A62T.

At over a hundred feet, Buxton is high for a British town, but coming down to it from the higher rough moors, it wears an improbably gracious aspect, with its eighteenth-century crescent and other self-consciously elegant buildings set amongst acres of fine green lawns. Another spa town, it was built by the fifth Duke of Devonshire, as yet one more hopeful rival to Bath. I had returned there to see the Micrarium, housed in what was once the spa's pump room. A relatively new invention – a method of projecting the image from a slide in a microscope onto large glass screens – it had won a special award in the 1985 Museum of the Year competition, and several people had urged me to see it.

It proved a wonderful experience, rather like looking into a kaleidoscope for the very first time as a small child, and knowing that you had been right all along to believe in magic. But the Micrarium was more wonderful than the finest kaleidoscope, for it revealed the true magic of the natural world. Huge transparent water fleas drifted across the screens, with babies developing inside them, popping out into the world at intervals. The intricate internal architecture of a flower, or the structure of a hair in the eye of a peacock's feather, could be studied in all their marvellous detail. A snowflake crystal revealed its fairy-tale beauty; and a host of other crystals could be seen growing and building the extraordinarily beautiful tapestries of life. Strangely, it was the fact that they were all real, unique and actual events, happening instantaneously, which made them seem so magical.

Children could easily operate the buttons that controlled both the magnification and the position of the specimens, without having to worry about the focus. The microscopic world was brought within the wondering gaze of any child tall enough to get its chin over the edge of the cabinets, and I would have considered the visit worth making just to watch the small intent faces, had I not been even more captivated by what they were seeing. It was one of the most enchanting things I have ever seen, and only hunger finally drove me out.

Another day I followed the Sett Valley downstream, riding the trail that had recently been constructed from the defunct Hayfield to Manchester branch railway line. At first it felt very strange to be there. The railway has always been such a forbidden place, somewhere strictly set apart with dire penalties for those trespassing upon it; even stripped of its rails and sleepers, it retains much of this sense of being separate. It wasn't like being on a natural path either, because it didn't follow the contours of the ground but had, in godlike fashion, evened out every rise and hollow, and flattened all but the gentlest of gradients. It had taken such herculean labours, such armies of Irish navvies, to build the embankments, to tunnel through the hills and to construct the viaducts and bridges of these marvellous feats of engineering, that it all seemed a little out of proportion for them to have become the haunts of machines that do not need rails and can so easily go up and down hills. Nonetheless, it is clearly far better that they are preserved for recreation than that they should revert back to fields, or become rubbish tips, and all that mammoth labour be wasted. Moreover, since they are so flat, and since they so often pass through the best scenery in Britain, they make the country easily accessible to families, and to cyclists who are too frightened to venture on the roads.

I enjoyed my ride on this section from Hayfield to New Mills, but I also felt a little cut off, and kept wanting to leave the track to see what was going on in the steep little villages that the line skirted around. I was seldom entirely sure of where I was in relation to anywhere else. In the end I got quite lost trying to find a way into the Torrs Gorge, which I had come to see.

The fast-flowing water of the Sett had powered many mills in the eighteenth and nineteenth centuries, the ruined remains of which dotted the valley floor, but none of them was so spectacularly placed as those in the Torrs Gorge, in an area of sandstone, where the River Sett and the River Goyt cut out for themselves a series of beds about a hundred feet deep during the first Ice Age.

Here, where the power of the river was concentrated, a unique troglodyte community was created during the Industrial Revolution, living and working in the subterranean gloom of the deep gorge. Torrs is now a theme park, above which towers the later Victorian town of New Mills, itself a living museum to another vanished era. There was an uncanny feeling in the canyon, as though one were on a time-warp that reached far further back, and had its roots in a darker history than that of the last two hundred years. Mill ruins, crude weirs, cobbled ways, bridges and aqueducts have all been tidied up and linked together with walkways, and tourist leaflets paint a romantic picture of the times. Up above, the solid, no-nonsense viaducts of the later town appear positively ethereal from these Stygian depths. For all the attempts at prettify it, the feeling of a brutish existence comes across at Torrs. It would always have been a world of half-light and shadows, but when it was full of screeching clattering machinery it must have been a hellish place, like Bedlam. An awful din would have beaten constantly back and forth against the cliff faces, and the red lights of the fires would have thrown monstrous shadows leaping after the echoes, amongst the swirling smoke and the soot. Conditions for men, women and children, ill-fed, poorly-clothed, and working desperately long hours in such a place, cannot have been much better than life in the salt mines, or on the rowing benches of Roman galleys. I found the attempt to present it to tourists in a romantic light rather sinister and disturbing.

Above, in the streets of the later mill town which climbed steeply up and over the brow of a hill, there was an even stranger emptiness. This too was now a dormitory village, with few signs of life, the inhabitants away earning their living elsewhere. Uniform rows of cheaply built back-to-back housing had sprung up overnight, as indeed had the whole utilitarian town. It was all of a piece, an exercise in expediency with none of the charm that comes from the overlap of styles and centuries. Without its covering of soot and smoke, it seemed a naked sort of place, like a plant that has been growing under a stone and, suddenly exposed, finds the light too strong for it.

I discovered a café open in one of the streets, and followed the lead of the man ordering before me who said, 'Are ye reet loov? I'll have a buttered barm. Ta, loov.' The exotic sounding 'barm', though it was served with a friendly 'Ere y'are, loov', turned out, disappointingly, to be no more than a buttered roll. Afterwards I went into an optician's to see if I could borrow a pair of thin pliers to free a part of my torch that had jammed. The assistant was a native of Hayfield, and as we struggled together to work the bent part loose, she told me how she viewed her part of the world after spending a few years away, working in the South. She appreciated her home town all the more for having left it, she said, and was prepared to earn far less in order to stay there. She endorsed all the positive things I had discovered about Hayfield. The only problem, she said, was that no one local could buy a house there any longer. Prices had shot up, and she herself, newly married, was living in one of an isolated row of former quarry-workers' cottages, stuck away out on the moor, miles away from anything except the busy main road. She couldn't get anywhere without a car, she said, which was a pity, because, like me, she liked bicycling, and thought the track from Hayfield would be a grand way of getting to and fro from work.

Striking camp the following morning, I found that I had stayed long enough for the tent to have left a distinct, slightly yellowed impression of its shape in the long grass of the meadow. I felt rather glad to be leaving it there as a small token of my temporary occupancy. It was an ephemeral mark and would have quite disappeared in a day or so, unlike the impression that Hayfield had made upon me.

CHAPTER SEVEN

Mill Towns of Yorkshire

Between the vast sprawl of Greater Manchester to the east, and the six or seven industrial towns that merge into the huge conurbation of West Yorkshire, a narrow breathing space of open moorland remains. Radio masts, television relay stations and electricity pylons encroach upon the highest places of this stretch of the Pennines, and at its narrowest point a motorway slashes brutally across it, swallowing hundreds more of its disappearing acres. All the more precious because it is so closely hemmed about and threatened, this slender corridor seems to offer an obvious open route north for a cyclist or a walker. The Pennine Way finds a path through, following the line of the high tops into Scotland: but for the bicyclist no such northerly way exists. Every road in the area seems to have the single intention of getting travellers off the moors and into one or other of the urban complexes as directly as possible. I was equally determined to wriggle my way through without becoming embroiled in either of them.

I could not avoid Glossop, for it lay on the only road north out of Hayfield. The sole industrial town of north Derbyshire, it has managed to remain just clear of Manchester's groping tentacles, and still has the moors lapping like a sea around it. I rode straight through with hardly a pause, and yet it left an indelible impression. It looked at first sight an unattractive hard dark town, with streets of small terraced houses, all of the same unflinching grey uniformity. But before I was halfway through it, my eye had begun to adjust to a different scale of values. There was a formalised air about these rows of identical dwellings that ended abruptly at the moor's edge, and had front doors opening directly off the pavements. They possessed something of the innocence and freshness of a child's drawing. The towering chimneys and cranes, factories and mills, and dark-brick chapels rising above the streets, filled the top half of the canvas and gave the scene a force and character of its own. It was a Lowry townscape, which had to be viewed from another perspective.

Uncompromisingly utilitarian though it certainly was, it seemed a far better place to live than most inner-city high-rise estates. There was an openness about Glossop that came perhaps with the fresh bracing wind blowing off the moors. In those rows of small companionable houses it was hard to imagine evil fermenting, cruelty to children being concealed, people afraid to go out after dark, or claiming not to know who their neighbours were.

I rode on across the empty moors into a day that was becoming increasingly unsettled – thin sunshine alternating with banks of scudding cloud sent great shadows racing over the ground, the colour flooding back as each wave passed. The wind, blowing for once against me, soon made me hungrier than I had been for a very long time. I was glad I had had the forethought to pack some emergency rations before striking camp that morning. With the last of the Hayfield real eggs, I had made an omelette, and fried some potatoes left over from the night before. Half of it I had eaten for breakfast, and the other half I had put between two pieces of bread. I ate this workmanlike and hugely restorative 'egg and chip butty' sheltering from the wind behind a drystone wall on a hillside. Below me the long line of reservoirs in the drowned valley of Longdendale looked black as ink, with a fringe of white-splashed waves around their margins. Another frantic cuckoo was calling somewhere on my left, while to my right a skylark spun threads of song that were torn away on the wind.

I stayed no longer than it took to eat, for the weather was fast deteriorating. It grew colder, greyer and damper as the cloud descended, throwing off little flurries of rain here and there. I was almost glad of the stiff climb up to the summit of Holme Moss for the opportunity to warm up. A steadily worsening prospect met me as I reached the top and could see what lay ahead to the north. The weather was doing nothing to improve the appearance of the straggling built-up area on the fringes of Huddersfield into which I had no choice now but to descend, there being no other road. To find a reasonable way through looked even more difficult on the ground than it had on the map. Not that I really minded leaving moors which had grown ever bleaker as the weather worsened. Weather makes a difference to one's appreciation of any area. Like most people, I much prefer sunshine, but I can enjoy rain too as long as a strong wind is not blowing it into my face, as it was on this day.

If cycling does have a drawback (and I find it hard to admit that it has any) it is because the rider is so adversely affected by a headwind. Walkers don't mind it nearly as much; coming down a mountain leaning into a strong wind is an exhilarating experience. But for a cyclist, a headwind constantly saps the energy and makes progress anything but a pleasure.

Tired as I was with the climb, it felt so arctic at this altitude that very soon I was hurtling down through the hairpin bends, clad in a full suit of waterproofs, which included a pair of grotesque fluorescent orange galoshes that were too large and an awful nuisance to get into the toeclips, but which did keep my only pair of shoes dry. The tyres made a loud swishing sound on the wet tarmac, and the rain was once again half blinding me as it trickled into my eyes off the edge of my hood.

The road signs were confusing, making it difficult to keep to my planned route. I had constantly to stop and consult the map, which as a result became more and more sodden. By the time I reached Meltham I was tired and dispirited, and I had decided that I did not care very much for this particular portion of England.

I had planned to stop at Meltham and get my weekend supplies. It was in an area of steep little hills which rose up spitefully just around blind bends, where my speed was down to a walking pace and the effort to get up the incline was all the greater. It was only 2 pm, but a bored assistant in the slovenly little supermarket – strange how every tinpot little grocer's in the country has become a 'supermarket' – told me I was lucky to find anywhere at all open after twelve o'clock on a Saturday in Meltham, and there was certainly nowhere serving teas. This did nothing to improve my opinion of the town, and by now thoroughly disgruntled, I took my few nondescript purchases, packed them in the panniers, and walked on to give my aching calf muscles a change.

I was trying to decide whether the faint drizzle warranted donning my waterproofs again before riding on, when my attention was caught by a woman in a bright yellow jumpsuit, who made an arresting and exotic splash of colour against the soot-blackened houses. She was weeding a tiny flowerbed and, looking up, saw me watching her. We each called out some pleasantry, and in the sort of instant sympathy that attracts people to one another, we were soon locked in conversation, and I was invited in for a cup of coffee.

It was an old weavers' house that they had not long moved in, Sue explained after we had introduced ourselves. Owing to the hilly nature of the land, there was an entrance from the street into the lowest floor, and another into the next level up from around the corner. Sue urged me to put Evans in the basement for safe keeping and we went upstairs. It was clear that the house was undergoing extensive refurbishment, and Sue apologised for the mess – not that there was much, just the strange contrast between rooms that had been totally transformed and were gleaming with newness, and those that hadn't yet been touched and looked as indeed they were, of a totally different ethos. I had just been invited to stay the night when Sue's husband, Darren, came into the room asking whose was the 'super bike' in the basement. When he heard that I was on a cycle tour of England, he too invited me to stay the night. I liked him immediately, as I had Sue – it would have been difficult not to warm to so affable and enthusiastic a person.

'Let me show you round our bit of Yorkshire. It's lovely around here when you know it,' he said. I accepted gratefully, and after supper Darren got out his battered Mini and drove us around the area as he had promised. He was determined, he said, to make me see this part of England in which he had been born, and to which he was strongly attached, in more favourable terms than I had so far expressed.

The villages round about which hugged the edge of the moor had all been part of the weaving trade – not cotton, as in Lancashire, but wool. Each had at its centre tall slender mill chimneys, inordinately high in order to gain sufficient draught to work the great engines. The workers' cottages, many of them built by the mill-owners, clustered about the high weaving sheds and the spinning-mills, as once the houses of peasants had clung to the curtain walls of castles, or hemmed in the great cathedrals. Everything was built of stone, blackened by years of sooty deposit, and buildings recently repointed were now marked with stark white lines. Winding up the hillsides between the houses were narrow cobbled streets, so steep that they must have been extremely perilous to negotiate in icy weather.

We sped along at what seemed a furious pace to one who had become accustomed to a bicycle's speed, making for the show places like Diggle and Delph, Uppermill and Moorside. Because Darren wanted to show me all the good points of the area, we saw too much too swiftly, and I was left with only generalised impressions. Built on strictly practical lines, the villages had become attractive in a way they can never have been in the industry's heyday. Money can transform almost any property into a desirable residence. These villages, which were once little better than industrial slums, now show an entirely different face. A fortune is being spent by civic trusts all over Britain to preserve and restore the past of various localities, but nowhere more so than in this part of the industrial North. Perhaps this is what gives people like Darren such a pride in their area – if it is worth spending so much money on, and if tourists flock to see it, then it must have value.

Nothing that I visited gave me more assurance of living in an affluent society than these rows of weavers' houses and workmen's cottages that were being snapped up as soon as they came on the market. Darren pointed out the stone mullions in the windows that were a strong selling feature. When glass had become readily available in wider sheets these mullions had mostly been removed to give more light; now people want to put them back in the interests of authenticity – like original fireplaces, plaster cornices and panelled doors in other places, 'original features' are the rage everywhere. Darren said he was going to cast mullions out of concrete for their house and then treat them with soot to tone them in with the rest of the stonework.

The whole area was an open-air museum displaying the achievements of the industrial age – canals, tunnels, locks and railways, all restored and preserved in a condition of cleanliness and an atmosphere of charm they had never possessed when they were serving their intended function. Tourism is the big business of today, however, and people come here in their thousands to have these relics of another era served up to them in an acceptable and hygienic form. The groaning and the grime have gone, and what remains is not history, but something that feeds the persistent nostalgia for a past that is perhaps more imagined than real. To the people who lived and worked in these places, our prosperity would seem like a miracle, and yet we of today have a sneaking suspicion that we might have lost some quality of life that they possessed.

We returned to Meltham via Saddleworth Moor, where the bodies of the tragic child victims of the Hindley-Brady murders had been hidden, and in some case still remain hidden. It was the quickest way back and not part of the sightseeing tour. I doubt if Darren or Sue would have mentioned it had I not suddenly associated the name with the horror of the events. They told me that for people living round about it is still too awful a series of crimes to be rational about. From time to time, they said, services are held out on the moors in an attempt to help people to come to terms with it – a sort of exorcism. Strangely, but with an awe-inspiring aptness, there was an extraordinary sky overhead as we crossed the moor – a deep jagged hole had opened up in the banks of lowering clouds, and a yellow and red sunset streamed through it, like an Old Testament vision of the pointing finger of God.

I got lost immediately and repeatedly after leaving Meltham the next morning. I ascended a steep hill, plummeted down the other side and found myself in a succession of steep one-street villages that had a footing on the moors and another on the edge of busy roads. At every turn I was either staggering up or slithering down a precipice; there wasn't so much as a pocket handkerchief of flat ground anywhere. Trying to follow byways, I suffered a period of total confusion when I seemed to have strayed into an unending maze of allotments and cul-de-sacs. When I finally found someone to ask where I was, it turned out to be Slaithwaite, only a few miles from where I had set out several hours before.

Confusion struck once again when, having rediscovered my correct line, I came to an area that did not tally with the map. This is a simply horrid experience for a navigator, a Kafka-like situation in which the world of ordinary everyday things has been overturned, where chaos reigns and reason is confounded. The knowledge that I and the map were both right, and that it was the terrain that had been altered (in this case a new fast road had been built since the map was drawn) was slow in coming. For a while I fully believed I had slipped into a sort of limbo.

Having regained my trust in the natural order, the next problem was how to cross this six-lane barrier, and I jinked about for quite a while on roads that ended abruptly at the motorway's edge, and whose only use now was for the illicit dumping of refuse. Presumably the rubbish was heaved out of cars passing along the motorway – a new sort of sport perhaps! Old bedsteads, three-piece suites, piles of oozing plastic bags and assorted smelly junk made a strange contrast to the featureless acres of the expensive new road.

An old gentleman eventually stopped his car and directed me to a tunnel beneath the motorway. I couldn't think what he was doing there on a road that went nowhere – perhaps he was one of the illegal dumpers – but I was very glad he had appeared when he did. But my troubles were by no means over, however, because when I came out of the tunnel on the other side, I found I was on the approach road to a race track with the 'brmm brmm' of highly charged engines revving up, and a line of low-slung go-cars rolling down towards me. A red-faced man with an armband and a red flag rushed out and asked me angrily what I thought I was doing. He was not at all mollified by my plea of total ignorance of the area, and clearly thought I was a new breed of hooligan. I was given a stern warning about what would happen if I was ever again caught 'contravening safety regulations' before being directed onto a grassy track which led through several locked gates and stiles to the other end of an amputated road on the north side of the motorway. So tired was I with overcoming all these problems and with having to unload panniers and lift everything, including Evans, over the gates and stiles, that I gave up looking for a rational route, and took the first direct road I could find towards Hebden Bridge and lunch. Fortunately I found a canal running parallel and was able to ride on the towpath for a good part of the way, and so avoid the worse of the Sunday traffic.

Hebden Bridge was quite a tourist mecca and had a good few pubs along its pretty riverfront, many of them relics of coaching days and most of them packed to the doors. The one I selected was less crowded because it was the stamping ground of the local tough teenagers. Both boys and girls sported the same rigidly brutal style – leather-clad, ear-ringed, wildly coiffured and tattooed, chain-smoking, gap-toothed, their only adjective 'f-ing', and with an apparent desperate need to be disapproved of. It was currently a warm day and they were drinking pints of dark flat beer with ice in it. I felt sorry about their neglected teeth, but apart from the wreathes of noxious cigarette smoke they generated, they bothered no one.

With Hebden Bridge I had reached the centre of this strange part of the southern Pennines. Ringed as it is by industrial towns, this rough hilly area is arguably more valuable now as a leisure amenity than ever it was when every river valley was poisoned by the smoke of the 'dark satanic mills'. Now that the clattering machinery has been silenced, and it is no longer necessarily the case that 'Where's there's muck there's brass', the gaunt buildings fit surprisingly well into the natural hard landscape of moor, river and rocks. The canals, railways and reservoirs in which the area abounds, and which were all built for industrial purposes, now provide the descendants of exploited mill-workers, amongst others, with countless opportunities for outdoor activities. How would William Blake have seen this greening of the land in his scheme of building a new Jerusalem, I wondered, as I stood watching a newly-clean river flowing beneath the stone bridge.

If I found Hebden charming, with its old pack-horse bridge and its coaching inns nestling among the mills of the valley floor, it was only a prelude to a much greater delight. Clinging to the steep slopes of the moor above was a cluster of ancient houses called Heptonstall, to which I was able to ascend with comparative ease, thanks to the help of a strong young man who volunteered to push the laden Evans up in order to impress his girlfriend.

Heptonstall had been perched on its hillside since Saxon times. A township mentioned in the Domesday Book, it had struggled on in obscurity through the various vicissitudes of history until wool gave its leading inhabitants the opportunity for unprecedented wealth. In its century of prosperous flowering it had become an architectural gem, diverse and beautiful in an entirely small-scale and domestic way. Each house differed from its neighbours, but also harmonised perfectly with them and with the surroundings, and the quiet cobbled square of weavers' cottages was as charming as anything to be seen in the area. Taken altogether, it was not surprising that it had become another open-air museum. Its salvation, from the point of view of the present inhabitants, is that the cars belonging to the thousands of visitors have to be left down at Hebden – which is no more than poetic justice, seeing that it was Hebden Bridge that had eclipsed Heptonstall when the Rochdale Canal was opened in 1804.

By the time I had wandered around Heptonstall, together with several hundred other visitors, and had found the grave of its most infamous inhabitant – the notorious coiner 'King' David Hartley, hanged at York – I was more than ready to decide where I should pitch camp for the night, and to end a day that seemed as though it had gone on for a very long time, and had witnessed rather too many

difficulties overcome and too many inclines surmounted. My map
showed a wide area of moor before another industrial belt began, and I
decided to find somewhere to put up the tent in this open stretch.

It was easier said than done. I went on towards Hardcastle Crags
looking for a likely spot but finding none. I turned my back on the
road to Haworth and Brontë country, for the traffic was all going that
way and I had seen enough of other tourists for a while. A new lease of
energy came with the pleasure of cycling along an empty moorland
road in the clean fragrant air. On and on I rode over the unpeopled
Heptonstall Moor and Widdop Moor, finding nowhere that seemed
suitable to stop, for there was no natural cover, and I did not consider
it safe to camp alone in full view of a public road (Saddleworth Moor
had cast something of a shadow over my usual carefree attitude).

Only when I had crossed the border out of Yorkshire and was in
Lancashire did things look more promising. There was now some
evidence of agriculture, though no farmhouses were to be seen. The
road was about to start its descent to Burnley and Nelson when I
decided that there was nothing else for it but to dispense with
permission, and to turn off into any likely-looking place that offered
some privacy.

The first open gate I came to led into a very large field of rough
pasture that dropped away out of sight into a hollow, and was full of
thistles and rather old cowpats. I wheeled Evans in and found a spot in
the shelter of a hedge well out of sight of the road. The tent was up and
organised in less than five minutes, soup was bubbling on the stove,
and I was experiencing that lovely glow of contentment that comes
from having established a shelter for the night by my own efforts.
There is nothing quite like making a home where there was nothing
before but the bare ground, and where there will be no trace of my
temporary habitation next day after I have moved on. There was a
tribe in ancient Israel known as the Rechabites who would not build
houses, even centuries after they had settled in their promised land of
Canaan. God, they believed, wished them always to live in tents.
Bricks and mortar, in their eyes, were barriers to a sense of awareness
of Him, and Bedouin believe this too of their God, as perhaps do all
dwellers in tents. Certainly it is harder to be unaware of a wider world,
when separated from it by so fragile a skin.

I was thinking about the Rechabites as I lay in my tent in the
sleeping-bag after writing up my journal, when I thought I felt the

ground move. I was just in time to reach out a hand and pull back the tent flap, as the black and white pansy-like face of a large Friesian cow tried to thrust her way in. There were five or six other cows right behind her, all looking equally intent on crowding in to join me. As each one was twice the height of my little tent, the effect was droll, once I had got over the shock. Jokes about how many elephants can get into a Mini had taken on a new slant. I got up and herded them all down to another part of the field, hoping they wouldn't drift back in the night and trample on me, or get mixed up in the guy-ropes – cows are not the most comfortable of camping neighbours.

Later, lying in the tent in the soft light and warmth of a candle stuck safely in a multi-purpose cooking pan, I listened to a broadcast of Alexandra Boyd-Neel's *Tibetan Journey* on my tiny radio, which gave superb reception at that height. When it had ended and evensong had begun, I fell asleep with the earphones still in my ears and a cathedral choir singing the lovely anthem 'I was glad when they said let us go up to the house of the Lord'.

Several times in the night I awoke, once with the earphones digging into me, several times with the pain from an old shoulder injury that had been aggravated by the day's ride, and once when the cows came back and I had to get up and herd them back down the field again. Every time I awoke there was the lovely liquid sound of curlews calling, and once, very close, a snipe drummed.

CHAPTER EIGHT

The Lancashire Moors

The now familiar daily pattern of ups and downs began on a fine brisk morning in the Forest of Pendle. This is not a heavily wooded area as the name suggests, but a stretch of land that had once been a hunting preserve of the English nobility. Caught out by a sudden sharp incline, I fluffed a gear change and unshipped the chain, and after the messy business of replacing it on the chain wheel, getting black oil all over my hands in the process, I had to walk up until the slope flattened out a bit. A couple of spry old-age pensioners coming out of a camping site gate pounced upon me as though they imagined Pendle Forest was still hunting territory, and bicyclists legitimate quarry. They seemed eager to convince me that I was not getting the best out of life. Both of them had sets of false teeth that clattered unmusically as they fired off a rapid stream of rhetorical questions at me.

Why was I so heavily laden? they asked, sniffing at poor Evans as though he was giving off an offensive smell: 'Nasty things bikes; not safe; shouldn't be on the roads.' Before I had time to think of a suitable reply, they were attacking on another front. Camping was I? Tents were more nuisance than they were worth! Caravans, now they were ideal. They had a caravan; took it everywhere. They knew all the best camping sites. I could just see their caravan there over the hedge – lovely life! By this time I was feeling trapped, but they barred my way, and short of thrusting them aside I could see no way of escaping. Without a moment's pause, they were off on another tack. What did I think of this part of the world? they demanded suspiciously, as though, being a southerner, I might not view it with the right degree of respect. I said truthfully that I thought it was beautiful, but this was not enough. 'You'll not find anywhere better than round here, not anywhere at all,' they declared belligerently. Should they tell me the best places to see? They knew them all. I would have to see this, and I must not miss that. But what 'this', or 'that' might be I did not discover, because by that stage desperation had lent me strength, and I found I was practically running up the hill pushing the laden Evans as though he weighed nothing at all, while the clicking teeth and the busy voices slowly faded behind me.

I worked my way up and over the knobbly contour lines, through pretty agricultural countryside that was all small steep irregular fields and thick thorny hedgerows. A sparse scattering of farmhouses and modest halls were built of the same stone as those in the mill valleys I had left behind, but here there was no deep impregnation of soot, and the stone was an attractive pale grey. Below, richer flatter pastures edged a main road that seemed remarkably quiet. One glance at the map revealed the reason for this. With the advent of a new motorway, the road had become a backwater. By taking a sweeping line a mile or so to the south, to link the chain of towns from Blackburn and Accrington to Burnley and Nelson, the M65 had effectively released the area from the grip of heavy traffic and given back to the Forest of Pendle a large chunk of land with tremendous potential for recreational use.

The bare summit of Pendle Hill, a distinctive isolated outcrop of the Pennines nearly 2,000 feet high, dominated the skyline to the right. It had in former times a long and notorious association with sorcery and black magic – so much so that in 1612 ten women from the villages round about had been tried for witchcraft at Lancaster Castle, and sent to the gallows. I wasn't yet aware of this infamous history when a coven of leering black-clad pointy-hatted witches, all clutching broomsticks, met my startled gaze as I topped the very steep rise into Newchurch. This was one of the chief villages from where the poor wretches had been dragged to stand their parody of a trial, and their life-size effigies were now part of the attractions of a gifte shoppe selling whimsical souvenirs to tourists. It seemed a hard-hearted way to treat former citizens. But the attitude was quite in keeping with that of the landlord of Newchurch's only inn. This gentleman, with not one other customer to attend to, claimed to be unable to provide even bread and cheese for a hungry traveller because Monday was his wife's day off, and he didn't know his way around the kitchen!

There was nothing for it but to abandon all my hard-won elevation and descend to the main road at the valley bottom, where, after eschewing a pretentious roadhouse with banqueting suites and a menu that would have laid me low until nightfall, I found the delightful Bay Horse – a traveller's ideal halt. Over a plate of fine home-made steak and kidney pie and fresh vegetables – a bargain at £2.95 – and a glass of real ale, I felt moved to tell the landlord of my earlier attempts to obtain lunch. 'I'm afraid,' he said, 'that in this country people get civility mixed up with servility, and confuse service with being servile.'

Because of the detour for lunch I didn't take my intended route over Pendle, being unwilling to climb the same hill twice. Instead, I followed the valley of the Calder into Whalley, and not expecting anything but a dull urban scene, was delighted to find instead an attractive little town graced by the remains of a Cistercian abbey and a lovely thirteenth-century parish church with three tall medieval crosses in the churchyard. As always, I was grateful to find the church open when so many are closed because of vandalism and the difficulty of getting unpaid custodians. There was a woman there dusting the pews who turned on some lights for me so that I could see the intricately carved and canopied choir stalls and misericords that had found a home there after the abbey's demise.

North from Whalley I began my delayed ascent up to the edge of the Western Dales and the Forest of Bowland – another ancient hunting ground. Of the many rivers which flow south-westwards from the high Pennines, I had the lovely Hodder besides which to wind my way through a wooded valley, heavy with the scents of leaf-mould, wild garlic and cows. Trees towered over the landscape again, with the occasional rare elm reminding me of how much they are missed from the English scene since Dutch elm disease laid most of them low. So different a countryside from the previous day, this land had no need to be reclaimed because it had never been debased. Limestone underlies it, which makes the grass greener than that growing further east. The houses in the hamlets and villages are built of the same mellowed stone and are grouped together more informally than those I had passed through in Yorkshire. By no means a soft county, Lancashire seemed nonetheless very lush and pretty after the stern Yorkshire moors.

The Hodder Valley had been famous cattle rearing country for hundreds of years and it retained much of the feeling of eighteenth- and nineteenth-century rural paintings. One particular image of a large Friesian cow printed itself indelibly on my mind. It stood there as heroic-looking as a Minoan fighting bull, massive and quite motionless on a green knoll, with a shapely tree stump to one side adding interest and balance. Against a perfect backdrop of rosy clouds in a china blue sky, I could imagine it waiting there patiently while Landseer immortalised it upon a vast Victorian canvas.

I had planned to make camp for the night somewhere along the lonely Trough of Bowland, but when I came to Dunsop Bridge where I should have forked left, I suddenly felt a desire for human company and turned right instead, towards Slaidburn. Still following the Hodder, a narrower more winding road led up and down over small heathery hills, with little copses of ancient twisted trees and clumps of bracken. It was early evening now, with cattle and sheep calling from the distance; a hint of wood smoke hung in the air, and there was the feeling of being in another and altogether less frenzied time.

This sense of tranquillity increased as the road dropped down into a fertile little valley where the River Hodder joins the Croasdale Beck, with the pretty stone-built village of Slaidburn clustered around the confluence, shaded by enormous sycamore trees.

Slaidburn has two old inns. One of them, The Black Bull, is now a youth hostel, and here I booked a bed for the night. The building went back to at least the thirteenth century, new bits having been added on at different times, making a rambling building with a lovely jumble of tiled roofs. Nothing much had been altered since the late eighteenth century; it was somewhat decayed therefore, and the amenities were very basic, which made it all the more in keeping with the feeling of having strayed into a previous age. Evans was put away for the night in a crumbling stall that had once provided shelter for weary pack horses. It led off a grass-grown cobbled yard, with a few huge empty stone troughs around the edge, pink clematis growing against one wall, and wind-sown clumps of lupins, feverfew and hollyhocks among the stones. Eating a simple supper at a scrubbed table in the dark cavernous kitchen, I could well imagine myself a medieval traveller.

There were only two other guests, a probationary monk on a walking holiday, and Joyce, a woman of my own age, who was also bicycling. The novice monk disappeared after supper to say the office of Compline in the privacy of the men's dormitory, while Joyce and I exchanged stories in the manner of Chaucer's pilgrims.

The other inn was in a much better state of preservation. It was called the Hark to Bounty, a name it had acquired in the mid-nineteenth century, the landlord told me – before then it had been simply The Dog. In the year 1861, the story went, the master of the local hunt (who also doubled as squire and parson) was having a drink there when his hound Bounty had started baying somewhere in the distance, and the master's exclamation of 'Hark to Bounty' had stuck.

However it acquired the name, Hark to Bounty was a fine inn with a friendly atmosphere, good food and excellent beer, and a few comfortable bedrooms for passing travellers. Best of all, above the bar there was a banqueting floor with massive fifteenth-century oak beams and all the trappings of a Jacobean courtroom. Slaidburn had always had an importance that belied its size, partly because it lay on an old salt road. The only Assize court between York and Lancaster had been held there from the fourteenth century, and when the original courthouse had become too dilapidated for use, around 1670, the assizes were held in the inn. Few alterations had been made to the room since that time, and the magistrates' bench was still in place. The only significant difference was that the dock had been shifted from the centre to one side, where it now served the useful function of a bar – a change which would doubtless have pleased many of those who had once stood there awaiting their sentence.

The church was well worth a visit too, especially for its rare triple-tier Jacobean pulpit. As with so many English villages, the church was huge for the size of the place, so that one might suppose that the population had shrunk since it was built, though I do not think this was the case – the English have always had a propensity for building far larger churches than they need. Every country churchyard I had seen on this journey had been most beautifully kept, and this was no exception. With its seats and flowers and lovely views over the valley, it would perfectly serve the function of a park; which is how ancient Egyptians, Etruscans, Romans and others viewed the resting places of their dead – not as somewhere morbid and gloomy, but jolly places, the venues for picnics on feast days, where the shades of the departed could join in the celebrations. I met the newly installed incumbent, who told me that he was still treading warily as an 'off-cumden', which is what the locals call incomers. I gathered there were not many 'off-cumdens' in Slaidburn, as houses came up for sale only rarely. There was a fair amount of local work for the men in agriculture, forestry, and with the water board, so fewer people needed to move away. Perhaps it was this that gave the village its unusually settled and cohesive atmosphere, and its air of continuity. Even the village school, with the date '15 May 1717' written over the door, was still in use after nearly 300 years.

I awoke early the next morning to a truly summer's day, and cycled off amid the mixed din of baaing lambs, rude tractors, and the shouts of men going about their various agricultural tasks. It was a lovely start, but by the time I had retraced the four precipitous miles to Dunsford Bridge I felt I had already seen rather too many hills. Nonetheless the struggle up the long, lonely incline of the Trough of Bowland soon changed into something approaching enjoyment, the effort growing appreciably less once I was able to establish a rhythm. I am always grateful for the development of really low gears on occasions like this, for without them such hilly terrain would be beyond the scope of heavily-laden riders, especially those past their first youth – unless they are prepared to walk for miles. Once I had the pedals spinning properly, I could forget about the cycling and concentrate on the views over the miles and miles of wild fells.

I sped down the other side into a wide valley, with fields full of golden buttercups, the hedges creamy with hawthorn and spiked with ragged robin, camomile, dog roses and marguerite daisies, all seeming immeasurably rich by contrast with the fells. I was just writing down my impressions, leaning against a barn, with starlings flying in and out of the open doors carrying beaksful of sustenance for their young, when an old man shuffled up. He was eager to tell me all about his stroke and his subsequent bloodlessness – 'Always in the infirmary, me,' he said with pride. He didn't think I would make it to Lancaster – 'It's all o' twelve mile over the top, lass,' he said solicitously. Actually it was six. I said that I thought I had already been over the top. 'Nay, you seen nowt yet,' he replied. 'If you be going to Lancaster, you got the Jubilee Tower still to come.' I was so intrigued by the sound of this Jubilee Tower that I remained undaunted by the thought of yet another steep rise to toil up in the heat of the day. I asked him to tell me more about it. 'I don't know no more, nor yet whose jubilee it were, but 'tis there right enough,' he said. And so it was; a squat castellated tower, miles from anywhere at the summit of a taxing climb, a strange folly that seemed to have no reference to anything else at all. There were splendid views from the platform at the top, but no plaque at all to tell when it was built, or whose jubilee it commemorated – Queen Victoria's, I presumed, but it could equally well have been the squire of Slaidburn's memorial to his hound Bounty.

The glorious day grew ever more golden and unclouded. Sweat coursed freely down my face, for the terrain didn't relent until I was right down on the narrow coastal plain. But although hill followed closely upon hill, the hot sun seemed to relax all my muscles, particularly my shoulders, which tend to stiffen on a prolonged climb. My spirits soared, and being quite alone I was able to give vent to my elation in song. Not for the first time I reflected that whatever religion man follows, he is a sun-worshipper at heart. Sunshine affects our mood more than most of us would care to admit, and it colours our response to places – anywhere looks better by sunlight, even a slag heap.

My mood continued to reflect the day even in the bustle of Lancaster, which was undergoing extensive rebuilding, and which in any case had little more to offer than the chance to restock my food supplies. Going north from the town I had no alternative but to cycle along the dreaded A6. But even this was not nearly as horrendous as I had feared: much of the traffic it used to carry was now rushing along to the right of me, on the parallel M6. Twice in as many days I had found cause to be thankful for motorways – which made a change.

Like molten silver, the huge expanse of Morecambe Bay shimmered away to my left, the light striking blindingly on the radiant surface. I got off the A6 as soon as I could, turning into the little lanes that, together with a narrow railway line, follow the bay around Warton Sands towards the mouth of the River Kent. After weeks of moors and hills the seascape seemed strange and exciting. It made me want to stop and just gaze, for it seemed much too intricate a thing to be absorbed even at bicycle speed. In any case, I had come quite far enough for one day and it was time I stopped. The problem, however, as always, was to find somewhere suitable to pitch the tent.

It was an area that must have been quite marvellously beautiful in its natural state. The many small rivers draining into the bay have created a delta, where craggy wooded fingers of land thrust out seaward, separating the marshy creeks into diverse secret places, the haunts of a host of wading birds. At the tidal edge of this avian paradise, the mud gives way to a great expanse of golden sands that spreads, seemingly endlessly, with the ebbing tide. The light changes all the time, as it strikes off these varied surfaces of sea, wet sand, marsh, rock, and dark green foliage. For somewhere so close to large towns and a major holiday area, it had an unbelievably newly-made, pristine look about it.

Being well off the beaten track for either Blackpool or the Lakes, it doesn't suffer from crowds of visitors. Nonetheless it has attracted discerning settlers over the years, and although a large nature reserve protects the marsh birds, less has been done for the land itself, and bungalow developments straggle along the fringes of the sea. On and on I went, hugging the coast and looking for the perfect camping spot: nothing but an unbroken view, I felt, could do justice to such a scene. It took a couple of hours to explore all the possibilities of the small roads, each with its string of bungalows, or down-at-heel Victorian and Edwardian houses flanking more ancient fishing hamlets. The perfect places had been snapped up by developers long ago, and the less perfect were in the process of having new developments built on them. I was nearly at Arnside without having found anywhere suitable, and had almost decided to capitulate and go to an official site: but if I was prepared reluctantly to abandon my dreams of the perfect solitary spot with a view, I still had requirements about peace and privacy, and I had already rejected two unsuitable sites. The third one was very generous in the amenities it offered – washerette, cafeteria, toilet block and even an amusements room – and I thought it would have delighted the caravanning couple who had waylaid me in the Forest of Pendle. But I would not have enjoyed their pleasures, any more than they would have liked mine. When I camp, I like to be alone.

By this time I had more immediate needs than scenery to consider – a cup of tea being high on the list. Seeing a woman watering some hanging baskets of fuschia outside a modern bungalow, I asked her if she knew of somewhere I could pitch my tent. She immediately offered me the use of the huge field alongside her bungalow, occupied by a handful of her husband's pet Jacob sheep and a few hens. Adding to her kindness, she gave me the run of her bathroom and all the hot water I wanted – a luxury indeed, and one which after the Trough of Bowland I really appreciated.

For the sense of contentment I felt there, it was as good a camp site as I had found anywhere. The field sloped up towards some woods, so there was privacy as well as a view of the shining sea below, a few hundred yards away. In the short time it took to peg out the tent, release the valve on the self-inflating mattress and fluff up the sleeping-bag, the kettle had boiled, and I had a pint of tea to sip while I relaxed and watched little cotton wool clouds crossing the deep *lapis lazuli* sky. The four-horned Jacob sheep grazed on undisturbed by my presence, but the hens, recognising domesticity, had begun to gather stiff-legged and hopeful, with the sun full and golden behind them, shining through their crests and turning them into haloes. If the end of life is to learn how to be still and contented, as many philosophers have said that it is, then I thought this moment might well be a reflection of that state. I certainly wanted nothing else from life just then.

Dinner was a feast, thanks to the shopping I had been able to do in Lancaster: fried chicken, new potatoes and salad, with a glass of the wine that comes so conveniently in a can; yoghurt; cheese with bread (biscuits do not travel well); fruit; and coffee. I could prepare the entire meal without having to rise from the spot, for I had by now got my organising down to a fine art, and everything came to hand naturally. On my simple but efficient stove I fried the chicken in the frying-plate with a pan placed over it to prevent the fat spitting, and to enable it cook more quickly and evenly. While the potatoes boiled, the chicken went back on top, still in the covered frypan, which kept it warm and provided a lid for the potatoes. Water was boiling for coffee and for washing up while I ate.

Washing up out of doors is hardly a chore with all the diversions of nature around, and it is certainly much simpler than in a kitchen. A saucepan becomes the washing-up bowl. A few drops of detergent from the small plastic pill bottle, a quick rub with the third of a nylon scourer, a wipe over with the J-cloth and the pans are bright and clean again, ready for use as washbasin, candle-holder or whatever. The economy of effort is as satisfying as the food itself.

Janet, the lady in the bungalow, came by the tent later in the evening to ask me to come and have a cup of tea with her. She apologised for not asking me in for dinner. 'I'd have loved a talk,' she said disarmingly, 'I don't see that many people these days.' It was so lovely in the field in the cool dusk that I didn't really want to go back with her into the close, brightly-lit bungalow, so I offered her a glass of my malt whisky instead, and though she refused, she sat for a while and talked. She told me that she was looking after her ninety-three-year-old mother, and finding her life very circumscribed. 'It's all right for men,' she said, 'My husband's happy as long as he's outside; it's me who's stuck in the house.' She stopped herself abruptly. 'I won't get started on that,' she said, 'or there'll be no stopping me. One of these days though I'll get out and do something like you're doing.' She said this with such bitterness that I felt a twinge of guilt, fearing that I might have proved an unsettling influence, as the seafaring rat in *The Wind in the Willows* had been for Ratty.

As the conversation drifted on, it turned out that it was not so much looking after her mother that made Janet so dissatisfied with life. Her discontent seemed rather to be a common twentieth-century affliction – too much leisure combined with too much money. Both she and her husband had taken early retirement, she told me, and they had everything they wanted materially. She knew no one locally, having moved to the area a few years ago from a Midland town, and concentrated exclusively on the house and garden ever since. The large custom-built bungalow was fitted out with every luxury; a couple of expensive cars stood in the driveway; there was no shortage of money to pay for help with the aged mother. The real problem was that now that she had everything there wasn't anything left to look forward to, and because she didn't have enough employment, or hobbies to absorb her energy, she had lots of time on her hands to realise how dissatisfied she was. She wasn't just bored: she was facing the disturbing thought that having achieved everything she'd dreamed of hadn't brought the happiness she had anticipated. She was left with the nagging thought that 'there must be more to life than this', and the even more disturbing fear that perhaps there wasn't.

Isolation, boredom and disappointment – three of the evils of the affluent society were being compounded by sitting about in separate little boxes watching TV, and by driving around encapsulated in other separate little boxes. Janet's life was being lived at several removes, viewed through glass. On second thoughts I decided that it wasn't necessarily such a bad thing to be an unsettling influence. Even a mile or two on a bicycle through the lovely little lanes around her home could give her a whole new perspective on life.

Once I was tucked up snugly in my sleeping-bag, the sense of deep contentment I'd felt earlier returned. I lay watching thin streamers of bronze-coloured cloud drifting across the moon. Suddenly there was a great soughing of wings and four geese flew low across the field in a tight chevron. On they wheeled out over the estuary that was now the colour of dark pewter, flying along a wide moonlit swathe that stretched to the horizon.

CHAPTER NINE

The Southern Lakes

The pitter-patter of light rain awoke me at around six o'clock. Peering out at a low and heavily overcast sky, I snuggled deeper into my sleeping-bag, hoping for conditions to improve. Instead the sound grew to a heavy persistent drumming, and reluctantly I sat up and prepared breakfast, feeling betrayed by weather which yesterday had given every indication of having settled at last into full glorious summer. I plugged in my earphones to hear the news, and learnt that the latest motion to bring back the death penalty had been defeated, a blow for the 'flog 'em and hang 'em brigade' which somewhat cheered the day, and made my coffee and bacon roll taste all the better.

Striking camp in the rain means packing the panniers inside the tent, never a pleasant job as there is so little room to manoeuvre. Washing up, I could manage quite well in this excellent little tent; the only awkward moments came afterwards as I leaned across to tip the dirty water into the bare ground under the tiny porch; an incautious movement at this stage could saturate my entire home. This morning it went well, the ubiquitous second cooking-pan which doubled as the washing-up bowl when it was not being used as candle-holder, wash basin or anything else, depositing its half pint of sudsy water exactly where it should. I never cease to marvel at the worth of this multi-purpose piece of equipment – it makes me realise what a breakthrough the discovery of the gourd and the clay bowl were for mankind. Apart from the fact that my bowls are made of lightweight aluminium, there can be little difference in the use I put them to; another link with those early roving ancestors.

After washing up, I can begin to get everything into its correct container, and then into whichever of the four panniers it belongs. In theory I can do this blindfold, as each item has its precise place. But somehow this never quite works out. Extra things are acquired and have to be squeezed in somewhere; small items mysteriously disappear and turn up just as mysteriously in the wrong place. The

bulkier pieces don't get lost – the problem they present is
compressing them so that they take up the least possible space.
Stuffing the sleeping-bag into its sack is not all that hard, but
squeezing the air out of the self-inflating mattress and rolling it up
tightly enough to get it into its bag requires a certain amount of
contortion, and leaves me hot and flustered, particularly if I have first
gone through the claustrophobic business of wriggling into my
waterproof suit.

Special care was needed that morning to make sure that everything
was double-wrapped in plastic to keep it dry: no panniers are one
hundred per cent waterproof; rain will always find its way through
stitching and through the tiniest of pinholes. All this made the
process of packing up more laborious. However, as my present tent
is so much roomier than the ridge tent I used to have, I reminded
myself of how much worse it could be. Once I had tossed the tightly
packed panniers out through the door, and backed out myself, feet
first, on hands and knees, brushing away the crumbs and sand with
my J-cloth as I went, the worst was over. All that remained was to
take down the wet tent (counting the pegs to make sure I didn't lose
any), shake as much of the water off it as I could, and then roll it up
and stow it away. It was such a relief to be finally up and riding that
the rain seemed to matter less than it had done when I was thinking
about it.

It was hard going at first, pushing into a strong wind, but it was a
salt wind that veered and capered and gave a madcap exhilaration to
the day and a promise of better weather to come. The whole world
was on the march; great banks of pearly-grey translucent clouds
rolling in across the sea, gaining height rapidly as they met the
warmer land air. Torn shreds of cloud, caught in the down-
draughts, wreathed themselves around a broken tower, before being
whisked away again on an up-draught. A steady roaring came from
the trees, their tops bending, branches tossing to and fro, leaves
flailing and buffeting, straining to be off with the wind.

As I topped the rise at Arnside, grey shapes of distant hills came
into view to the north. Higher and craggier than any hills I had seen
so far on the journey, their dark silhouettes were separated from the
grey cloud about them by a slender glowing outline. The air was
warm and smelt of the sea, and the sky was not in the least
threatening in spite of the racing clouds. Around another corner and

the huge lovely expanse of Milnthorpe Sands appeared, pristine and fresh, newly washed by an ebbing tide. So swiftly was the cloud ascending now that beams of sunshine were breaking through, playing over the cliffs across the estuary, while my side still lay in shadow. The surface of the sea in between us looked like gently bubbling pewter – thousands of rounded facets catching the muted pearly light.

The wind, full in my face again, was blowing down the estuary, a palpable force, hard to fight. A few people were sitting in parked cars, reading newspapers, and a row of birds with ruffled feathers was busy at the tideline, each species oblivious of the other. Shelduck, oyster catchers, black-headed gulls, a tiny dunlin, a pair of hoodies, a single mallard, turnstones – all studies in concentration, each seemingly intent on the small patch of foreshore immediately beneath its pointing beak. But there was too much else going on to watch the birds. Suddenly, beyond the golden sands, the great precipitous mass of Coniston began to appear, as though a giant hand was peeling away the scudding clouds from its black rocky flanks.

I turned my back at last on the lovely estuarine world of shining pearly light, though the battle with the north-easter continued. Head down, eyes streaming, I made snail-like progress in a very low gear, until, after a mile or two on the A6, I crossed the River Kent and entered the Lyth Valley, where I had the shelter of the steep cliffs under Helsington Barrow.

The abrupt change to stillness was remarkable. There was still a great rushing of wind overhead, and an occasional torn green leaf cartwheeling down the road towards me, but otherwise all was tranquillity. There was no longer any lingering tang of the sea. I was among steep green fields, stands of timber, drystone walls and rich hedgerows. Ferns, celandines, clover, marguerites, yellow poppies, foxgloves, periwinkle, eyebright, vetches, birdsfoot trefoil, campion, nettles, ground alder, dandelion, bramble and a score of other flowers I couldn't identify growing in profusion beside the way, made a great wealth of colour and scent. A close, intricate landscape it seemed, but one that was certainly not over-peopled, and with very few animals.

The narrow green way passed through a few small hamlets tucked into the slope, with houses built above one another in tiers up the steep hillside. Each cottage garden was highly labour-intensive, stepped and terraced, and full of colour. I was invited into one where a couple had been hard at work weeding and planting. They had seen me coming and had called out to ask if I wanted to stop for a drink, adding that they were ready for a mid-morning break themselves. It was one more instance of the kindness and friendliness encountered by a lone cyclist. Apart from the always welcome refreshment, I find such encounters delightful for the glimpses they give into other people's lives.

Over mugs of tea and substantial slabs of sustaining fruit cake I learnt that my hosts had both taken early retirement and moved up here from Birmingham a year and a half before – she had taught and he was an industrial writer. Both were in their mid-fifties, and they felt that to have any chance of putting down new roots they couldn't have left their move any longer. About half the houses in the village were now owned by incomers like themselves, they told me, mostly from the Midlands, so it was not like trying to become accepted into an established group of people with a totally different ethos. They felt they were part of the formation of a new community, and were very happy about the amount of co-operation and friendliness there seemed to be between their new neighbours. Their own priorities were clearly worked out – a strictly utilitarian ordering of the house to allow them the maximum amount of time to cultivate the pretty garden, which was now their passion.

The great wind continued to tear the remaining cloud cover apart, until, after an hour or so, only a few wispy streamers remained very high in a blue sky. Out of the shelter of the tall cliffs every natural thing was dancing a different measure to the tremendous force. Over the hillsides long ripples of light and shade passed as the grass flattened and rose. The light, pendant branches of the silver birches streamed out horizontally, while broad-leaved trees like sycamores were one huge rustling undulating mass, their leaves standing on end, light undersides exposed. Saplings whipped to and fro, bending their heads almost to the ground at the fiercest blasts. Only the great Scots pines seemed hardly to stir, unlike the poor cyclist fighting to control a heavy load! But what a delight it all was too. No wonder children are bubbly and hard to handle on such bright days of high wind; it gets into the bloodstream and makes them want to run and dance, until it is almost impossible for them to stay still. I can remember how I used to think of the wind as a person when I was a very small child. I think I confused it with God, and imagined that if I could pray hard enough, it would pick me up and whisk me away out of harm's reach.

Once the sky was free of cloud the wind began to die away, coming round to the east at the same time, so that when I turned west to ride down to Lake Windermere it was no more than a pleasant breeze at my back. Having avoided the towns of Bowness and Windermere and arrived at the lake where the ferry crosses, I found it looking quite beautiful, like a serene early Turner, and not at all spoilt, as many reports make out. There were no 'rowdies' in motor boats – in fact there was hardly anyone about at all, just a few cars waiting to cross and a fisherman or two casting a line from the end of the jetty. Six fluffy grey cygnets swam to the steps with their immensely proud and stately parents, looking hopefully for a handout, but disdaining to linger when there wasn't one. They moved off, heads turning imperiously on those so elegant necks, as graceful a flotilla as one could see anywhere.

The lake water lapping at the shore brought an instantly-remembered combination of scents, less pungent than the all-pervading salt smell of the sea, but equally exciting. It had such an inviting beckoning feel to it that I couldn't resist, and taking myself off a little way down from the ferry I found a place to get undressed and go in for a swim. Cool browny green water folded itself about me, wonderfully soft, and so thick with algae and peat, and thousands of microscopic life forms, that underwater I could barely see further than my hand. All my tiredness sloughed off me like a skin, and I lay back enjoying the lake scene, gently kicking my legs to keep myself up.

This was Arthur Ransome territory, the setting for *Swallows and Amazons* and the other sagas of the Walker children and their friends the Blacketts, Dick and Dorothea and the rest – books portraying a world of straightforward real-life adventure, where villains were never very bad and certainly never frightening; a predictable world where children and adults had a clear role and always behaved decently. A generation of children between the wars eagerly awaited each new volume. They found themselves totally in sympathy with the characters and yearned for the day when they could make similar camping and sailing expeditions – delightfully freed, of course, from

the constraints of accompanying adults. It all tied in with the start of
the youth hostelling movement, and with an almost universal belief
in the intrinsic benefits of being outdoors. It was a time when
charities gave poor city children their first glimpse of the countryside, and made converts of them – to nature, if not to religion, as
had happened to Arthur Gee on his mission holiday in Hayfield.

Post-war generations brought up in a less trusting age have tended
to find Ransome's characters less convincing, harder to identify
with. And yet, now, in an era in which children are all too aware of
life's nastier realities, in which all too frequently they hear of the
dangers that surround them, with the media full of reports of child
murder, rape, drugs and other horrors, Arthur Ransome's books are
enjoying something of a comeback, sixty years after they were first
published. This has been attributed to the recent expansion and
interest in outdoor activities, but it has also been suggested that
Swallows and Amazons is read by today's children as escapist
literature, much as they will read space fiction and other fables. Sad
as it seems, few parents now feel able to allow their children the
degree of freedom that children like the Walkers enjoyed in the
Thirties.

Children, it appears, underneath the quasi-sophistication of this
materialistic society, can still relate to uncomplicated outdoor
experiences, especially when they include freedom from adults.
Perhaps they are also yearning for the lost innocence of a Golden
Age; though whether that world ever really existed, except for a
privileged few, is debatable. Safer it might have been in the Thirties
and Forties, war aside, but nasty things could and did happen to
children nonetheless. The main difference was that reports of such
things were not then so spread about as they are today by our huge
media network, avid for 'news'. Nor was it the custom in the
Thirties for parents and teachers to acquaint children with these less
pleasant facts of life, as they feel they must do now in the interests of
their safety. There is a very high price that today's child, and society
in general, must pay for this early knowledge of evil, and the
suspicion of people that goes with it – for trust, the psychologists
assure us, is the very basis of the growth of love. Books, like Arthur
Ransome's, that offer another range of possibilities and alternatives
are all the more valuable therefore, and I can only hope they continue
to be read and enjoyed.

As I floated further out in the lake imagining that the odd little movements I felt were fishes nibbling at a toe, I remembered that in the cold dark depths beneath me, lurked the strange and highly-treasured char. Windermere is as much as 200 feet deep in places and because its lower levels are considerably colder than might be expected, that most interesting of all Windermere's fish has survived. The char is more usually found in the Arctic, for he is a close relative of the salmon, and like him he is a salt-water fish who spawns in rivers. At some point in the earth's long evolutionary process, the char became landlocked in Lake Windermere and adapted to a fresh-water existence. His flesh is so highly thought of that there have been many occasions in the last few centuries when he was fished almost to extinction, 4,000 pounds being netted annually by the end of the nineteenth century. Before the days of railways and refrigeration, char were sent down to the tables of the great in London baked in pies, as costly a commodity as caviar. Even now whenever a few of them are caught, they are snapped up at once by the local hotels.

Char are no longer allowed to be netted, so fishermen troll for them from a slowly moving rowing boat, using an enormously long weighted line, which has several shiny hooked metal lures attached to it at intervals, so as to attract fish at different depths. I saw several examples of these unique tackles, each different and individually made, and later, at Coniston, I saw some actual char for sale, oddly enough in the butcher's shop. I didn't know what they were until I asked, and was most disappointed. I had expected something exotic – instead they were rather nondescript-looking, dark little fish, less than a foot long and weighing only about half a pound.

I waded out of the lake after my leisurely bathe, through thick shoals of minnows who were feeding on the plankton in the warm shallows. White-faced coots – the little clowns of the lakes and rivers – were zigzagging over the surface as though they were skating, heads bobbing as they went. There was a pair of shyer moorhens too, making sorties from under the overhanging foliage. Dragonflies hovered inches above the water, droning gently on stiff iridescent wings. It was such a limpid tranquil scene, with the long unruffled surface of the lake throwing back reflections of the sky, and the craggy fells rising up steeply all around, that I would have liked to stay. But the thought that, with the mid-day lull nearly over, the lake might suddenly erupt with noisy flotillas of pleasure boats, coach parties, and Ransome's 'hullabaloos' got me moving: I was lucky to have seen it like this, and I wanted to preserve the memory.

My last views of Windermere were from the small old-fashioned chain ferry that was carrying just three vehicles and Evans across the lake. Belle Isle, with its tall trees, hid the more populous upper reaches, while to the south were long quiet stretches of gold-flecked water.

Once on the other side, the lake vanished abruptly as I wound my way up to the low fells through the shadowy lanes of a forestry plantation. Above the tree line a narrow switchback road ran between low drystone walls. Behind the walls were small green fields, bright with buttercups and grazed by fat white sheep. A surprisingly quiet and idyllic little way, considering it was leading to the most visited house in all of Lakeland – Beatrix Potter's farmhouse at Near Sawrey.

Beatrix Potter had written her best work before she settled here at Sawrey, as the middle-aged wife of a local lawyer. What brought her from a conventional Victorian background in Kensington to this simple seventeenth-century cottage was, I like to think, something shared by Arthur Ransome's young characters – a kind of joy in being alive in such surroundings. She was shrewd, unorthodox, and a great benefactor to the National Trust (without her, one wonders if there would be a National Trust). Most importantly, she was a brilliant writer and artist in miniature. I had never read her as a child, and it was as an adult reading to my own children that I first came across her books. I was as captivated as they were, and have remained so.

Beatrix Potter's charming pictures have tended perhaps to overshadow her writing somewhat, but I find her stories equally as delightful; they are full of humour and have the same minute and meticulous attention to detail that she gave to the drawings. She was such a sly debunker of pompousness, and she had such an accurate ear for speech, that her prose rings clear as a bell – '"I am affronted," said Mrs Tabitha Twitchit'. Like many fine children's books, Beatrix Potter's deceptively simple little stories exist on many levels, and surely that is what accounts for their phenomenal and lasting success, rather than pure nostalgia for the lost world of the nursery.

For whatever reasons she is valued, the 80,000 or so annual visitors to Hill Top Farm pose a huge problem for the National Trust, who find it almost impossible to cater for them all. However, my luck held once more. There were no more than a couple of dozen people when I arrived, though even this number seemed a frightful crowd in the tiny cottage. When the coaches begin to roll in, as was happening when I left, it must be awful – and this was only early June. What it must be like in August doesn't bear thinking about.

In a real sense Beatrix Potter's books are the Lakes. She had known and loved them from childhood, when she spent long annual holidays there with her wealthy, oppressive parents. When she returned to her 'privileged' circumscribed and lonely life in a stuffy Kensington house, she was armed with scores of Lakeland sketches and lots of small live pets to keep her company and provide models for her sketchbook. Mrs Tiggy-winkle, Hunca Munca, Peter Rabbit: she knew them all intimately, and Mrs Tiggy-winkle travelled back and fro to the Lakes with her for many years. Brought up to be a dutiful Victorian daughter, subservient to her mother in all things, Beatrix Potter had no financial means of her own until her first two books, *Peter Rabbit* (initially rejected by several publishers, including Frederick Warne) and *The Tailor of Gloucester* were published in 1902, when she was thirty-six. *Squirrel Nutkin, Benjamin Bunny, Two Bad Mice* and *Mrs Tiggy-winkle* followed hotfoot, and a change of circumstance for their author now seemed possible.

She was nearly forty and still living under the parental roof when she bought Hill Top Farm in 1905. It did not give her an immediate independent existence. She was still the dutiful daughter of demanding parents, and the cottage was no more than a bolthole whenever she was able to get away from London. For the next eight years she spent only some three months there each year, in odd snatched weeks. Yet during those years she produced a further thirteen highly successful books, and started buying up chunks of the surrounding Lakeland property with the proceeds.

At the age of forty-seven, against the wishes of her parents, Beatrix Potter married William Heelis, whom she had come to know through the acquisition of her new properties – and that was more or less the end of her writing career. Now that she could at last live in her beloved Lakes, she had no time left over to devote to books. As Mrs Heelis she moved into Castle Cottage across the way and began on a new career of raising prize Herdwick sheep, a passion that would last for her remaining thirty years.

She turned Hill Top into her personal museum – the home, one might say, of her literary characters. She added to its traditional furniture with bits and pieces that came her way from a now fast vanishing period. Even without the associations it is a fascinating museum of seventeenth-century rustic Lakeland interiors.

The income from her books she continued to use for buying up Lake District farms, in order to save the land from the property developers. Beatrix Potter was a conservationist before the word became common parlance. She bought land to give directly to the National Trust (often anonymously), and the rest would go to them in her will.

When she died in 1943, at the age of seventy-seven, she had accrued £200,000 and 4,000 acres, and she looked, said her friends, like Mrs Tiggy-winkle in person – a battered old bonnet on her head, bundled up in layers of old tweeds, wearing clogs, and very, very small.

The clogs are still there in Hill Top, beside the open hearth in the stone-floored kitchen that one enters straight through the front door. It is a room with which one is immediately familiar, having seen it from many angles on many pages. The oak dresser, the long-case clock, the patty pans and fire-irons – the place is a shrine. It needs only the characters to enter – Tom Kitten, Pigling Bland, Jemima Puddle-Duck, Miss Moppet. If only one could hear above the excited chatter of visitors identifying this and that, surely there would be 'extraordinary noises overhead' from Tom Kitten, Mittens and Moppet, all supposedly 'in bed with the measles'.

Shrewd, perceptive Beatrix Potter to have her ashes scattered in some secret spot, and to leave this one evocative memorial to her life and work. And if it is a shrine, then the high priestesses are certainly the National Trust ladies who administer the place and guard the magpie treasury. They know every detail of every book and every detail of Beatrix Potter's life, and they employ a certain waspishness in correcting visitors' misapprehensions and incorrect identifications. Small wonder really, for the post is no sinecure. As one of these ladies assured me, a most vigilant eye has to be kept on every visitor and every tiny item, or the one will disappear into the pocket of the other. It is an aspect of the job that shocks her deeply.

I wondered whether I should tell her that it was ever thus with pilgrims. Once the holiest man in all of the Byzantine empire, Simon

Stylites, had lived on top of a pillar, which was as tall as Nelson's column. He had done this in order to commune with God away from the distractions of life. Within a year or two of Simon Stylites' death, pilgrims chipping away splinters of his marble shaft for souvenirs had reduced it to a little stump, small enough for a child to sit upon.

CHAPTER TEN

A Forest in Lakeland

After the emptiness of the roads I had been following all day, my arrival in Hawkshead was traumatic. A world which, up to that moment, had seemed all of a piece and singularly harmonious was, in an instant, fragmented and unreal. It was like straying onto a filmset where people were acting out their drama against a painted backdrop of entirely the wrong period; the two halves just didn't match. The pretty little period town – probably the best preserved in the whole Lake District – has narrow winding cobbled streets, ancient coaching inns and linked squares of grey stone and timbered houses. But it was so dwarfed by coaches and inundated by crowds of tourists as to have all but disappeared beneath their onslaught.

Hawkshead was once a market town and has a history stretching back into medieval times. The centre of a thriving woollen trade, its wealth was established long before the Industrial Revolution concentrated the cloth industry in the Midlands. Tourists bring wealth to the town now, and Hawkshead's shops were entirely geared to their needs. All the genuine pokey little village stores (many of them models for Beatrix Potter's illustrations) were selling a wide selection of the usual souvenir tat, including the very worst in whimsical tartan nick-nackery from over the border – though not necessarily the Scottish border, since much of it was made in the Far East. For the wealthier, or those who must presumably spend much of their holidays restocking their wardrobes, there was a large purpose-built store selling high-priced designer clothes and accessories, the plate-glass windows of which could have swallowed several of the little grey cottages. It was obviously necessary to have a large car park, and possibly the large modern restaurant next to it as well, but it should not have been beyond someone's wit to disguise their militant ugliness.

Lakeland's most famous son, William Wordsworth, was sent to Hawkshead's distinguished little grammar school in 1779, after his mother died. He was then nine years old, and reputed to be rather wild. Annie Tyson, the widow of a joiner, with whom he was put to board seems to have grown very fond of him, and was able to replace some of the love and affection he had lost with his mother's death. It had been assumed that Annie Tyson's house was in Hawkshead itself, and so the picture postcards and the signposts still maintain. However, in the course of her buying up of local properties, Beatrix Potter came upon papers which showed that Mrs Tyson had moved to a neighbouring village by the time Words-worth was boarding with her – a piece of scholarship which, if it was heeded, would cause the coach parties to have to walk an extra half-mile.

William Wordsworth, like the later Swallows and Amazons, was another who enjoyed considerable outdoor freedom early in life, roaming the fells and lakesides, and staying out half the night when he was still just a ten-year-old. Hawkshead was the only settled home he had as a child, and his attachment to it was strong. Even after he went up to Cambridge he returned to spend his holidays at Annie Tyson's house, and the remainder of his life was spent within a day's walk of the place. Wordsworth memorabilia are not all that plentiful considering the prosperity he has brought to the town. The only significant building associated with him is the little eighteenth-century grammar school, preserved as it was in his day, even to the desk he sat at, scored by generations of schoolboys' pocket knives; but I felt that his shades had departed the besieged town long since.

I soon escaped along a minor road on which I felt reasonably sure that no large luxury coaches would pursue me. It ran down towards the west side of Esthwaite Water, a small lake on which Wordsworth used to skate as a boy. No one seemed to be using the road today, and thinking that I might find somewhere there to camp, I cycled on beside the shallow reed-fringed little stretch of water until I was about as far south again as Hill Top Farm, and less than a mile away from it across the water.

A suitable camping place did not, for once, take long to discover. I enquired at a house standing alone in a neat little garden by the side of the road. It was all overhanging eaves and rustic timbers, and called, appropriately, Swiss Cottage. The owners had another garden which ran down to the water's edge on the other side of the road, and I was given the use of this for the night, together with a key to lock the gate. There was a rustic table and bench to sit at by the lakeside, a small shed for Evans – and for me too, should it come on to rain, for there was another table and chairs inside, and windows looking out onto the water. Mature trees and bushes screened me from the road and afforded shelter and privacy, and a soft mossy lawn overhung by other trees provided the most luxurious pitch I had yet encountered. This was grade one luxury camping. There was even an outdoor loo and a water tap beside Swiss Cottage, so I need bother no one.

Not that the owners, Mary and David Hawkes, minded in the least being bothered they told me later, when they asked me in for a drink. They had lent their lovely little lakeside garden to other cyclists, they said, and their feeling about it was that if you were lucky enough to live somewhere like this, it was only fair to share it occasionally with people who could appreciate it.

David Hawkes, a man of about my own age, was the District Forester at Grizedale Forest, a large area of about 8,000 acres between Coniston Water and Windermere, owned by the Forestry Commission. He spoke with great enthusiasm about his work there, urging me to make a detour and visit the forest the next day, adding that it had very good trails through the woods for cyclists. Having spent a great deal of my life in places where the Forestry Commission has ruined vast areas of ground with endless regimented squares of low-grade timber, I had acquired a deep antipathy for the organisation. The last thing I wanted to do was to spend time cycling through these particular stands of boring gloomy spruce trees, but I could hardly say this to a man who had been so hospitable to me, and whose whisky I was drinking. I murmured something non-committal and changed the subject.

The sun had all but disappeared behind the Langdale Pikes when I got back to my idyllic camping site again. As the last flushes of yellow and pink faded away in the darkening sky, catspaws of wind began to ripple across the surface of the lake, bending the tops of the reed beds at the water's edge with soft little susurrations. There was a peninsular jutting out to my left, and I swam out beyond its inky shadow just as a pale carpet of moonlight began to spread out over the water. A moorhen squawked its indignation at my invasion of the territory and made off. Wingbeats of unseen birds passed low overhead: there were splashings and ripplings, and a variety of calls from all around as birds landed on the lake, or settled down in the reeds for the night. As silently as I could, I made back for the dark shore and the darker little rounded hump that was my cosy nest.

Feeling virtuously clean after my second bathe of the day, and smelling pungently of lake water, I lay in my sleeping-bag watching the first stars appear in a sky that still had fading scraps of duck-egg blue in it. The land birds too were going through their last little flurries of activity before settling down for the night – a scrap of a thrush's song here, an answering note there, a rustling in the trees and bushes, until, finally, a deep silence prevailed everywhere. There seemed to be a pause as though nature was also putting up her feet after a hectic day, and with the stillness there came again that sense of absolute contentment. The silence lasted for about as long as it takes to breathe in and out once, and then the wind returned from the north-east, sending little waves splashing against the shore, masking the small stealthy sounds of timid nocturnal creatures beginning to go about the night's affairs.

'Awoke at 4.30am.' runs my journal 'to a blare of birdsong. Sky red, turning to yellow. Shoulder painful.' And as soon as I read the cryptic line I can see Esthwaite Water – dark brown, flecked with white, the waves still vigorously slapping and splashing on the mud and shingle, and the reed beds swaying and sighing. A fat thrush stands about three feet away to the left and a robin two feet to the right, both helping me to eat my breakfast. The robin stayed put throughout the slow packing-up that followed, flying to new low vantage points as I moved, regarding me with an unblinking scrutiny, head quizzically on one side.

Fine warm mornings like this are one of the chief joys of camping, and waking up on such a morning with the dawn chorus seems entirely proper. A friend of mine used to divide people into 'larks' and 'owls'. Larks functioned at their best early in the day, while owls were naturally more alert at night. I think I am a mixture of both; if I had to choose, I would settle for mornings, but I can also enjoy staying up far into the night. What I could most easily dispense with is the afternoon, the deadest point of the day for me. The Mediterranean practice of a long mid-day siesta would suit me very well. On this particular morning, by 8.30 a m, when I was ready to set out, I had already had four hours in which to absorb one small corner of the Lake District. It is no wonder that it is so engraved upon my memory – or that I so often feel like curling up for a sleep after lunch.

When I went to say goodbye and thank you to the Hawkes, David had already left for work, but Mary was still around, clearing away breakfast before she too went off to her job in the Forest Visitors' Centre. She said that David had been disappointed not to have seen me before he left, as he had been hoping to persuade me to change my mind and visit Grizedale. He hadn't wanted to disturb me however, in case I was still sleeping. 'Do come,' said Mary impulsively. 'It's worth seeing.' Not wishing to appear churlish, I said I would.

Almost as soon as I turned onto the forestry road I was glad I had changed my mind. This was nothing like the usual area of regimented low-grade timber, but an interesting and varied landscape. Even the spruce had been planted with some attempt to make their lines harmonise with their surroundings, and on this sunny morning they looked quite pleasant. A half-hour's ride along empty morning roads brought me to the Visitors' Centre, which alone would have been worth the detour. Everything here spoke of attempts to make the forest available to the general public, while at the same time providing a habitat for wild life, of which there were several endangered and rare species already breeding there, such as crossbills and polecats. It was all a far cry from the locked gate policies of the Forestry Commission which I had been used to only a few years before.

The Centre was also the hub of the forestry operations and was housed in buildings of a former estate which, although not old, had a pleasingly mellowed appearance. The walled garden was used for plant propagation and was lined with specimens of the bewildering large family of fir and pine, all neatly labelled, but all so similar that I didn't think I would ever learn to tell most of them apart. At one end was the most attractive children's playground I have ever seen. It had been made by a sculptor out of timber grown in the forest, and each piece was enchanting, as well as providing exciting opportunities for play. There was a giant robin with a slide concealed in its back; a hedgehog made of graduated lengths of tree trunks set on end; and much more in the same vein.

A purpose-built exhibition room with good audio-visual aids explained the history of the forests from earliest times. In imaginative displays it showed their growth, destruction and rejuvenation, and the industries associated with their different periods. There were lovely forest dioramas, with lots of stuffed animals and birds (all victims of natural causes, I gathered, unlike their Victorian forerunners) and diagrams to identify them by. I always enjoy these exhibits for the realism of the taxidermy and the settings, coupled with the sheer numbers of creatures in such a small space, predators and preyed-upon, all amicably cheek by jowl. It lends an air of fantasy, a glimpse into an ideal world – rather like Isaiah's vision of the lion lying down with the lamb. They were popular with the children too, who were now beginning to roll in by coachloads with their teachers.

Mary Hawkes, presiding at the counter of the excellent book and gift shop – no tourist tat here – took time off to show me the elegant little theatre – the Theatre in the Forest – which had a year round programme, ranging from an 'evening with Ken Dodd' to string quartet recitals. By this time I was quite ready to echo Ken Dodd's commendation, writ large on the billboard – 'I didn't know forests could be like this.'

David Hawkes then took me for a guided tour of some of his favourite places, after which I was close to forgetting how much I had previously disliked the Forestry Commission. I was interested to hear his views on today's forestry problems – the inheritance of years of poor management and short-term commercial interests in tree-planting that have wreaked such havoc in marginal lands throughout Britain. Many authorities suggest that the leaching of the soil which has resulted from such poor husbandry might well prove irreparable in some places. I found David had less pessimistic views. He seemed to think that harmful practices had already been abandoned just about everywhere, and that a start had been made on reversing the damage. On the desirability of phasing out low-grade timber in favour of restoring indigenous broad-leaved forests, he also had different views to those of most conservationists. He thought there was room for both, and his arguments made me aware of some of the more recent complexities which I had not considered. I might not have been totally convinced by his arguments, but I couldn't have doubted his enthusiasm for forests in general and for Grizedale in particular.

Grizedale was fortunate in never having been totally denuded of its native oaks and other broad-leaved trees, as so many re-afforested places were, so the problems here were less acute anyway. It possessed great natural beauty, but what was even more outstanding was the way in which that beauty had been made available to the general public without detracting from it. 'Trees are for people' was Grizedale's policy, and the results were impressive. A network of paths and roads opens up most of the forest to walkers, and quite a considerable amount is available to cyclists as well. Little of it remains static for long – paths change as new areas are being felled or replanted, for it is still primarily a commercial forest. The dynamic atmosphere of the place was, I felt, due in great measure to this interaction between working and leisure environments. If that policy could be taken as a general one right through the Forestry Commission's lands, as David claimed was happening, then it indicated a new sense of accountability in this erstwhile stiff-necked and high-handed organisation, which I could only rejoice in, even while I still had difficulty in believing in the change of heart.

But the real delight of Grizedale for me was its sculptures, and the role they played in the interaction of the visitors with the forest environment. They were scattered amongst the growing trees, over an area of several square miles. If I say that many looked as though they had grown there, it is by way of a compliment, for each of them had been created for its particular site and were meant to be a part of the forest, so that there were no plinths or fences to separate them from their surroundings. The creations of individual artists who had been granted a working residency at Grizedale for a few months, they varied tremendously in scope and style, though all had arisen from the forest environment and the artist's relation to it. Everything had to be made out of the natural materials of the forest, so that they would decay with it, at the same rate. Some pieces were naturalistic representations of forest life – a marvellous family group of wild boars in a mud wallow; a stag newly-alerted in a clearing; three human figures from a distant age deep in conversation. Some were witty or plainly humorous. Some were vast works; some quite small. Still others were highly abstract, dealing with the spaces, and relating to distant hills, and to the fabric of the place. Others gave a sense of age-old worship. All were tremendously exciting within their context, and lifted forest wandering to a new dimension.

I watched some of the youngest visitors exploring the trail closest to the Centre. Their joy in running and playing among the trees after being cooped up in car or coach was clear, and their laughter rang out infectiously. And their reaction to the stag sculpture, the first they came upon was also lovely. Many seemed to think that it was real at first, and their faces went through a range of emotions from awe to fear that it might run off before they had properly seen it. As each child came in sight of it he or she abruptly stopped stock-still, and then beckoned excitedly to his or her companions to come quickly and look.

One of the artists, Don Rankin, had created his sculpture in the playground of the local primary school. Working with the children, he had constructed a fort along the top of a natural rock face that edged the playground. It was made entirely of small flat pieces of local slate, laid as in drystone walling. Hugging the contours of the rock as though growing out of it, the battlements, towers and curtain walls were as breath-stopping in their own way as my first sight of a crusader castle on a desert hill in Syria. I was not surprised that it continued to delight the young pupils. Every so often Mr Rankin returns, and together he and the children construct another stretch of it. It would be hard to imagine a better introduction to art.

The lunch that followed this impression-packed morning, which had already lasted eight and a half hours, was worthy of the occasion. Since I had not been able to replenish my supplies at Hawkshead, I couldn't picnic, and went instead to Grizedale Lodge, a small family hotel just up the road from the Centre, noted for its food. I had an interesting soup made from fresh lovage, and a local trout which had been newly caught and tasted as a trout should, for like the Hayfield hens it had fed upon the sort of food nature intended for it. A short rest beside a hedge in a green field with Dvorak's cello concerto coming sweetly through my earphones and I was ready to cycle through the forest paths to Coniston.

I had to stop at a fork to ask a couple of forestry workers if I was on the right track, and one of them asked in turn if I was Bettina Selby, because he'd heard from Mr Hawkes that I had been visiting Grizedale. It turned out that he was a keen cyclist and knew my name from reading some of my articles in magazines and was glad of the opportunity to 'talk bicycles'. He hadn't long been with the Forestry, and he said he and his wife were still counting their blessings over their removal to the Lakes. What a change from Coventry, and what marvellous cycling! You could go for miles on these tracks and never meet a soul. It was a different life here altogether, lived at a different pace. He would never go back to city life.

He was right about the forestry roads. Apart from a casual encounter with three friendly muddy hounds who lolloped out of the trees – they should have been on leads – and jumped all over me as though they were half-heartedly attempting to bring down a deer, I saw no other life that wasn't indigenous to the forest. It was like being back a couple of hundred years, when all roads were dirt tracks. Peak after peak kept appearing as the road topped each new ridge, each peak looking totally individual and different in outline from its neighbours. It was all so varied there was no chance of becoming used to it, or of taking it for granted.

It wasn't until I was out of the shelter of the forest and had reached Coniston that I realised how cold the day had grown. Changes come quickly in the Lakes, and the unseasonable north-easter had been busy piling up yet another impressive sky, full of grey moisture-filled clouds. Since there was a youth hostel in Coniston with soft beds and lots of hot water, I booked in and gave myself up to a night of luxury.

One indolence leads to another, and having inspected the rare but untempting char at the butcher's, I decided I couldn't be bothered cooking dinner, not even in the comfort of a hostel kitchen with a proper stove and a wealth of culinary aids, and went out to explore instead.

Coniston was a workmanlike little village, attractively combining economy with good local building materials. There were very few pretensions to elegance, since it had arisen essentially as a centre for copper-mining, an occupation which had been carried out in the immediate area for centuries, ceasing only after World War I. Many of the cottages had been built without mortar, employing the same superb dry-walling techniques with flat slates that Don Rankin had used in his model castle. These slates were not the uniform colour of Welsh or Ballachulish ones, however, but varied from a soft green through to a grey that was almost black, so that there was a pleasing liveliness to the houses too. High craggy hills reared up very close all around, with the Old Man of Coniston a hoary bastion to the west. A few superb specimen trees – several cedars and giant redwoods – grew in the sheltered gardens of the larger houses on the outskirts, particularly in that of the youth hostel, which had once been rather grand, though who had owned it and planted the trees I did not discover. The size reached by trees in these sheltered places indicated how splendid the natural forests must once have been.

Until the days of macadamised roads, Coniston Water was the main highway to the area from the south, and along its length has come huge quantities of charcoal from Grizedale Forest for the smelting of iron ore. A straight five-mile stretch of sheltered water, it was also where Donald Campbell made his last attempt on the world's water speed record in 1967, when *Bluebird* turned over at 300 miles an hour and broke up. Neither Campbell's body nor the bulk of the wreckage of *Bluebird* was ever recovered from the lake's depths.

I had been intending to walk down the lake to see the famous views from Ruskin's house, Brantwood, but in view of the lowering skies I followed instead a sign 'to XVIth Century Inn 150 yards'.

This turned out to be an excellent choice even though it was actually nearer 300 yards, and straight up the side of a precipitous mountain. I found it a rare pearl amongst inns when I panted up to its front door – open log fire, stone-flagged floor and genuine beams that were not hung all over with phoney horse brasses. There was a friendly informal atmosphere around the large scrubbed tables in the public bar, and people talked to one another as they tucked into excellent soup and crusty bread and good ale. I must have done my share of talking too, enthusing apparently over the joys of a bicycle tour, because many months later I received a card with a signature I didn't know, posted from some remote village in Africa. It read: 'Remember the pub in Coniston? Took your advice, bought a bike and here I am. Wonderful.' I have absolutely no recollection of giving any such advice but I wondered if the sea-faring rat looked over my shoulder as I read the card.

CHAPTER ELEVEN

Storming the Passes

A single small black arrowhead drawn across a road on the map indicates a steep gradient, and more than one a hill of extreme and continuing steepness. There were a dozen of these little black barbs ornamenting the route I proposed to take westwards towards the coast, which suggested that Wrynose Pass would present quite a challenge, especially as the last six chevrons were placed close together in the final half-mile.

It was a particularly lovely morning when I set out, with Lakeland wearing its picture postcard guise – Coniston Water serenely blue, the tall trees along the narrow valley bottom in full fresh leaf, and great thickets of mauve rhododendrons flowering profusely on the lower slopes of the fells. The softly luminous morning sky, with just a few fluffy puffs of cumulus clouds sailing gently across it, gave promise of a hot still day to come. Every detail of the hills stood out clearly, looking even closer than they had the previous night – an integral part of the immediate landscape and not at all remote, as mountains usually are in Scotland.

My first climb came early on the main A593, along which I was hurrying in order to get clear of it before the coaches started to crowd the roads on their way to the hallowed centre of Words-worth's cottage at Grasmere, and the cosmopolitan delights of Ambleside. The turn-off for Wrynose Pass came a mile beyond the summit of this first warming-up ascent, by which point I had lost all my hard-gained elevation and descended again to my former height above sea level, and had immediately to begin climbing once more.

The minor road was in no hurry to settle down to any particular direction, but dipped and twisted and turned in the most delightful manner, presenting a different view of the hills every few yards. This helped to take my mind off the remorseless upward trend – four chevrons in just over a mile. Thanks to my low gears I just managed to keep the pedals turning, and didn't have to walk. Nevertheless, when I arrived at the summit of that particular climb, in the

charming hamlet of Little Langdale, I must have looked quite hot
and puffed, because a woman working among the flower beds in
front of her pretty drystone wall cottage said, 'You set yourself
down there, my dear, while I get you a nice cold drink.' The lemon
barley water and the easy chat about pansies and hollyhocks and the
lovely weather were wonderfully restorative.

Two chevrons pointing the other way squandered most of my
latest gains, and brought me cool and windswept to Fell Foot and the
meeting point of two waters running down from the high tops. This
was the sort of place I could have lingered in for a long while,
listening to the larks spinning their threaded songs as they swung
higher and higher into the sparkling blue, and watching the dippers
bobbing their long tail feathers over the streams. But already the
exhausts of the day's first cars were beginning to taint the fresh
mountain air, and it seemed best to go on before their numbers
increased even more alarmingly on that narrow unfenced mountain
road.

With the restocking I had done in the Coniston shops, Evans and
his gear now weighed about ninety pounds, far too much for these
hills. My store of energy had already been depleted by the earlier
climbs, and in any case the cars left me little room to take the
corners. It was not long before I was off and pushing, bent almost
double, arms at full stretch, body parallel to the ground, feet flat on
the tarmac for maximum purchase. On the extreme one-in-four
gradients only my toes could maintain contact, the calf muscles
shrieking with the unaccustomed strain. Sometimes it was all I could
do just to hold the bicycle stationary against me as I stood gulping in
oxygen – together with the unwanted carbon monoxide – and
waiting for a new lease of energy.

Pushing a heavily-laden bicycle up a steep hill is desperately hard
work; much better to stay in the saddle and keep riding up in a really
low gear. On these long unrelenting gradients, however, it would
need a Tour de France rider to keep the pedals turning, and I doubt if
even he could have done it laden down with the luggage I had
aboard. Had I been on a similar hill in Scotland, a driver would have
stopped and suggested taking the panniers to the top for me; I was
even offered such assistance by a Bedouin once, when I was climbing
out of a remote deep wadi in the deserts of southern Jordan. But
going up Wrynose Pass on a hot day, choking in the dreadful pall of

exhaust gases from the overworked cars, now bumper-to-bumper, no one thought to do anything but wave, or call out such pleasantries as 'My God! It's all we can do to get up here by car!' The irony was that even with all that expenditure of effort, I could still have enjoyed the ascent for the tremendous views of the peaks and fells that were opening up all around, but that the noise of the revving engines and the choking fumes spoilt everything.

Nor was that the end of my bitterness towards motorists on this particular day. For when I finally reached the top of Wrynose Pass each side of the unfenced mountain road was littered with parked cars for hundreds of yards, the ground torn and rutted by their wheels. The occupants were wandering off in all directions to enjoy the high places that they had reached by no effort of their own, leaving every lovely prospect framed by a parking lot.

The wildest and most spectacular landscape I had seen so far in England spread out all around. Far below, from where I had come in what seemed a surprisingly short time, was the valley of Little Langdale, a jigsaw of small fields, tenderly green in contrast with the rock and the grey-green herbage of the heights. Ahead, beyond the Three Shire Stone that marked the spot where the boundaries of Lancashire, Cumberland and Westmorland touched, was an inviting ribbon of road twisting down to another meeting of waters.

At the bridge the ways divided also, with the old Roman road continuing on over Hard Knott Pass – ten feet higher than Wrynose, and meriting seven little chevrons on the map. An even narrower way snaked away to the left. The stream of cars, like an endless line of toiling ants, was moving inexorably up to Hard Knott, but nothing seemed to be turning left. Consulting the map, I saw that this left fork led down through the Duddon Valley to Ulpha. From Ulpha I could head right on another lane over Birker Fell, to rejoin the Roman road at the foot of Eskdale. This way it would take at least twice as long to reach the same point, and if I took it I would miss the remains of the Roman fort on Hard Knott – but these were small sacrifices to make if I could escape the traffic.

Once I had entered the Duddon Valley, the change was as immediate as turning a knob on a radio. From the roaring of engines and the squealing of brakes, the fumes and the dust, I moved into a chorus of birdsong, the music of a merrily gurgling beck, and the faint purr of Evans's tyres on the smooth tarmac. The pot-pourri of evocative valley scents was just as suddenly unstoppered – hot sun on rock, water, resinous trees, grass, heather, and a hundred other subtle scents of growing things. The stony summit of the Grey Friar and the steep faces of Seathwaite Fells were on my left, while on the right Harter Fell rose serenely above the woods that clothed its lower slopes. Now I had the peace and freedom to enjoy what was there, the day as suddenly assumed a splendour that made me want to join in the bird chorus with my own 'Te Deum'. The only vehicle I saw in the next hour was a battered old van with a well-mannered collie dog hanging out of one of the windows.

It took me considerably longer than an hour to cycle the five miles to Seathwaite because the way there called for so many stops to look at views and waterfalls, and small happenings like a hawk hovering above the trees, or a bird splashing in a puddle in the road. I stopped to boil a kettle at the side of the little river, and as I sat there drinking coffee, my eye was caught by the sudden iridescent blue sparkle of a kingfisher, flashing out of sight over the water almost before I had registered its presence.

Seathwaite almost didn't exist, it was so small, but it had a simple little church with a newspaper story about a previous incumbent, 'the wonderful walker' framed upon a wall. I felt this could have been an object lesson to tie in with my recent thoughts. The 'wonderful walker' had been the parson in this tiny church for sixty-three years, on £5 per annum, and had reared a large family, eking out his livelihood with a little sheep-rearing. His life spanned the mid-eighteenth to the mid-nineteenth centuries, and he died aged ninety-three, after a 'frugal life with no moments wasted in recreation'. He had apparently walked tremendous distances preaching the gospel, at a time when walking wasn't thought of as 'recreation'. After his death the large flat stone on which he had sheared his sheep had been converted by his parishioners into a sundial, which stood before the porch door as a reminder to others that time flies.

There was a small inn close by where I had lunch of soup and bread. It was a lovely old building, low and stone-built, with flagged floor, stone fireplaces and old oak settles, all quite unspoilt. Incongruously, it was reverberating to loud heavy rock music, and even in the garden, to which I fled, the ground seemed to be throbbing with the beat. The soup, though, seemed rather good, and being unable to identify the taste, I enquired what it was. The large heavily blonde lady behind the bar – just moved in from Birmingham, and finding it a bit quiet – told me it was 'half homemade and half out of a packet'.

For a short while after lunch, when I had turned right to come back to my route, I was once more pushing Evans up one-in-threes and one-in-fours towards the summit of Ulpha Fell. Doubled over and practically on all fours, with my face close to the road, there were, surprisingly, some compensations. I was climbing in the shadow of a wood, and by turning my head sideways I could gaze straight into the variegated bells of foxgloves – marvellously beautiful from that angle, with their cool freckled interiors. Ants too, busy underfoot were scurrying along with excessively large burdens. Small birds darted in and out of the undergrowth with a rustling and shaking of twigs. My silent approach took every creature by surprise. Several rabbits sat casually burnishing their whiskers until I was almost upon them, when with one startled look they were gone.

Often all I see of wild life along the road are the mangled remains of those mown down by traffic – badgers, moles, weasels, stoats, rabbits, cats, dogs, birds, hedgehogs. No driver ever seems to consider stopping to move a slain creature to the side of the road, so it stays there, and other vehicles drive over it until eventually it is just a flattened piece of fur or skin and feathers. Sometimes the creature is not quite killed by the first assault. I move the corpses off the road if they are not completely flattened, as it seems more fitting that their small bodies should enrich the ground that nurtured them, but I resent having to finish off badly-damaged creatures that a motorist has left to die in agony.

With so much to observe it seemed only a short while before I was able to ride again. The height gained gave me the benefit of a strong breeze that had sprung up from the south, which took me effortlessly over the lesser gradients. At the summit, a mere 889 feet, I didn't feel like rushing straight down the other side into Eskdale: with the sun so hot, the high fells were a great place to be. There was a track marked on my map leading to a small isolated lake called Devoke Water. A decaying barely decipherable notice at the start of the rough boulder-strewn way read 'No Fishing or Camping', but I thought that if I found the place irresistible, I would probably be tempted to ignore the last injunction, at least for a few hours, as by now I was feeling my afternoon torpor stealing over me.

The track ended in a stone-built boat house, by the side of which a Volvo estate car was parked. Two men were out in a rowing boat, one at the oars, the other flogging the surface of the water with long snaking casts, and clearly catching nothing – it was far too bright a day, I would have thought. The small round lake was hidden in its own bowl of low hills, and I had no trouble in finding a spot sheltered from the southerly breeze. I set up the stove, made coffee and fell asleep with the empty mug still clutched in my hand. When I awoke, the boat was at the other side of the lake, far enough away for me to slip into the brown water and swim away the day's perspiration. There was a curious lack of sensation to this bathe, so close to body temperature was the shallow water on this hot day. Only the small wind-driven waves and the wide expanse made it pleasantly different to a warm bath.

When I had regained the road I had to stop for another long halt because the peaks were so arresting, razor sharp against a totally unclouded sky that was as blue as the bluest delphinium. There were a host of skylarks here too, sounding like a scattered choir tuning up. There were also numbers of white ewes, each of which, curiously, had a dark brown lamb by its side. Even more curiously, each lamb had an identical comic little face, like a monkey's, with a white ring around the muzzle.

It was nearly seven pm when, with the sun at my back, I left the lovely panorama of hills and began the long descent to Eskdale Green. As I rounded a steep bend long golden beams shone full on some gaunt grim structures and tall belching chimneys far below. Where should have been the first sight of the open sea was Sellafield Nuclear Power Plant, set squarely and horribly on the edge of this Cumbrian paradise.

It came as a complete shock, though I knew what it was immediately. I pulled up and stared at it, in an attempt to see it just as a complex of buildings, shorn of all the controversy and argument that surrounds it. But I failed, for rather than being simply an ugly blot on a beautiful landscape, it still looked to me as intrinsically evil and threatening as it had at first sight. On around another bend and it had vanished, and very soon I was down on the valley floor among green fields, pine trees and rhododendrons. I crossed the lovely River

Esk, on the other side of which was a welcoming inn with tables and chairs outside and smells that promised good food.

The evening was still wonderfully warm and golden, and far too lovely to think of going inside. A couple invited me to join them at their table; they had passed me earlier in the day in their car, they said, and had been intrigued by my bicycling alone. They bought me a drink, and while we waited for food we chatted about the weather and about this and that, until I happened to mention the awful view of Sellafield from the fells. This was something of a gaffe, though I couldn't have known that he was a nuclear power installations engineer. He was very much on the defensive, and bitter about the general public's attitude to nuclear power. Quite a few people round about listened to his defence of Sellafield, and a number of them contributed their thoughts on the subject; it was obviously a frequent and inexhaustible local topic. There seemed to be a clear division between those who worked at the plant and those who did not.

'There was cancer here before nuclear, it just wasn't talked about,' said one.

'You should have seen conditions here before it came, there was no work hereabouts. It's brought a lot of good, and I for one am glad of it,' said another.

'What can we do?' asked a retired farmer's wife rhetorically. 'We don't want it. But we can only move away, and we've been here all our lives. We don't want to go.'

There was much more in the same circular vein, and whenever anyone brought up a specific instance of damage or illness that they thought was due to the presence of the nuclear station, there was someone else to shrug it off as nonsense.

For dinner there was delicious Cumberland game pie and salad, followed by the sort of cream-laden pudding I thought I could afford to eat after the day's expenditure of energy. In spite of all the talk of Sellafield, it was out of sight and, mellowed with food and wine, the thought of it no longer seemed so sinister. It would by no means be the last I heard of the controversy, however. As I moved through this part of the Lake District it pursued me like the smoke from its chimneys.

As the sun finally set and the light faded, midges began their virulent forays, and I wandered off to find a place to sleep. There was a camp site nearby, but to judge from some of the campers who were in the inn it would be a noisy place. They had a crowd of obstreperous children in tow, whose idea of fun was squirting each other with shaken up cans of fizzy drinks as they raced through the bars. I wanted somewhere more peaceful, and headed for the open fells. I had left it rather late however, and I kept wandering up blind alleys, defeated by wicket gates and empty barred farmhouses. I ended up pitching in the semi-darkness, on a patch of ground under a yew tree in a farmyard, by kind permission of the elderly couple who owned the place.

Morning revealed me camped in the middle of what had once been a wonderfully self-contained little world of farm and mill. The mill had ceased functioning nearly a hundred years earlier while the farm had ended its working existence some decades since. Within the large enclosed cobbled yard was a plain square Georgian farmhouse, occupied by the old retired farmer and his wife. An empty cottage of a similar period faced the farmhouse across the yard and caught the full glory of the morning sun. Various sad empty barns and outbuildings completed three sides of the square. On the fourth side was the three-storey dilapidated mill, which I gathered was soon to be converted into a dwelling by some people from the South.

A slope at the rear of my tent led down to a ford across the little mill stream, which ran between steep banks behind the mill from a huge mirror-still mill-pond above. This stream, so near to the farm and yet so completely hidden from it by overhanging trees, seemed like a secret place. The remains of an old stone road were clearly visible, crossing the stream and petering out on the far side in a wood clogged with thick undergrowth. Nothing on the whole defunct farm was as evocative of another more rural age than this fragment of road – shades of country waggons such as Constable had painted rumbled across it into the cool dim shadows beyond. There would have been a great to-ing and fro-ing once, for the mill was large enough to have ground all the grain in the neighbourhood.

In the sun-dappled water, with swallows and sand martins skimming the surface after the flies that hovered there, I could have my morning wash hidden from human eyes. I also tried to get some of the blue ink out of my shirt, which had an enormous stain spreading from the pocket where my pen had come undone. I scrubbed away, and slapped it vigorously on a flat stone as they do in India, all without much success, and finally I threw it over a branch of the yew tree to dry while I made breakfast and struck camp. So hot was the morning sun that the shirt was ready to wear before I left, and the old farmer who had come out to chat, and to inform me, hopefully I thought, that the empty cottage was for sale, laughed at the stain and said I looked like a Chernobyl sheep – for sheep affected by the nuclear fallout were all daubed with blue dye.

I asked the farmer about the road across the stream, but it had fallen into disuse many years before his day, he said, when the mill wheel had finally stopped turning. Not, 'mind you', that he hadn't seen plenty of changes here in his lifetime. His wife, who had come to try to urge me in for a second breakfast, joined in and said they had indeed, they'd seen the full circle. From getting the place into shape after the war, they had seen it all go back again. It had been a good mixed farm, but it had been a struggle to repair the field drains and to get the land into good heart. It was work you couldn't 'leave go', or you were back where you started in no time. He had near broken his back on it, but they had no one to come after him, not that it would have made any difference if they had. This sort of farming was finished now: too small. I could see twenty such in as many miles – good farms all empty now, or gone for holiday homes. 'Oh yes,' said the old man, whose dim blue eyes had taken on a more and more remote look as his wife spoke, until he appeared to be gazing back to a time that he could see quite clearly in his mind's eye: 'Oh yes, another world altogether now.'

CHAPTER TWELVE

A Wilderness under Siege

The north of England was still enjoying the settled spell of halcyon weather when I reached the wildest and most majestic part of the Lake District. Wast Water, the deepest of all England's lakes, lay profoundly still under radiant skies, mirroring in deep shadows the awesome cliffs which sprung vertically from its southern shores. Going up to Wasdale Head along the northern shore was once again like riding through an eighteenth-century painting. Tall oak woods overhanging the narrow winding road gave a deceptive luxuriance to the scene, belying the shallow flinty soil. Carefully-built stone walls, a few green meadows, and the lawns and shrubs in the gardens of a baronial lodge made a park around the lake, wonderfully verdant in its contrast with the stark towering hills all around. There was a carefully orchestrated feeling about the wild and the cultivated aspects of nature here that seemed, at first, to be almost too self-consciously romantic, almost too Wordsworthian, to be quite believable.

A little further, and the aspect changed totally again, becoming altogether awe-inspiring. Gone were all attempts at cultivation. Closing in more and more of the sky on either side were the mightiest peaks of Lakeland – Great Gable at the head of the narrowing valley, like a monarch with his courtiers about him; to the right, Scafell Pike, at 3,206 feet the highest mountain in England, and Sca Fell, only a little lower at 3,162 feet, both of which I had been skirting around for days. On the left, Pillar, Kirk Fell, Red Pike and Haycock appeared and receded one behind the other, and were hidden by lesser, more immediate peaks as I rode on up the lake side.

The steep sides of the hills around Wasdale Head, slowly eroding over the millennia, have spilled their rocks in great fan-shaped scree and boulder fields. The lower slopes had been cleared of the debris in the past, and walled into little fields – memorials to man's indomitable will to survive in the face of almost insurmountable obstacles. It was ground that could never have yielded more than a starvation living, even before the introduction of sheep had degraded the land still further. Sheep, unlike cattle, put nothing back into the soil by way of useful manure; instead, they rob the ground of its mineral nutrients, and their close cropping inhibits the growth of finer grasses, debasing the sparse pasture even further. Now the sheep have the whole place to themselves; no one attempts any other kind of farming here.

At the head of the valley is the inn which became famous when climbing began to exert its appeal over the Victorians, around the middle of the nineteenth century. Here was the cradle of the sport, and the bars of the small hotel are filled with mementoes and photographs of the first 'tigers', just as the nearby church – which completes Wasdale's claim to the triple record of highest mountain, deepest lake and smallest church – has buried in its graveyard men who lost their lives challenging the peaks.

Before the advent of climbing and tourism, Wasdale Head Inn had been a simple farm on the packhorse route over the Styhead Pass to Borrowdale – the lovely old packhorse bridge is still in place over Mosedale Beck, just below the hotel. It was the ideal spot for a clearing house in the profitable seventeenth- and eighteenth-century smuggling trade – tobacco and brandy in, and plumbago out, plumbago being the soft valuable graphite that was mined in the hills, and which carried a high export duty. In the increasingly ordered times of the early nineteenth century, the inn, with its disreputable past hanging over it, was regarded with no great favour by the local authorities, and the first landlord was prosecuted for illegal trading before finally being granted a licence and settling down to a more respectable way of life.

The result of its changing fortunes has produced a building of simple charm, with a variety of heights and levels, as bits have been tacked on here and there at different periods of its growth. It is now the small, comfortable sort of hotel that I would choose to stay in if I were not camping. In the little hall, just the other side of what would have been the original front door, I found a splendid oak bread cupboard measuring about five feet high and several feet across, which could well have dated back to the sixteenth century. It was a carefully-made arrangements of doors and drawers that was probably needed to protect the bread from rats, and another piece from a distant period that was instantly evocative.

Behind the hotel's modest façade sprawled the bars that catered for the extensive lunchtime trade – walkers, campers, motorists and climbers made the place something of a junction. Pub meals are a recent improvement in the English way of life. Where once, and not so long ago, a traveller in remote areas could perish for want of sustenance, especially on a Sunday, it is now possible to find food at a reasonable price where there is no café, shop or restaurant for miles around. As the profit margin on meals is greater than that on beer, there is a healthy competition to attract customers, which results in curious food cults, like the *chili con carne* which the family at the next table ordered. With this, as with most pub meals, a salad garnish – usually consisting of one lettuce leaf, half a tomato, and a slice of cucumber, is *de rigueur*. Unfortunately, the greengrocer's van had broken down that day, the waiter explained, so there was no garnish. 'No salad?' exclaimed the family in chorus, sniffing loudly, with an incredulous air of disbelief: 'we'd better go somewhere else, then.' What's twenty miles in a motor car after all, especially when a principle's involved? Off they trooped, two indignant parents, with their two pasty-faced overweight children casting hurt and accusing glances over their shoulders as they went.

I lunched outside on bread and cheese – another ubiquitous pub dish, known as 'ploughman's lunch' – with the Armstrongs, whom I had met earlier in the day at Santon Bridge. I had nearly run them down as I came speeding around the corner after a precipitous descent from a shoulder of Irton Pike. They had been standing in the middle of the road, just around the bend, admiring the Bridge Inn, and after they had thanked me for braking in time we had started a conversation, which we continued over lunch. The inn which they had been examining so intently had once been a run-down old pub kept by Mr Armstrong's great-great-grandmother, and he was as pleased as Punch to have found it still standing. He had recently retired from accountancy, and begun to explore his family history, a hobby that had obviously become his chief joy, though I think his wife had some reservations about it.

They were on their way north by slow degrees, stopping along the way to pursue Mr Armstrong's historical researches. Their destination was the Scottish Borders and a gathering of the Armstrong clan – an ancient cattle-reiving border folk, with whom they would join forces for a great visiting of reiver castles and strongholds. 'Even coming from America, fancy,' said Mrs Armstrong, who was longing to talk about how awful it had been on the M6, but kept being interrupted by Mr Armstrong relating some new detail of his researches. He had traced his immediate family back through several generations, and was proud of them all, even the one who had served a six-months' prison sentence, and had subsequently falsified his age to conceal the fact. Mrs Armstrong chipped in every so often with 'The lady doesn't want to hear all that old history.' But I certainly did, and they were a pleasure to share a meal with, both so enthusiastic about life, and enjoying themselves so much.

Santon Bridge had provided another pleasant encounter when I had called at the little post office in order to send home the maps and books I had finished with – anything to lighten the load. I had hoped to buy a large envelope there for the purpose, but the post mistress had none. Instead she produced a large brown paper bag, sellotape, scissors and sticky brown paper and, as though time had no significance, helped me to parcel the things together. Finally, when it was judged to be secure enough, she made us both a cup of tea before waving me off with a 'Drop in again when you're passing.'

It seemed bizarre that in the wildest part of the Lake District it should be difficult to find somewhere peaceful for an afternoon rest. But wildest here did not mean most remote. There was a large National Trust camp site at the head of Wast Water, and although it was important to have it there to discourage uncontrolled camping, together with the inn, the inn's camp site, and the parking for climbers and walkers, and the usual run of people motoring around, it made for an enormous amount of traffic going up and down the narrow road beside the lake. I thought how much better the Americans organise their national parks, such as Yosemite, where visitors have to leave their cars in one central area and then get taken about on a free shuttle service. A place like Wasdale, which has no through road, would be ideal for this type of traffic control.

Even so, sleep I did by the water's edge under the hot sun; and the sound of a nearby cattle grid, which banged up and down every few seconds as each car passed over it, became the beat of horses' hooves, fitting in with all the recent talk of reiver castles and border raids. It was not a restful sleep, and in my dreams the wild steed I was riding through the burning stack yards, with a fiery cross going before (it was all very confused, the more sensational kind of historical reconstruction) had somehow become Evans with his palm cross being raced at speed up and down impossible gradients.

I awoke to find that the black surface of the lake had been turned to a sheet of silver by the angle of the setting sun, and that the great towering amphitheatre of hills was the softest rosy pink. It was all extraordinarily beautiful, and seeing it like that so suddenly I felt moved to tears. Part of my meagre travelling library is a slim booklet containing some of the offices of the Church. Although I don't use these services of psalms and prayers in any regular way, on occasions like these, when some sort of response to the sheer wonder of the creation seems absolutely necessary, I find it helpful to read through one or other of them, as formalised channels for my thoughts and feelings. The Psalms in particular seem so rooted in a response to nature that they are often especially appropriate, as Terce proved on this occasion (though it was nearer the traditional hour of Compline), with Psalm 119 'Teach me O Lord the way of thy statutes' and its lovely line 'And I will walk at liberty'. I read it through as the sounds of evening were coming across the water – a single cuckoo muted and rather ghostly, and exuberant skylark song rising up above the twittering of starlings. At my back green woodpeckers called unseen from the woods, with their unmistakeable echoing chuckle sounding clearly above the dull roar of motor cars and the clashing of the cattle grid. It seemed a curious coexistence.

The motor traffic died down eventually, and I sat on by the lakeside far into the evening, quite under the spell of the sudden profound stillness. Not a ripple stirred the water as the sun slipped further and further round, sending longer and longer shadows up the valley. The surface of the lake changed slowly from silver, through a steadily deepening pink, to blood red, and finally to black. I probably would not have moved even then, but for the tormenting midges, for the moon rose on a scene that was every bit as lovely. I took Evans and scrambled a little way up a track, where earlier a Lake District warden checking in fell runners completing a day-long race had indicated that no one would bother me if I bivouacked there for the night. I didn't bother to pitch the tent, but just placed it under the sleeping bag, with a fold of it over the top to keep off the dew.

Next morning Wast Water was quite changed again. A fresh little breeze was ruffling up the surface, destroying the rapt stillness of the previous night. This new morning was full of vigour, and I no longer felt inhibited about swimming. Raucous gulls wheeled and dived – flashes of dazzling white against the dark scree slopes, and incandescent as they flew into the eye of the sun that had only just soared above the ridge, throwing an instant river of blinding golden light across the lake. It was easy to imagine Jacob's angels coming up and down such a ladder.

An hour from this solitary idyllic scene and I was cycling along a road lined with nodding yellow poppies, within a stone's throw of where Sellafield was spewing its visible effluent into the lambent blue sky, while its infinitely deadlier poisons were steadily accumulating unseen elsewhere, to provide a legacy of horrifying risk and danger for the next million years. I would not have come anywhere near the plant if I could have avoided it, but the only road around the hills led me down to Gosforth before I could turn north, and that was barely a mile from Windscale. Beyond the black pall of smoke, in the far blue distance, was the tall cone of Snaefell, on the Isle of Man, and here, between the loveliness of the Lakes and that far ethereal shape, lay this hideous excrescence, this monster in our midst. Every inch of it was ugly, and every inch of it was pregnant with menace.

It seemed to pursue me around every bend of the road until I could at last turn my back on it at Calder Bridge, and head north on a little road that climbed steeply over the skirts of Lank Rigg, at which stage my mind was more engaged by the demands of the terrain. I made rather heavy weather of the taxing gradients until I stopped to tighten a cable, so that the chain no longer jumped off the cog in low gear. After this simple mechanical adjustment I was able to settle to a rhythm, and the effort became easier. There was no one about except an unladen cyclist who passed me without a sideways glance. This seemed so untypical that, calling on a reserve of energy, I went up a gear and chased after him, and we rode on together for a while. He was on a training run for a forthcoming race, but was having a bad day, which was why he had been feeling too grumpy to say 'Hallo'. Once he had recovered from his pique at being overhauled by a female on a heavily-laden bicycle, he professed himself glad of 'a bit of company' and even offered me a swig from his water bottle, as I had forgotten to fill mine. He had worked at Sellafield for thirty-six years, all his working life – 'There wasn't any choice in the matter,' he said, 'I went in straight from school.' I asked him if he would do the same now. 'No, I would not,' he replied emphatically. 'But I'm trapped now, so I try not to think about it, like most folk round here.'

It being once more a Sunday, I was concerned about finding supplies, but the cyclist directed me to a small store at Ennerdale Bridge, where the prices were noticeably lower than anywhere else I had been in the Lake District. The owner, who appeared to be on very good terms with all his customers, told me that he did all his own marketing, which was the only way a small local shop like his could run at a reasonable profit while keeping the prices low enough to ensure that people would not want to rush off to the town for everything. Freight charges in this part of the country were apparently much higher than in most places, because the mountains meant everything had to come by such a roundabout route. In the old days, before all freight came by road, goods had arrived by sea, which had been both quicker and cheaper.

My guide book claimed that Ennerdale Water, having no road around it, was the loneliest of the lakes, and I thought it would be nice to make the short detour and have an early picnic lunch there before proceeding north to Loweswater. The book clearly needed revising. I had no sooner set up my stove and brewed coffee than the hordes descended, and it became like Southend on a bank holiday. First a large gang of local youths burst upon the scene, hollering and swaggering, and heaving great stones into the lake to impress their girl friends, who traipsed after them in a self-conscious, giggling clique. They were followed by a stream of uninhibited family groups, accompanied by their dogs, both adults and children throwing stones into the water to encourage the dogs to swim. They also pelted an already battered notice, which read NO FISHING SWIMMING OR BOATING – STRICTLY PRIVATE WATER AUTHORITY. Others began inflating flotillas of rubber boats.

'Coom on, our Nelson', 'Hey oop, our Ben', rang out the encouraging cries, and 'Watch oot, yer gummock!' as a dog shook the excess water from his coat onto his owner's bare torso. It being a hot day, the English menfolk, as is their custom, had shed half their clothing, exposing large expanses of reddening white flesh. Huge beer bellies overhung trousers which seemed supported only by faith, aided by frequent upward hitching of the waistbands. Two such men, with an hallooing young boy and a girl in tow, came and

stood at the water's edge close by, and with uncouth utterances and
threatening gestures began to force the children into the lake, driving
them further and further out by dint of flinging huge stones into the
water close beside them. The boy soon got away, but the girl just
stood there soaked and shivering, and as she cowered and shrieked,
with the men looming over her, boulders poised menacingly above
their heads, the scene took on an awful biblical aspect – the incipient
stoning of the woman taken in adultery. But just as the tension was
no longer bearable, attention switched to the dog, and the erstwhile
victim was ordered to drag it into the lake by its collar and lead. It
was a King Charles spaniel, too fat to put up much of a fight. Its
soulful brown eyes bulged even further and a faint whimper came
from its throat as it concentrated the rest of its puny energy on trying
to keep its head above water. At what seemed the point of despair,
the order was given to release it, and it raced back towards its
tormentors on a burst of renewed hope.

The constant yelling of commands, and the threats, tears and
shrieks which accompanied these tribal ablutions, were all a bit
wearying, especially after the idylls of the last few days. I quickly
packed up and headed north on a narrow road lined with
late-flowering hawthorn, which took me high over empty open
fells.

I was soon glad that I had been reminded to fill my water bottle,
for the day grew ever more scorching, with the sun beating straight
down, and dehydration can occur quickly when pedalling a bicycle
in those conditions. The white quartz dressing on the road was
blinding, and I felt tired having missed my usual afternoon nap.
Then, as I slowly walked Evans up a steep stretch of the lonely road,
far blue hills that could only be southern Scotland swam into view. It
was a moment of elation; suddenly I felt very much the traveller, and
London and home seemed an immense distance away.

At a place called Lamplugh I came upon an ancient church, much
restored, with little in the way of other buildings near it, except for
an old farmhouse behind a grand arched entrance, with a coat of
arms above it and the date 1565 AD. A little further on was a rough
bridle track leading off across the moors, signposted 'corpse road to
Loweswater', which meant that the church and its burial ground had
once served a wide and scattered flock. I was unable to resist this
'corpse road', partly because of its name and associations, and partly

because a green track stretching away out of sight is always a temptation. A people who could remain self-sufficient in all the necessities of life for months at a time still needed a route that would remain passable in all weather conditions, in order to transport their dead to burial in hallowed ground. My respect for the strength and tenacity of the Cumbrians who had used this precipitous rough way for that purpose grew after I had wheeled Evans over it. The track took me high up onto Burnbank Fell and Carling Knot, above Holme Wood, where, if I needed reward for the hardship involved in the route, I received it in the thrilling sight of a pair of peregrine falcons riding the light airs above the wood.

Two middle-aged women stripped down to bare essentials (as I was myself by this time) gestured lazily for me to join them where they lay sunbathing beside a cool stream. They were both returned exiles of almost exactly the same age as one another, who had been born and brought up in adjacent Lakeland villages, but had first met only recently, after returning from working in the South. Both had decided that they were prepared to accept a much lower standard of living if they could get back to the Lakes they had missed so much. They acted as volunteer wardens for the Lake District National Park in their spare time, helping to maintain paths, preventing unofficial camping, and keeping a watch on rare nesting birds and the like. They told me that in spite of a twenty-four-hour watch being kept on the nest while they were rearing their young, these peregrine falcons had lost their chicks to a thief who had managed to get away unseen with them. The fact that some Arab countries will now pay many thousands of pounds for young hawks makes their protection very difficult.

I hurried as fast as was possible on the unrideable corpse road, down to Loweswater, which had been tantalisingly in sight all the while that I was toiling round the hillside under the boiling sun. Another half-hour and I was floating in the green restoring lake – soaking the water in though my pores, or so it felt – in company with an armada of Canada geese swimming in decorous order one behind the other, and a few dotty coots scudding wildly hither and thither. The water was cold and refreshing, and I emerged with a glow of virtue at having completed my ablutions for the day. All that remained was to find somewhere to pitch the tent and think about dinner.

A suitable pitch again proved elusive. The village of Loweswater was beautifully situated on slightly raised ground between two lakes. There was a church, a pub, and a handful of houses, but I could find no farms as such, and most of the fields looked abandoned. The only likely door I discovered was opened to my knock by a young man who had just rented the place for a fortnight's holiday. After a half-hour of wandering up and down pretty narrow lanes, a couple stopped their rather battered Volvo and asked if they could direct me somewhere since they could see I must be looking for something. When I had explained my need they suggested I should park myself wherever I found an open gate, since the fields were indeed unworked at present, and going to rack and ruin. They had once farmed here themselves, but were now on a bigger place at the north end of Bassenthwaite Lake, and they invited me to come and visit them there when I passed next day. Thus encouraged, I did what I would have been loathe to do otherwise, for fear of some irate farmer coming to turf me off in the middle of the night: I wheeled Evans up through a field of thin long grass to a rocky knoll on the other side of a rotted fence, where I put up the tent with its back to the shelter of the rock, and looking out on yet another peerless Lakeland view, this time over Crummock Water.

It was 8 pm, with the sun still bright and hot, as I tried to raise the energy to go off to the pub for dinner. Lying on my stomach in the tent, I was at eye level with the grasses which had reached their full age, their heads heavy and drooping under the weight of their seeds. Infinitely small transparent winged creatures made the perilous ascent of the stalks. Framed in the V of the entrance was the blue of Crummock Water with the steep fells of Grasmoor rising up behind it, and a face of Loweswater Fell to the left, clad in an ancient oak wood of small gnarled trees. Straight ahead, the lower peaks concealed Buttermere, beyond which was Great Gable, to the south of me now – only about nine miles away as the crow flies, but a hard day's journey the way I had come.

I realised too late that the pub specialised in puddings, and having waded through a huge and rather boring Cumberland sausage in the interest of sampling local delicacies, I was *hors de combat* and could indulge no further. The pub clientele was a mix of visitors and people who lived round about. I sipped my beer slowly and listened to a discussion instigated by two young men who had just walked the Cumberland Way – a route that leads right across the Lakes. They had been appalled to find young local people swimming in the sea off St Abbs' Head, only a few miles up the coast from Sellafield's outflow. 'Even the fish in the shops was advertised as being caught in the North Sea,' said one. 'Well, people don't glow in the dark yet, that's the trouble – not even the Chernobyl sheep do that,' said a local farmer, joining in. 'Don't they read the newspapers up here then?' asked the visitor incredulously. 'Yes, as much as anyone,' replied the farmer, 'but they're bored with it. Every time someone gets defoliated and compensation's paid there's a stir, and then it all blows over again, and people forget about it. Half of the things that go wrong get hushed up anyway. Nobody really knows what's going on. The young people don't believe the scare stories any more.' The young nuclear-wise southerners shook their heads in horrified disbelief.

Coming back to the tent, deep in thought, something alerted me just in time to see a small brown leveret crouched motionless in the long grass almost at my feet, its ears pressed tightly against its quivering sides and its eyes wide and moist. I longed to stay and stroke the frightened furry little form, but I resisted, and moved on quickly to spare it any more fear. It didn't stir, even though I passed within inches of it. I remembered suddenly that the farmer's wife in the Volvo had said that when she had first caught sight of me on the laden Evans, she had thought immediately 'Oh the freedom of it.' It was small perfect experiences like this with the leveret that made me conscious of that freedom. And it was that sense of total contentment with the present moment that stayed with me through the night, rather than the dark thoughts about Sellafield.

CHAPTER THIRTEEN

North to the Borders

I had reached a point in the journey where each day seemed more marvellous than the last. I had not the slightest doubt that this owed as much to the weather as to the scenery, conditions making camping out the most perfect existence imaginable. Although nothing could have exceeded the beauty of Wast Water, sitting in a meadow high above Crummock Water, washing the breakfast pots with Delius's 'Apallachian Suite' coming through the earphones of the radio, I thought this morning crowned all others in terms of sheer zest in being alive. So strong was the need to share this feeling of complete happiness that I interrupted the cleaning chores to record it in my journal.

It was a morning of great clarity, which gave tremendous depths to the long vista of hills beyond the lake, and brought every detail of the scene into razor-sharp focus. I shared it all with a few sheep, a herd of somnolent Friesian cows, and half a dozen scattered cottages that blended into the colours and contours of the land. The radiant morning, the scenery, the music and my response to it all, combined to begin the day on a note of celebration.

The clear skies kept their promise of early heat. By 10 a m it was too hot for comfort on the open main road, but running parallel and a little higher to the west was a perfect lane for that sort of day, which the map showed I could follow as far as Thwackthwaite. The moment I turned into it and rode into the pools of deep shade cast by the tall trees arching over the narrow way, it was as though the heat had been abruptly switched off. The overall dim green gloom was lightened here and there where the trees and bushes thinned out and let in patches of dappled light. Cool airs eddied around, stirring a complicated pot-pourri of fresh scents. Most trees were now past their first green delicacy and in full leaf, but the leaves were still fresh and perfect, as yet unmarked by the ravages of summer. Few cars passed, perhaps because this close secret world was essentially a boring road for motorists who could see nothing but the thick high hedgerows pressing in upon them. At bicycle speed, those same hedgerows were a riot of heavy-headed blossom, while at their feet buttercups spread out their petals flat and wide to stray sunbeams, and tall foxgloves hung heads crowded with richly ornate bells.

Birds darted out of the hedgerows on either side, only inches in front of my wheels, and would have joined the other corpses had Evans been a car, for they had absolutely no notion of caution, intent only on food-gathering for their growing broods, which I could hear cheeping vociferously from the undergrowth.

A glimpse of white through the trees brought me to a halt, and there was a lovely Arab mare with her colt – dark eyes and muzzle lifted questioningly; long streaming tail and mane rippling out on the breeze. She had come to drink at the stream on the other side of the hedge, and having drunk she gave an imperious toss of her peerless head, shaking off a shower of sparkling crystal drops. Still marvelling at the splendour of her as she turned away, there was a sudden scurrying in the leaves, and a red squirrel passed just feet away without seeing me, the sun shining through his thistledown tail and his ear tufts as he flowed effortlessly from tree to tree.

'Ah, much the same problems as R. L. Stevenson had with his donkey,' said the National Trust lady brightly at Wordsworth's birthplace in Cockermouth, as I was casting about for something solid to which to chain Evans while I toured the house. It was a strange and unlikely analogy, I thought, except for the punctures poor Modestine received in her rump from the donkey prod, and they were far greater in number than ever Evans got in his tyres. But as it was an attempt by the N.T. lady to be friendly, I forbore to comment. It was also, I thought, an attempt on her part to enlist my tacit support over the matter of some other visitors who had asked to bring their dog inside because it was so hot for it to be left in the car. She had said, 'So sorry, rules you know,' and 'What a shame,' and 'Poor dog,' and other placatory remarks suitable for the dog-loving British public. But when they had gone off in a mild huff, she had snorted indignantly, 'Some people! We tried it, you know, once. We used to let them bring their dogs into the garden, and then, when we were holding a special function, one of them let their dog do something near the refreshment table. She didn't come and tell us or we could have done something about it.

You can't have that sort of thing going on, can you? But that's visitors for you.'

Wordsworth was born in 1770 in this solidly prosperous North Country house, with its comfortable unpretentious rooms and its modest garden leading down to the river. Six years earlier, Fletcher Christian, who led the mutiny on the *Bounty,* had been born close by, and attended the same school for a short while. Perhaps Cockermouth bred wild boys, for both had that reputation. I used to feel that Christian had probably had a rough deal until I came to have some business dealings with one of his immediate descendants, after which I found my sympathies had shifted to Captain Bligh.

Cockermouth was being heavily assaulted by a major road-widening scheme, and was terribly noisy and dusty in consequence; otherwise I am sure it would have been the peaceful sort of market town I like. It was not consciously preserved, but had lots of old shops, and odd corners to poke about in. Little had yet been sacrificed in the name of progress, so that the layers of history still existed naturally and unselfconsciously in the everyday working fabric of the town.

When I enquired at the baker's where I could find meths for my stove, I was told first where not to buy it – 'not at that new-fangled camping place that charges too much'. Going instead, as directed, to the old-fashioned hardware store, I found a dark Aladdin's cave, long and narrow and lined with hundreds of oak drawers of nails and screws. Tools and bales of wire and suchlike hung in festoons from a ceiling blackened with age and the soot of oil lamps. The brown-overalled assistant drew me a whisky bottle full of meths from a drum that stood among other strong-smelling drums and barrels in a corner, and then wrapped it in a piece of brown paper, and tied a piece of string around it – a transaction that took all of ten minutes, and which was none too long to take in what could have been another Beatrix Potter interior.

In an old warehouse, off an even older ramshackle courtyard, I came across an unusual museum containing a large collection of ethnic dolls and antique toys, and downstairs, extensive Hornby o and oo railway layouts that could be operated by visitors. But even while I was thinking what an enchanting place it was, and how sensible to have something to attract the men and the boys as well as the girls, the German lady who owned the place was telling me how awful it was to have such a museum where no one appreciated it. She said she had started it in the Home Counties where it had done well, and had moved it up here because she and her husband had wanted to live in the Lake District. But now, although she loved her house out on the fells, she couldn't wait to take her collection back to the Home Counties and leave this 'cultural wilderness'. She seemed rather angry about it not having worked out, but I thought that, nice as the museum was, it was also probably a bit esoteric for an out-of-the-way little market town that was hardly a mecca for tourists.

More in keeping with Cockermouth was the weekly livestock sales which I passed on my way out of town. They were held under a wide expanse of corrugated roofing, a very large, no-nonsense concrete area divided by metal hurdles into an endless series of pens. It was the tail end of the sales, and the last few bunches of yellow daubed sheep were being hurried in and out of the pens with bewildering rapidity, bleating piteously, their eyes appearing to be looking in all directions at once. A small collie puppy on a string was learning his job of keeping them on the move, amid the incomprehensible mutterings of the auctioneer and the shouts and signals of a handful of men ranged around the barriers. Everything reeked of urine, sheep grease and fear; I found it a sad place, especially when I thought that I might well have seen those same sheep grazing happily on the fells. After only a short while I left them to their fate, and hurried on to Wythop.

Wythop Hall, on the west bank of Bassenthwaite Lake, was where Michael and Joyce Shield lived – the farmer and his wife whom I had met at Loweswater. They had invited me to camp at their farm so that they could show me what a real Cumberland village atmosphere was like. As it happened, I didn't meet very many of their neighbours, because it was a community of widely-scattered houses, rather than a village as such. But I gained the impression from those I did meet, and from the Shields themselves, that everyone knew everyone else in the surrounding few miles, and that an easygoing spirit of co-operation and support existed that would have made it a very pleasant place to live, if it wasn't for the perpetual nagging fears about the Monster – I had soon discovered that 'the Monster' was a common way of referring to Sellafield, and not just the name that had sprung naturally to my mind.

I found Joyce Shield waiting for me at the stretch of rough track that led to the isolated farm, after I had toiled up the series of precipitous lanes from the flat river land around Cockermouth. She had expected me to arrive about teatime, and had walked down to meet me – a courtesy which made me feel very welcome. Joyce was a pleasant-looking, softly-spoken woman, with children about to leave home, and an interest in life that was beginning to extend beyond the confines of the farm. We found we had much in common. She was still fascinated by the freedom of my bicycle tour, and said she would love to do something similar if only she dared. I am never sure what 'dare' means in this context, but suspect that it has to do with overcoming fears about mechanical and physical inadequacies, and appearing eccentric – none of which is in the least important, bicycles being so easy to maintain, and everything else falling into place as the journey unfolds. But I find it impossible to convince people of this, for the only way of finding out is simply to set off and do it – and that, of course, is the hardest part.

Dwarfed by the much larger modern barns and milking sheds crowding around it, the solid old farmhouse where we were joined over tea by Michael Shield, could well have dated back in part to the fifteenth century. Its situation was splendid, but the interior had the purely functional, rather characterless air that often distinguishes tenant farms. No matter how much a farmer may be prepared to improve the land he rents – especially if he thinks he will reap the benefit from it – few people will lavish more care and money on a house that doesn't belong to them than is strictly necessary to keep it efficiently habitable.

Most of the twelve hundred acres which made up the farm was rough fell grazing. The lowest part was the fertile valley where the farmhouse stood, at around the 700-foot contour line – a valley that had been farmed continuously since Roman times. It was very different country to the rest of the Lakes; still hilly, but with more softly rounded contours, and with no high peaks closing it in, it had a much more open aspect.

Bassenthwaite Lake, which bordered the property to the north-east, is the only stretch of water in the Lake District to bear the name 'lake' – all the others are called 'water' or 'mere', which makes for difficulty when the main village in the area is called by exactly the same name, as is generally the case. The shores of Bassenthwaite are well wooded at the northern end, with Wythop Woods, nearest to the farm, being of particular interest, and protected by a preservation order. It is an ancient oak forest that has been coppiced for generations for the production of charcoal, and this has given the trees a characteristically strange twisted growth, like the enchanted woods of fairy tales. I had noticed similar smaller stands of coppiced oaks in other parts of the Lakes, without knowing the reason for their gnarled appearance. But these woods at Wythop are quite unique, as they have remained undisturbed since their charcoaling days were over, and many people come there to study them. Recently, some nesting-boxes had been installed there, and now the woods are doubly interesting, having been colonised by scores of the pied flycatcher, an attractive little migrant that has been growing increasingly rare.

The Shields ran a flock of 1,000 Swaledale sheep, and a herd of about 70 cows and 100 calves. They also kept a small domestic flock of geese. Michael took me on a tour of the place after tea, and I was shown where he had re-drained some of his fields, coming upon the original Roman drains during the operation. Michael's love of farming is, he says, tempered by present-day issues, and he says, he has become more and more preoccupied about what exactly he is producing on his land – something he feels to be increasingly uncertain. The subject of Sellafield and its possible effects upon livestock was one of the first things we talked about, and the one to which we kept returning. If his lambs are likely to be carrying some ghastly long-term inheritance, he wants to know about it. As a food producer, he considers it is his responsibility to know, but he feels that the whole subject is surrounded by a conspiracy of silence. With so many local men dependent upon Sellafield for their livelihood, it appears that people, like himself, who ask uncomfortable questions at meetings tend to get hushed up; their questions go unanswered.

Since the Chernobyl disaster forced the subject of nuclear contamination out into the open, he feels that things are worse, as there is now something outside the area to blame for the incidents that do come to light. But why, he asks, is there a sharply-drawn line, on one side of which sheep are no longer tested, while on the other they are perpetually monitored (his own sheep, I gathered, were no longer under review). And why is it that contamination is attributed to the effects of Chernobyl, when the line is so ominously close to Sellafield? All hard questions that Michael feels

must be asked, but which he can readily understand people wanting
to turn away from.

The topic of 'the Monster' was continued at the pub to which we
went for dinner. This was a place frequented only by locals, and it
was interesting to see the mechanisms and jokes that had been
developed to cope with the subject – like the name 'Monster' itself.
As the farmer at the previous night's pub had claimed, the young
men in particular tried to avoid the subject if they could, and if
challenged directly about their views would try and turn it into a
joke, saying something like 'Are you asking me if I believe my bits
will drop off?' But once the laughing had subsided, and the topic was
out in the open, then – at least on this occasion – everyone had
something to say. All sorts of fears were aired, and all sorts of dire
possibilities considered. Most anger seemed to be directed towards
the reprocessing of other countries' nuclear waste – 'the filth of
Europe that other countries don't want dumped in their own
backyards.' It was clear that people felt powerless to do anything
about it, or to gain positive reassurance – which contrasted very
much with the bright television advertising there had been recently,
showing Sellafield keeping open house to the general public, and
eager to answer all queries.

I had not realised until then how wide an influence on the whole
area Sellafield had, and how many people it employed. We were
twenty miles away from the plant, but very many people from the
immediate locality were doing contract work there; a local man was
shipping in gravel for 'Pad 4' – the latest high-level waste
containment area. They reckoned that the work on that structure,
and on others that are planned to contain the high-level waste from
the expanding nuclear industry, would continue well into the next
century, with a lot of local people getting rich in the process.
Accidents bringing the stuff in were a real and constant threat, they
thought – whether caused by terrorism, train crashes, or
complacency. These people had considered them all, and their fears
were not allayed by anything anyone had yet said. You had no
choice but to 'swallow their line' or clear out of the area, was the
general conclusion; there wasn't really any other alternative. It
wasn't a problem that would simply go away, since far too many
vested interests were at stake. Many people, they said, simply
refused to believe there was any danger because it was easier that

way. One local man was said to be making a fortune from storing low-level waste that was supposed to remain toxic for only twenty years. He was said to have been given grants to build sheds, and the stuff arrived there by lorry in great drums. He was apparently using his new-found wealth to build bungalows alongside these sheds. On the way back to the farm, we drove past this private-sector storage place. There were three buildings there – huge, brooding places, like great hangars, fifty feet or more of unrelieved corrugated steel, and in their shadow were the newly-built bungalows – giving another new twist to the old Northern saying, 'Where there's muck there's brass'.

Nonetheless, and in spite of 'the Monster', I packed up my camp in the little orchard under the ancient twisted oak wood with regret. I was about to leave one of the most beautiful areas of England, which I had been given the inestimable good fortune to have seen in such idyllic circumstances. I said goodbye to the last of my Lakeland hosts and sped off down the little lanes, losing the height I had gained so laboriously the previous day, while fat little rabbits looked over their shoulders as I passed and devil-may-care birds darted out of the hedgerows, almost between my spokes. A large fish leapt in Bassenthwaite Lake as though saying a last 'goodbye' – not such a strange fancy this, as I learnt subsequently, for it was here on a visit that Tennyson had written *Morte D'Arthur*, in which the mystic arm rises out of the water to seize the sword Excalibur: if an arm, then why not a fish to bid godspeed to a traveller? Emulating the locals, I too cast my pebble into the water; it bounced once across the surface, which probably meant something.

Another chapter of the journey was beginning, I felt, as I headed north again over bare open fells. I was glad of the motion and the speed as I crossed summit after summit of the countryside that John Peel and his hounds had ridden over in pursuit of the fox. With the wind at my back, and a hot sun overhead, it was exhilarating going, and I kept on and on, ignoring all turn-offs to possible lunch places, until I was so hungry that I had to stop, by which time there were no more pubs to be found. The open landscape shimmered under a blanket of heat, and there seemed to be not the slightest patch of shade anywhere in which to sit and make a picnic. After vainly casting about for a further half-hour, seeking a suitable wayside tree,

I found instead a curious small building, which I subsequently discovered to be an automatic telephone exchange. It stood there beside the otherwise empty road, miles from anywhere, looking like a cross between a wendy house and a public lavatory. There was a miniature garden the size of a tablecloth in front of it and an incongruous little footscraper beside the doorstep, over which the building cast its own slight shadow. I decided this would make a tolerable stopping place, and feeling a little like Goldilocks, I pushed open the low gate in the picket fence, wheeled in Evans and set up my stove by the front door.

Half expecting the Three Bears to come rolling in at any moment, it was not quite such a shock to be disturbed by a truck pulling up, driven by a man who had come to cut the minuscule lawn. He was not at all put out by my occupation, however, and one look at the sparse low grass convinced him that it wasn't worth unloading his mower. Instead, he sat in his cab eating his sandwiches and 'passed the time of day'. He was an ex-miner who had set himself up with his redundancy money, and now made a considerably better living as a self-employed gardening contractor, cutting other out-of-the-way lawns. He visited this tiny patch six times a year; twice a year he sprayed it to inhibit the growth, and he cut it about four times, for which he received £400. It seemed an awful lot of money to care for so few blades of grass, though it would doubtless have cost the owners more to send out an employee to do it. If it were mine, I think I would have considered having it paved.

From my elevated luncheon halt, it was a long cool glide down to the low lands around the Solway Firth, across which the River Eden snaked its way towards the sea, winding through the ancient and much fought-over capital of north-western England, which for centuries has stood as a bastion against the Scots. A red sandstone city, glowing on such a day, Carlisle still retains something of its unique character, in spite of the costly sacrifices it has made to the age of the motor car, and the cult of the shopping precincts. But as I rode in, I hardly recognised it for the splendid medieval town I used to pass through before the days of motorways, when it had been an important last stop before Scotland.

After my long sojourn in country places, I felt at a loss among the traffic scurrying around the bewildering new roundabouts and one-way systems, and among the smartly dressed townspeople hurrying along the wide pavements. Suddenly aware of my travel-stained and unkempt appearance, I locked Evans to a lamp post, and went in search of a haircut and a launderette. Failing to find the latter, I bought a shirt from an Oxfam shop, paying a lot less for it than for the haircut.

Feeling cleaner and rather less conspicuous, I made my way across the precincts and into Carlisle's red sandstone Cathedral of the Holy and Undivided Trinity, a building which has undergone considerable changes since it was first erected by order of Henry I, in 1122. It was grey sandstone then, but drought, fire and changing architectural and ecclesiastical fashions, have resulted in an almost total rebuilding of the original structure, and the present truncated red church dates largely from the fourteenth century. Its small size made it rather homely, and I liked it very much, particularly the blaze of medieval colour on the ceilings and the ornate woodwork. I said as much to one of the guides who had caught my eye. This led to a conversation and a stroll around various other cathedral treasures, and so a relaxed and pleasant half-hour passed. I was just about to leave when the guide asked my name, and suddenly we were both aware that we knew each other, having spent two very significant weeks of our lives together on the remotest island in the kingdom. It was the most curious of coincidences that we should have bumped into each other like this, because she only spent one hour a week on duty at the cathedral, and I happened to have chosen that very day and hour to make my visit.

After evensong, I went home with Margaret, so that we could catch up on the intervening years, and reminisce about the two weeks we had shared on St Kilda – a speck of rock, about half a mile square, far out in the Atlantic, beyond the Outer Hebrides, with the highest sea cliffs in Britain and a unique bird population. Until the 1930s, the island also had a unique human population, which had lived by harvesting the sea birds. There had been an infamous evacuation of these people, and it was in order to preserve aspects of their culture that about eighteen volunteers, including Margaret and myself, were out there on a working party for the Scottish National Trust. All of us were similarly infected with island fever, but we did not necessarily have many other interests in common. We had lived cheek by jowl, in primitive conditions, and knew one another only by Christian names for the most part. Neither of us had made any attempt to keep up an acquaintance with the others after we had left the island. But now both Margaret and I were delighted to meet again, and I happily agreed to stay the night.

We talked till well past midnight, and I went to my room quite exhausted. But even so it was a long time before sleep came, so curious did it feel to be lying in a high, soft, yielding bed. It was like first stepping ashore after a long voyage, when the ground feels insecure. Even stranger was the sensation of there being a solid roof over my head, and walls around me, cutting me off from the night sky and the sounds of the natural world.

CHAPTER FOURTEEN

Wall Country

Rediscovering an old acquaintance so unexpectedly made all the difference to my enjoyment of Carlisle. For one thing it resulted in my spending more than just a single night in the same place, something I had not done for quite a while. On a journey, I find it all too easy to get into a pattern of moving on each day, forgetting how important it is to take time off now and again simply to relax, to rest tired muscles and recharge energies. I was more than ready for such a break, and once I had got used to Margaret Coulthard's soft spare bed, I found it kind to the sunburn and the aching shoulders, so that I was refreshed enough even to remain unperturbed by Carlisle drivers' cavalier attitude towards bicyclists. More importantly, Margaret's enthusiasm for her home town got me properly primed for looking at it.

Carlisle has been in existence as a settlement for a very long time, and has doubtless seen mysteries in plenty. None, however, have been more perplexing than the question of what happened to the Ninth Roman Legion. Somewhere in the vicinity of Carlisle, which was then an important Roman supply base, the entire crack troop of some 5,000 men, together with their baggage, their cavalry, and their eagle, disappeared without trace. Whether it was this event which caused the widely-travelled Emperor Hadrian – the most indefatigable of Roman builders, whose triumphal arches and fortifications litter the classical world – to decide upon the construction of the famous Wall is a matter of conjecture. But the scope and extent of Hadrian's Wall, which stretched from the Solway Firth to the Tyne, was such that it effectively kept the northern part of Britain separate from the rest of the country; a state of affairs which lasted officially until the two crowns were united under James VI of Scotland and I of England some 1,500 years later. Unofficially, as far as Scots seeking devolution are concerned, the two countries are still separate, and Luguvalium or Carlisle, established by the Romans as a permanent border town, remains so to this day.

There is no evidence of the Wall in Carlisle itself, nor of any other Roman structure, except for a little sunken shrine by the entrance to the museum, and some interesting stones inside. The original Roman fort has been built over, layer upon layer, throughout the centuries. Extensive archaeological excavations to explore these successive cultures were under way in the cathedral graveyard, and some of the Roman heritage was coming to light in the form of cobbled roads, coins, and pots of fine Samian ware.

Details of the Saxon past were also being uncovered in the dig, about which the archaeologists were much more excited. Roman history is reasonably well documented, but the Dark Ages, which followed the Roman withdrawal from Britain in the fifth century, are as yet only a subject for historical conjecture, particularly in respect of this remote north-western corner of England. Saxon graves had recently come to light here, together with coins minted at York in the ninth century, and expectations of even more significant finds at deeper levels were running high. When I took my turn to peer down into the excavation pit, there were several brown skeletons being laid bare for all the tourists to see, with young workers carefully brushing away the earth from around the bones. It seemed tough luck even on barbarians to have their peace so rudely disturbed after so many centuries.

I also found history vibrantly present in Carlisle's splendid castle, the fiery red sandstone walls of which suited its character far better than they did the cathedral. Since the Normans had built their massive keep here in the twelfth century, choosing a higher piece of ground than the Romans had for their fort, Carlisle had become a shuttlecock between advancing and retreating armies. Both Scots and English had had a hand in enlarging and strengthening the castle, turn and turn about. Perhaps it was because of these frequent conquests, which continued far into the eighteenth century, and the thousands of prisoners who had been lodged in the dungeons awaiting execution, that the place has such a grimly workmanlike and evocative atmosphere.

Although the moat is now dry, entry is still made through the daunting castle gatehouse, beneath a massive spiked portcullis. Inside, the castle is a maze of dark passages, spiralling stone staircases, and chambers which strike chill even on a warm summer's day. The dungeons are particularly gruesome, with an added touch of gratuitous cruelty in the presence of the 'licking stone', which for some reason slowly oozes moisture, and which was supposed to be the only source of water available to the prisoners. Strange human and heraldic figures had been carved into the cell walls over the centuries; some of them rather fine, reminiscent of much earlier Celtic and Pictish traditions. Perhaps a precedent had been set by one particular prisoner, and others, seeing the work had added to it in kind. Or, perhaps, the carvers were illiterate, and where other prisoners might carve their names or initials, they left these enigmatic figures as their memorials.

Out on the battlements in the welcome sunlight, it was a relief – as it must have been to any prisoner granted the privilege of walking there – to gaze outwards over views extending far beyond the Solway Firth into Scotland, across the war-ravaged miles over which so much history has ebbed and flowed. I have both Scots and English blood in my veins, and so my sympathies are inevitably divided, but even if this were not so, I would find it impossible to feel no pity for Mary Queen of Scots, brought here after her defeat at Langside, when her own country had rejected her, but still hoping that her cousin, Elizabeth I would support her – if for no other reason than to uphold the divine right of kingship. She was not yet officially a prisoner of the English crown, but once she had passed beneath this grim portcullis she was never to be free again until Elizabeth had signed her death warrant nineteen years later, in far-off Fotheringhay.

Mary's descendant, Bonnie Prince Charlie, captured the castle during his attempt to restore the fortunes of the Stuarts in 1745; and when that forlorn attempt was crushed a year later at Culloden, the castle dungeons were crammed to suffocation with Scottish prisoners. Of the 382 men imprisoned here, 127 were led out to their execution, and the gates of Carlisle were hung all over with their severed heads and quartered bodies.

One evening, Margaret took me in her car to explore the fascinating area of the Solway Firth. The tide was out, and the vast gleaming area of muddy sand was left newly exposed, the hunting ground of numerous wading birds. The tide comes in there like an express train, and treacherous quicksands constantly shift their course. Nonetheless there was always a route across the wide expanse for the fit and strong, as long as they had the services of a reliable guide who could find the ever-shifting route, and it was a favourite way for armies and border raiders to slip across – including, no doubt, Mr Armstrong's ancestors. Hadrian's Wall had extended right along the coast to guard this back-door approach, but it is not easy now to trace its course, except where the villages of Burgh, Drumburgh and Bowness stand on what were once Roman forts. The church at Burgh could be mistaken for a fortress, for its massively strong battlemented tower is modelled on a Border peel tower, and was built as a refuge to which the villagers could retreat during the frequent raids and skirmishes, with its only entrance from inside the church, a low tunnel-like entry secured by a strong iron gate. All the other old buildings and houses in these ancient townships on the sea's edge were also tower-like, presenting tall, immensely thick, windowless façades towards Scotland and, like Burgh church, all largely built of the fine dressed stone from the Wall.

A mile from Burgh church was the lonely monument to Edward I, who had died while encamped there in 1307, when he was almost seventy years old – a rare age to have attained in those times. But then Edward I was an extraordinary monarch, one who seemed to have embodied most of the attributes expected, but seldom found, in those who had fought in the Crusades. During his thirty-five-year reign his most passionate concern seems to have been to make the various parts of Britain into a single nation. He had been preparing to lead his army across the Solway Firth to put down the latest revolt by the Scots, who had recently risen again, this time to the standard of Robert the Bruce, when the illness that had already kept him for months in a nearby abbey finally killed him. The body of the indefatigable old campaigner was laid in Burgh church before being carried all the way back to rest in Westminster, beneath the inscription 'Here lies Edward the First, the Hammer of the Scots'.

The picture of a great army with banners and pavilions encamped with a dying king in these lonely salt marshes, miles from anywhere, was like a misty page from Arthurian legend. The whole area is one great nature reserve now, a welcome landing-place for many species of migratory geese coming south with the first blizzards of winter on their heels.

Further on, we stopped to watch three or four fully clothed men standing up to their chests in the water of the Firth, holding posts

between them from which heavy nets were slung. I had seen similar
tackle leaning against cottage walls and knew it for a haaf net – a local
method for fishing salmon that went back many centuries. An old
man told us that it is not an occupation that is much favoured any
more, being too much like hard work and very cold, though he
believed the haaf net was still the best way of catching salmon.
Margaret said that if they did catch any, no one round about would
eat them for fear they were irradiated; the old man agreed, saying
that the catch was flown straight away to France. Both assured me
that Cumbrian people will only eat fish guaranteed caught in the
North Sea, just as any lamb they buy must be stamped New
Zealand.

On a pleasant evening like this the Solway Firth would seem to be
one of the finest treasures Carlisle has on its doorstep – a panorama of
enormous skies and wide lonely spaces, where sea merges impercep-
tibly into land, and where a great variety of duck, geese, waders and
divers can be seen. It is a setting of great delicacy of tone, where the
eye is led on naturally from the particular to the infinite. A long
jagged skein of black shag undulating across the vast sky like a
Chinese dragon comes to mind when I remember this evening; and,
equally memorably, a ghostly barn owl, pale and unreal, silently
flapping across the last of the sunset with strong deliberate
wingbeats. And behind these two images stands the most obscene
intrusion, which my memory attempts to blot out because it seems
so alien to that primordial scene. Chapel Cross nuclear power station
is sited slap bang across the water on the Scottish shore, so that from
no point on the English side is it possible to avoid the sight of its ugly
gaunt structure and its huge cooling towers, pouring out its dark
smoke into the clear air.

Margaret, who like many people in these parts, is a 'nuclear
watcher', said that hardly anyone comes out from Carlisle any more
to sit on the green benches set up at intervals all around the estuary of
the River Eden, once a favourite place to spend a summer evening.
The grass at the water's edge is still the prized turf of a thousand
bowling greens of England, but the numbers of birds have greatly
diminished over recent years. Her thick file of newspaper cuttings
include many which claim that the Irish Sea, of which the Solway
Firth is part, is the most radio-actively contaminated in the whole
world, as well as being the most poisoned by sewage and industrial

waste. Among the myriad reports of leaks, near accidents, unexplained illnesses, and anything environmentally detrimental connected with Sellafield, was one particular blaze of publicity about Chapel Cross. Reports in the *Guardian*, *The Times* and the *Observer* in December 1979 stated that an earthquake which had reached 5.5 on the Richter scale, and which had been felt over a hundred miles radius, had its epicentre within a half dozen miles of Chapel Cross. Nuclear power stations are not built to withstand earthquakes.

From Carlisle I decided that my route, like that of the Wall, would run eastward through the Border Country. It was impossible not to be fired by the idea of this most marvellous of all Roman monuments, and not to want to take a closer look at it when it was so near. A sense of adventure marked the departure, a feeling of treading the limits of civilisation, beyond which the Romans had marked their maps '*exploratores*'. I left in the teeth of a mild but annoying north-easterly wind, heading for a town called Brampton, which Margaret thought I should visit on the way. The sense of being in shifting border country was enhanced by finding I was on the edge of several maps, which made route-finding awkward. The obvious way was a narrow but busy road from which I detoured as often as I could, finding circuitous little lanes to the south that ran close beside the River Gelt, and which once led me, possibly illegally, through what had been the extensive park of a large country estate.

By coffee time I had reached Brampton, and was able to enjoy a wealth of local information from one of the ladies who ran the local tourist office on a voluntary basis, and who was taking her mid-morning break at the next table. Brampton, I learnt, was a small market town with strong Bonnie Prince Charlie connections, as he had made it his headquarters for the assault upon Carlisle. A memorial I had passed on my way in had recorded some of the aftermath of Brampton's brief importance: the inscription read:

> This stone is placed to mark the site of the ancient Capon Tree under whose shade the Judges of Assize rested and upon whose branches were executed Oct XXI MDCCXLVI for adherence to the Cause of The Royal Line of Stewart – Col James Innes, Captain Patrick Lindesay, Ronald Macdonald, Thomas Park, Peter Taylor, Michael Deland.

'Capon', I discovered from my well-primed informant, probably referred to 'capon justices', so-called from the custom of these travelling magistrates expecting to be given nicely fattened fowls for favours shown when they were on circuit, dispensing 'justice'. That the tree, a large oak, had been used to hang members of the rebel army was doubtless intended to be a warning to the people of Brampton as to whose side they were supposed to be on, something about which they had clearly felt ambiguous.

The solid little house in which Prince Charles Stuart established his headquarters is still preserved, with a plaque to differentiate it from the other modest houses of the same period in the attractive unpretentious central square. But the treasure of the town is undoubtedly the unusual nineteenth-century church of St Martin, which is filled with superb stained-glass windows designed by Burne-Jones and made by William Morris, both of whom had been friends of the Howard family, who had sponsored the building. The glowing jewel-like colours and the beauty of these windows has created, over and above their value to the church, a magnificent art gallery, as unexpected as it was delightful in so small and obscure a town. The themes of the windows were also interesting in depicting Victorian values as distinct from medieval motifs – no Nativity, Crucifixion, Resurrection or Judgement here, but instead, Childhood, Paradise, the Good Shepherd, and various virtues and biblical heroes.

The tourist office lady had urged me to visit the old church, which lay a mile from the present town and which had been built inside a Roman fort on the Stanegate – a road that pre-dated Hadrian's Wall, and ran to the south of it. Only the locked chancel remains now in the centre of a graveyard full of ancient stones, but the position is lovely, with wide views over a rough and varied countryside, and I felt again those stirrings of adventure that seem to be a constant accompaniment to a traverse of the Wall country. As Lord Macaulay wrote of the area in his *History of England*, 'No traveller ventured into the country there without first making his will.' Although it is probably a good deal safer today, motor traffic aside, that sense of it being a place apart, a no-man's-land, remains.

The north-easterly wind was steadily gaining strength and since I was riding straight into it, it was cold as well as energy-sapping. Fortunately, by lunchtime I had dropped down to the shelter of the

Irthing Valley, to where the serene ruins of Lanercost Priory, whose walls once sheltered Edward I, stand in a favoured spot among tall trees by the water's edge. I ate my bread and cheese there, sitting on a wall by the rich meadows, watching the swallows swooping under the lovely arch of the medieval bridge, and afterwards I crossed over to explore the priory.

The ruins are particularly well-preserved. The nave has been divided from the rest and serves as the parish church, the east window of which looks onto the great ruined chancel, where the monks once sung their daily offices. It is one of the very few monasteries of England where worship has continued to be celebrated since its foundation in around the year 1166. This is largely thanks to Sir Thomas Dacre, to whom the priory and its lands were granted after the Dissolution of the Monasteries in 1536, who either didn't choose, or else had no need, to rip off the roof and turn the place into a building quarry. Through marriage, the property passed to the Howard family, of whom George Howard had been a competent painter and a friend of the Pre-Raphaelites, a fact which had accounted for the design of Brampton's new church, and for three more smaller but equally wonderful stained-glass windows by Burne-Jones and William Morris that glowed from the mellow sandstone walls of this church, in long narrow medieval embrasures.

Both artists used to stay at Narworth Castle, half a mile away from Lanercost, a place I wasn't able to visit because it was closed for repairs. From what could be seen of the exterior and the grounds, it was easy to imagine what a source of inspiration it must have been to Victorian artists. It had been in existence there as a rude fortress even longer than the priory, and was built in its present form in 1355. Everything that could be expected of a romantic Border stronghold was there, embellished with all the art and antiquities that a wealthy cultured family had lavished upon it over the centuries. Lanercost Priory was fortunate in having had Narworth as its patron.

The original west front of the priory, with its splendid ceremonial entrance, is now the everyday doorway of the present church. It must be the grandest front to any parish church: the loveliest too perhaps, so delicately is it carved, in the simple Early English style. At the apex is a thirteenth-century statue of the Virgin and Child, which bears such a close resemblance to the 'Angel Choir' at Lincoln that scholars think that Edward I may have brought a Lincoln sculptor with him on his first visit here in 1280.

The guesthouse where Edward and his queen, Eleanor, stayed is close by the church door, and is used as the vicarage now. Scottish and English forays constantly disturbed the peace of Lanercost between the turbulent years 1280 and 1350. Edward brought with him the problems of his entourage – some 200 people who had to be fed and housed. Once the English king and his army had finally departed southwards, Scottish retaliatory raids would follow, with fire and sword, destruction and pillage. I was pleased to read in a pamphlet about the priory's association with Edward I; that it was from here he had set out to his death on the Solway Firth wove another thread into my journey, just as coming upon Prince Charles Stuart's route had done.

I was so charmed by the church, and by the well-kept ruins which were in the charge of English Heritage, a body who somehow manage to preserve a more relaxed atmosphere than is usually to be found in National Trust properties, that I lingered there for a long while. There were many unexpected touches – like the tomb of a Dacre baby girl, with the effigy of the child modelled in red sandstone on the top, looking as though she was asleep with a flower in her hand. In the course of wandering about, rapt in the broad sweep of history that had flowed through the quiet place, I struck up a conversation with the guardian, Jennifer Waldron, who was doing a fine job, mowing the extensive lawns when she wasn't selling tickets or answering visitors' questions. As there was a paucity of visitors she invited me to take a cup of tea with her, and later, at closing-up time, she kindly allowed me access to a flight of stairs that led to the top of the north transept walls, still standing to roof height, where an airy traverse afforded quite amazing views after the low confines of the water meadows. We discovered that we had many interests in common, and she invited me to spend the night at her house, in order that I might see a little known part of Cumbria – an invitation I gladly accepted.

Jennifer lived a few miles away in a small hamlet of four tiny terraced cottages, perched high on a hillside of the Tinsdale Fells. A bleak spot it seemed at first sight, especially after the greener pastures of west Cumbria. In this land 'East of Eden' – so-called not for any biblical association, which would indeed have been appropriate, but because it was east of the River Eden – acres of thin moor grass were scarred by the remains of old mine workings and quarries, and by the waterlogged, overgrown paths leading up to them. A rough stony track took me up the hill, ending at the little terrace. There was an unfinished look to it all, as though it had stopped just short of becoming civilised. It had in fact developed only to the extent that the exploitation of the few small local mines and quarries had proved viable, and all these were now worked out, or had been abandoned. The various enterprises had been served by gravity-operated railways, and it was on these that the most famous railway engine ever built – Stevenson's Rocket – had ended its working days, a fact that immediately added a touch of romance to the place.

The Waldrons, with their two teenage boys, had bought a house here because it was all they could afford when they decided to come and live in Cumbria. The four of them were as cramped as sardines in their tiny two-up, two-down cottage, but they were planning to have an extension built on very shortly. They also had a very long garden at the front of the cottage, where once the quarrymen had made ends meet by growing vegetables for their families. At the foot of this garden, shrouded by old currant bushes and wind-tormented trees, was a very comfortable modern caravan, and it was here that I had been invited to stay. At first, seeing how pushed they were for space, I thought the boys would be using the caravan, and were moving out on my account – something I wasn't prepared to accept. But it turned out that I would be disturbing no one, as the boys absolutely refused to sleep there. 'Too spooky; you'll see,' they warned. 'There's this branch that creaks and rubs against the van, right by your head, all night. It's horrible.'

After a restful night, in which the branch had creaked and groaned on every occasion when I had been awake to hear it, but without carrying a single spooky or horrible overtone, I decided that I must be inured to such experiences after my nomadic wanderings with only thin tent walls between me and anything that might be likely to go bump in the night. The boys were disappointed by my lack of susceptibility.

The following day Jennifer was free, in lieu of having to work on Sundays, and she and her husband Kevin suggested that they take me for a tour of the surrounding area in their ancient car. We drove out on a lonely road south, alongside my old friend the Pennine Way,

which, on this stretch, followed the course of the Romans' Maiden
Way, alongside the infant River Tyne. Alston was our first stop; a
folksy little sign informed us that, at 900 feet, we were in the highest
market town in England. It was all steep cobbled streets, and had a
decidedly flat-cap image, but very comfortably and self-consciously
so, having been carefully upgraded with help from the Manpower
Services and the local tourist board, with every attempt made to
preserve the North Country flavour of the place. It was full of
attractive little corners, with shops demonstrating local crafts –
cheese-making and the like. This side of Cumbria was in the process
of being developed to attract visitors, in competition with the Lake
District, and had recently been declared an area of outstanding
natural beauty – there can be few places left in Britain today which
do not now have this official seal of approval. In spite of feeling that
its charm had been acquired rather too quickly for it to appear quite
natural, I liked it a lot more than somewhere like Hawkeshead
because it had not yet become tourist-jaded, and because there was
such an air of enthusiasm and involvement there. Many local cars
carried stickers reading 'We Love Cumbria but Sellafield Breaks Our
Hearts'; something I had not seen further west and nearer to 'the
Monster'.

Although British Rail closed the branch line from Haltwhistle to
Alston in 1976, the town now has the highest narrow-gauge railway
line in Britain, and the station presents a far livelier scene than would
be found on many working lines. All had been beautifully restored to
a state of cleanliness and charm that has been absent from BR's
platforms for many years. The booking-hall, a refreshment room
and a bookstall were manned by a host of friendly ladies and
children, while outside on the platforms, along the lines and in the
engine sheds, scores of men in boilersuits were milling about,
tapping wheels and wielding oilcans, and looking blissfully happy.
They were all volunteers, working on the restoration of a small
section of the defunct branch line, and refurbishing the rolling-stock
to run on it.

I was told all about the project by a sprightly white-haired
gentleman called Mr Eddie Dyke, who seemed to be in charge of the
operation. I found him working on a carriage, and although he was
as engrossed in his task as everyone else there, he courteously
straightened up, took a neatly folded duster from the pocket of his

beautifully laundered boilersuit, soft with repeated washings and, having carefully wiped his hands, proceeded to explain about the delights and the problems of setting up a two-foot gauge railway. The engines apparently can no longer be found in England; each of Alston's three had been painstakingly tracked down and acquired from Portugal, Poland and East Germany respectively. There had been no difficulty, however, in finding volunteers for all aspects of the work, such is the magic of steam; currently they had 300, only five of whom came from Alston. About a mile and a half of the former line is open again, and on it some 16,000 passengers currently take a nostalgic steam-powered journey each year.

Mr Dyke had been a member of the small consortium that had originally tried to buy the complete line from BR, and keep it operational, but in spite of the £18,000 they had raised, BR had ripped up the track. This caused a certain amount of bitterness, but they had not let it deter them; they just had 'to rethink the possibilities'. As a tourist attraction, Mr Dyke feels that the new narrow gauge railway has been well worth all the effort. 'It might even pay its way, one day,' he says, his eyes taking on a far away look, 'who knows? it could even run all the way to Haltwhistle again.' There can be few such cost-effective hobbies providing so many grown men with such dreams of glory.

We finished our day not far from Jennifer and Kevin's hamlet, at a village called Tinsdale, which I felt so enthusiastic about that I might well have bought a house there, had there been one for sale. It was in the throes of celebrating a centenary, and an exhibition had been mounted for the occasion in a rickety little hall. The story of those hundred years was told with all the simple graphic detail that can be provided by a few dozen early photographs and some everyday period objects. It showed the thriving little community of 1888 enjoying the fruits of a new social awareness that was beginning to change the conditions of the working man and his family. Small local industries were flourishing, new buildings were going up, and a co-op and a reading-room had been built. But it was a brief flowering. Even before the First World War, the slow industrial decline had already begun, and people had begun to drift away in search of jobs elsewhere; the place had begun to take on a bedraggled appearance. By the 1960s, the pictures showed a ghost town, with houses derelict, roofs fallen in, and the gardens reduced to rubbish dumps.

The village itself was the present-day part of the exhibition, and as we walked around it was clear that Tinsdale thrives again, although on a totally different footing to its nineteenth-century heyday. No longer tied to a narrow range of industry, its strength now lay in the diversity of its inhabitants, and in the fact that it was not work which had brought them here but the place itself. People had moved in from all over, and they followed a very wide range of callings: I met an archaeologist, someone who made kits for home-brewing, a carpenter, a wood-turner, a puppeteer, several artists and craftsmen, teachers, a journalist, and scores of children.

There were no pretty houses as such, and yet the whole village had taken on an air of charm and attractiveness from the way in which each building had been renovated, and the way each fitted in with its neighbours. It may be that most of the people who had moved there had done so, like the Waldrons, because it was cheap. Certainly the restorations looked as though they owed more to hard work than to large expenditures of money. Diversity was combined with harmony, and it looked as though a great deal of thought and ingenuity had gone into it all, but without the result being over-contrived or desperately self-conscious. It also seemed to have been achieved without the sacrifice of individuality. Any stray patch of ground had been planted with trees, bushes, vegetables and flowers; the flowers spilled over into window boxes, and into pots beside front doors that opened straight onto the yard or the dirt street. This helped to soften the hard lines of the rows of uncompromisingly square workmen's cottages, and the long, otherwise unrelieved terraces.

Even more exciting was the sense of commitment that extended beyond the bounds of the village into a concern for the wider environment. The Tinsdale Community had already created a nature reserve centred on a small lake nearby, and were now planning to plant more trees and generally improve the surrounding countryside. The village was like a green eye in a parched desert, and it was good to think of that greenness spreading out from it a little further each year.

Thinking over the day as I sat in the caravan with the sky still light, though it was barely an hour to midnight, I watched the sheep settling down in companionable huddles, taking advantage of the few wind-tortured hawthorn trees. They were pastured in a sour, poorly-drained meadow; many of them were lame in consequence, and few of the lambs were thriving. I gathered that they were the remnant of someone's last sorry attempt to farm the place. Taking it all in all, I didn't feel that the immediate area was one of outstanding beauty, but, nonetheless, I found it a place of exciting possibilities. The industrial nineteenth century had added many scars to a land that had been subjected to ravages as long ago as the Bronze Age. The tribes which had settled here then had hacked away at the forests, exhausting the soil and moving on. They had left a legacy of marginal lands, which succeeding generations had further despoiled until it was fit only for the sheep, whose grazing had further degraded it. What the area was rich in now was its wonderful abundance of open space. The bones of the land had a great potential for beauty: they just needed fleshing out a little.

This age has the leisure and the knowledge necessary for the healing of debased land to a far greater extent than any previous generation. All that is really needed to make the transformation is good will, and a faith in the future that makes it worthwhile to consider reshaping things for the benefit of generations to come. After meeting the new inhabitants of Tinsdale, and seeing what they had achieved in a comparatively short time, I felt that a real beginning had been made in one small part of this neglected landscape. A single curlew called, a last fluting trill before the light finally died, and I suddenly felt glad that the sheep were not my responsibility, that I was still fancy-free and would be cycling on in the morning. But I was also very glad that I had taken up Jennifer's offer to see what this area of England was like, where the River Tyne has its source in the last of the English Pennines, east of Eden.

CHAPTER FIFTEEN

The Frontiers of Empire

It was a glorious June morning when I set out next day towards the Wall. In the early morning sunshine the thin scoured moors seemed altogether a different, brighter place. The wind had returned to its summer quarter in time to help me on my way, and within a short time I was in richer land, coasting down empty fragrant lanes, between hedgerows full of birdsong, down to the river valley and the crossing of the Irthing. Narworth Castle came suddenly into view around a sharp bend in the road, a gilded romantic picture straight out of legend. There was no wind at all in the lane but the tall trees in the castle park were tossing their heads, and rooks were peeling merrily off the tower battlements like torn pieces of a black flag. A last shadowy glide under the towering oaks to the medieval bridge, and there once more was Lanercost Priory brooding beside the still river, with woolly sheep grazing round about it in the lush green meadows, the very symbol of peaceful prosperity. Apart from the chancel roof open to the skies, the Dissolution and the succeeding centuries might never have happened.

Another very different world met me at the top of the escarpment. The gentle breeze was now a force to be reckoned with, and I was very glad it was at my back. Beyond the ridge that ran eastward along a craggy irregular contour, was a wild empty-looking country stretching away to the north; the sort of country where the wind is never still, and where it has left its mark permanently on the coarse parched grass and the few gnarled trees and bent twisted bushes. Such details hardly registered at this moment, however, for my attention was immediately gripped by the Wall itself, which the ridge carried along its crest. A broad swathe of masonry, it marched implacably onwards into the far distance, with the remnant of the ditch on its northern side emphasising its height and line. What previously I had thought of in terms only of its historical importance, I was now seeing in its physical reality, and the effect was at once exciting and astounding. Hadrian's Wall is among the most famous monuments in the world, and even in its present state of truncated ruin, it is easy to see why this is so. It is still extraordinarily dramatic in that rugged landscape; so orderly and regular, it gives the impression of unlimited power and infinite resources. I wondered what my barbarian ancestors north of the Border had thought of it; no mean stone-workers themselves, the Wall must nevertheless have daunted them somewhat. It must have made them realise something of the staggering might of the Roman Empire that was ranged against their world. Odd to think that it was the barbarians who triumphed eventually.

At Birdoswald, a few miles further on, I was to have some aspects of the Wall explained to me by an archaeologist, Tony Wilmott, whom I had met the previous day in the remade little village of Tinsdale. Tony was one of those rare and fortunate men who was not only doing precisely what he had set out to do with his life, but was very conscious of how lucky he was – his being a profession that offers surprisingly few such opportunities. He was in charge of an extensive archaeological dig in the large Roman fort at Birdoswald, funded by Nuclear Fuels – 'archaeology is a very respectable field for sponsorship,' Mr Eddie Dyke had told me wryly the day before, lamenting the fact that Alston's railway project had been too low-profile to attract Sellafield's generosity. For Tony Wilmott, Nuclear Fuel's money meant an army of skilled workers to uncover the enigmas of history on which his skills could get to work – skills very similar to those of a detective: painstaking, piece-by-piece historical deciphering, with now and again a jackpot gratuity, like the uncovering of the tomb of Tutankhamen, or finding the Treasure of the Oxus, or the Sutton Hoo burial.

His 'hire a digger' force of workers was milling about all over the site in jeans and wellies, pushing wheelbarrows along precarious planks, or squatting in holes, brushing away dirt from some inconspicuous piece of debris. They were like the itinerant skilled artisans of former ages, moving on from job to job as one project ended and another began, hearing of fresh opportunities through their particular grapevine. Some of them were students or ex-students of archaeology, unlikely ever to get to the sort of position that Tony had attained; others came from different academic disciplines, or from none at all. They were mostly young people who had been bitten by this particular bug, and could at present conceive of no other existence which would give them half the satisfaction: it was a little like the thrill of prospecting for gold, they told me, in that you never knew when you would suddenly come across something of special significance. Most thought they would eventually find employment in some totally unrelated field, but until ambition or opportunity moved them out of the archaeology circuit, they were prepared to put up with an existence of minimal comfort and low monetary reward. This sizeable band was camping in the baronialised house that a nineteenth-century gentleman had made for himself from the small farm that had sheltered within the walls of the ruined fort.

I arrived on the site at the same time as various rival archaeologists and a few new diggers, and was taken on a conducted tour with them. The talk was all very technical and way above my head. To me the site was little more than a jumble of stones, ditches and muddy lakes – drainage always seems a major problem on archaeological sites. I gathered that important new theories were being formed from all this unexciting looking evidence, which, if proved, would overturn all existing theories about the medieval history of the area. I didn't need to be an expert to realise that no real information was being given away, and that a delicate verbal fencing match was in progress, with searching questions being cleverly turned, and secrets closely guarded. It was evident that this branch of archaeology was as highly competitive, and as jealous of its reputation and discoveries, as that I had previously observed operating in the field of Egyptology.

What I could appreciate about Birdoswald was the marvellous view from the fields at the back of the fort, where the land falls away steeply into a hidden valley 300 feet below, enclosed in an ox bow of the River Irthing. Lovely woods, still in new leaf, clothed the flanking hillsides, while the sheltered wheat fields in the great sweeping bend of the river were just beginning to turn gold. It was a place whose existence could never be suspected from the Wall, but I was sure that many Roman legionaries serving their time in Birdoswald had hopefully earmarked those fat acres for their retirement.

When the experts had left, Tony gave me a straightforward introduction to the world of the Wall, which was to prove very helpful in looking at the other sites, as well as at the Wall in general.

The information was no different to what I could have gleaned from books, but Tony's enthusiasm and his long familiarity with the period made it all much more interesting. I enjoyed it all, even the joke at my expense when we stopped to chat, as though by accident, by one particular portion of the Wall, and Tony was able to point out that I was resting my hand on something 'rather indelicate'. It was a crudely exuberant representation of male genitals which Roman soldiers had carved there, as they had apparently done in many other places along the Wall, as tokens of good luck. The symbol, used with such archaic innocence, was a timely reminder that the Romans, no matter how thoroughly modern they might seem in so many ways, with their laws, books, engineering skills, roads, sanitation, hygiene, administration, communications and so forth, were nonetheless part of the pagan world, with an ethos fundamentally different to our own.

Hadrian's Wall was built about 125 years after the birth of Christ, but it was well into the fourth century before Christianity began to bring about any profound change to the thinking of the Roman world. Curiously, it was from this far outpost of the Empire that the first nominally Christian Roman Emperor would come. Constantine the Great was born at York, the base camp for the Wall, and it was from here in 306 AD that he left to make his successful bid for the Empire, and to initiate the great Byzantine age.

I met a few people walking the Wall – seventy-three miles from end to end. Far more were touring around by car, and walking the odd stretch; but as it was not yet the school holidays, I often felt I had the whole area to myself. Weeks, months even, could easily be spent exploring it all, and I saw only a fraction of what there was in the excellent museums and well-documented sites. Forts, inns, temples and bathhouses displayed their few remaining courses of stone on the closely-mown grass, leaving it to the visitors' imagination to construct their past glory from what they had gleaned in the museums. It was hard work, and I can sympathise with the reconstruction school of archaeology. There was a wonderful latrine that I would never have fully appreciated without the help of pictorial reconstruction – the soldiers had sat companionably side by side over holes set in long slabs on either side of a narrow room. Beneath the slabs, permanently running water had washed everything away through a culvert, to emerge far beyond the walls of the fort, where it could be used for manuring the fields. Sponges had apparently served the Romans for toilet paper, and they had rinsed these out in channels of running water that passed in front of the seats. The sponges were carried round on little sticks and there was even a socket provided in front of each seat for holding them. I found it strange to think how many centuries would have to elapse before our civilisation came up with anything like as hygienic – and there are many areas of the world today which would find the Roman latrine more acceptable than twentieth-century Western lavatories.

In the museums, all manner of reconstructed scenes and recorded talks were designed to give visitors a sense of the Roman past, but it was, as usual, the actual artifacts, the little trifles of everyday life, that made the inhabitants of these long deserted settlements seem suddenly real to me – a tent peg, a scrap of cloth, a betrothal medallion, sandals dug out of a bog, a lady's slipper stamped with the maker's name – 'Lucius Aebitus Thales, son of Titus'.

The Romans had kept the area of the Wall strictly separate from civilian life by the equivalent of a perimeter fence – a continuous wide ditch flanked by mounds, called the *vallum*. Purely military in purpose, the Wall followed the line of the highest ground, where there was little shelter, in order to keep as wide a watch as possible on any barbarian movement in the north. Small mile castles were built across the wall at regular mile intervals, with two turrets in between, so that no portion of the Wall would be left unpatrolled. Even in the warm spell that I was enjoying, it was not difficult to imagine how desperately bleak a place it would be in winter.

Contrary to popular notions, the Wall, the ditch to the north of it, and the *vallum* were not built with slave labour, but were constructed by the legionaries themselves, and each stretch had a commemorative stone to show who had been responsible for it. I pitched my tent on a stretch built by the Century of Gellius Philippus – almost on top of where turret 35a would be if it had not been replaced by the intriguingly-named Sewingshields Farm, so called after the stretch of the Wall from which it was constructed. No one seems sure of the origin of this name; some authorities claim it should be Seven Shields, which is what Sir Walter Scott called it in his poem, *Harold the Dauntless*, but I read somewhere that the name comes from Old English and means Shiels of Sigewine – presumably a Saxon's farm.

The present day Sewingshields Farm has the original centurial tablet, inscribed 'GELLI PHILPF' standing in the porch, along with the wellies, dried geraniums, and an accumulation of defunct tools. The heavy sloping roof of the old house sports a luxuriant natural garden of mosses and waving ferns, for the farm is completely overshadowed by a narrow strip of tall trees growing on the section of the Wall that was taken down to build the farm. It is the strangest sight – the Wall ends abruptly, as though sliced through with a knife, and begins again where the farm buildings cease. Mr Murray, the owner, was quite happy for me to camp there among the trees, so my little tent soon stood directly on the line of the Wall, the tent pegs sliding easily into the thick leaf mould that covered any stones which might remain.

It was a fine place to spend a night on the Wall, on one of its highest and craggiest sections, with wide views northwards over a valley steeped in legend and rich in prehistoric remains. Somewhere in the cliffs beneath was believed to be the hidden opening to yet another cave in which King Arthur and his knightly court lie spellbound, waiting for someone to come and blow a horn to release them. From the tent it was just a few feet to where the Wall started again – a lonely place to walk as the sun was setting, and where I could well imagine coming upon a ghostly Roman legion. All I actually saw, however, were scores of little brown rabbits scuttling headlong down the cliffs at my approach.

Morning on the Wall was so cold that the sheep in the fields below didn't bother to stagger to their feet until nearly eight o'clock, and I delayed striking camp until Mr Murray came past to see if I had survived the night. He came driven in state like an ancient British chief, with his two grandsons, aged seven and nine, as his charioteers, handling the balloon-tyred motor tricycle and trailer with the easy competence of boyhood. It was a useful vehicle for crossing the rough fields, much less expensive to run than a tractor and much less damaging to the land; but old Mr Murray could not get the hang of it at all, according to his son, and had to rely on the skill of the boys.

I was invited into the farmhouse for a second breakfast, and to meet all three generations of the Murrays who worked the Sewingshields lands. A few miles back I had crossed into Northumberland, notorious as the last stronghold of male chauvinism, but this clan seemed most definitely to be a matriarchy, with old Mrs Murray giving out orders left and right, particularly to her daughter-in-law. As no one seemed to be unduly bothered by the spate of commands, and as the atmosphere was essentially good-humoured, I decided that no one took Mrs Murray too seriously.

I was evidently welcome as a fresh audience, and having got me sitting down and anchored with a large mug of tea, Mrs Murray lost no time in bringing out photograph albums and several large and impressive charts of her family tree. She had been born an Armstrong, and was yet another member of that clan to be fascinated by her roots. She attempted to acquaint me with an array of departed Tulleys, Armstrongs and Murrays through the bewildering web of their convoluted genealogies. The photographs however were an unalloyed delight, giving a glimpse into late-Victorian and Edwardian life in the Borders that seemed almost as divorced from the present day as the Romans. It was not just the solemn little girls in frilled white dresses and black stockings, posed decorously at the church picnics, or the boys in their thick stiff knickerbockers, little round caps and Eton collars, that made it all seem so different. The composed serious little faces looked out of a landscape that had changed to such an extent as to be unrecognisable. The countryside of those days had supported a population several times that of today. On land where only sheep are now farmed, people had practised a mixed economy, and had been largely self-sufficient. The area had known a fair amount of poverty and hardship in the early part of the century, but it had also known the interdependence of a community who had shared their labour and their outings in a way that the 'nuclear age' has lost entirely.

General Wade had wrecked a lot of the Wall after the 1745 Rising by building his military road with the stone – a feat that most experts consider a great waste of time, since the Roman road, and the older Stanegate, were already running parallel, and both of them far better roads. I felt I could endorse this, as I pedalled along the general's road, dropping into the great hollows caused by the subsidence of the ancient earthworks over which it ran. But with the strong wind behind me it was all great fun, like riding a giant roller coaster. It was a lovely ride as far as Chollerford, where the road crossed the North Tyne. Here the Romans had built the large fort of Chesters to guard the crossing. The huge abutment of their bridge can still be seen on the east bank, one of the most impressive memorials in the area.

Less satisfactory was the matter of getting something to eat. Because it was Sunday, people were out in force, and the inn at Chollerford was thronged with cars. When I asked if I could have lunch, I was told that it was extremely unlikely, and in any case I would have to wait until 2.30. This was serious. I had not had a proper meal for a day or two, and there were few supplies left in my panniers. I had been burning calories extravagantly since early morning and was so hungry that I began to regret refusing Mrs Armstrong's offer of a second breakfast. A small man in a cloth cap drinking by the bar said I should go to his favourite pub – I would get 'a lovely meal' there. I was to tell them that he had sent me, and he gave me careful instructions on how to get there.

It was quite a distance to this recommended gastronomic haven, over a number of sharp little hills, and my legs were beginning to feel the effect of the glass of beer I had drunk at Chollerford. I struggled up the last slope, and thankfully chained Evans to a drainpipe, hastening inside in a glow of expectation. The air was blue with cigarette smoke, so I had to wait a while until the room swam slowly into focus. The buzz of conversation ceased immediately; twenty pairs of outraged male eyes swivelled in my direction; twenty vast beer stomachs, constrained under identical sleeveless singlets, heaved up from the tables in disbelief. I had the impression that no woman had ever before dared to penetrate this male preserve. Not only was I not welcome, I felt that they were restraining themselves with difficulty from rising *en masse* to eject me forcibly. The huge bulk of the barman thrust itself threateningly even further across the counter. He seemed barely able to bring himself to reply to my query as to what there was to eat, but croaked, in a surprisingly small voice for so large a man – the effect of the cigarette smoke, doubtless – that there was 'Nothing, nothing at all'. Remote corners of Moslem lands have yielded somewhat similar experiences; the only thing to do is to retreat with dignity.

Back at Chollerford, my guide to a good lunch, who was still on the same perch at the bar, professed himself surprised at the reception I had received. I was not convinced that his motive had been without mischief, but as he had clearly downed a good few pints by then there seemed little point in remonstration. The inordinately late lunch I was finally able to wring out of the inn wasn't very good in spite of the price, but by then I would have eaten anything, and the lateness of the hour meant I would not need to bother about any more food that day.

By the time I had finished eating, I felt disinclined to head north as I had planned. Three miles south at Acomb there was a youth hostel, and I thought it might be a good idea to spend the night there, and indulge in some of the luxuries the Romans had enjoyed, like a hot shower. I had not had many opportunities to wash during the last thirty six hours – which shows just how much the area around the Wall has deteriorated since the Romans went home.

It was a happy decision, because on the way I came across a lovely little village called Wall. Perched on the edge of a hill, with a huge outlook to the east, charming old cottages were clustered around several small greens; they had been built very solidly and close together for protection in troubled times. No two of them were the same, having all been altered, or modernised at different periods. Over the oldest of them was a lintel which read 'Feare God in Hart RK MK', with the date 1631 above. The owner, Mrs Huddleston, opened the door when she saw me studying the inscription and invited me in to see the rest of the house. The injunction over the threshold was a 'marriage lintel', I learnt, but the house pre-dated the inscription, being a 'bastle' or tower house, the traditional domestic building of the area in earlier times, designed to withstand attack from border raiders – the Armstrongs and their ilk. The walls were six feet thick, and it was roofed with massive stones that couldn't be set on fire. Originally the entry would have been at first-floor level, with a retractable ladder. There would have been no windows at all on the ground floor, and the few there were higher up would have been very small.

More light had been allowed in as times grew more peaceful. From the outside it looked at a casual glance no different from many other charming stone-built cottages. Inside it was different again. Mrs Huddleston was proud of the hard work she and her husband had put into it over the forty years they had lived there. Apart from the deep window embrasures and the steep staircase, they had created a neat cosy interior that could be mistaken for a 1930s three-bedroomed semi.

Wall is now a village of old folk, said Mrs Huddleston. No younger people could afford the prices of houses there. With Newcastle less than twenty miles away, the village had become part of the commuter belt. When she was young there had been sixty children in the village school. The railway had been an important factor in village life, something that linked one with the outside world. The village had joined in corporate outings to the town or to the seaside, eagerly anticipated events that helped to preserve the sense of community. Walking across the fields with the children and grandchildren to wave to passing trains had also been a regular excursion. Then the railway was withdrawn, the school was closed, and the village as a living community began to die. She took in B & Bs now, as much for the company as for the money.

If it ever comes on the market, I am sure Mrs Huddleston's bastle house will not remain as it is now for very long. The tiled fireplaces will be ripped out; the beams which appear tantalisingly from the lowered ceilings will all be exposed again, and the place will be 'restored' to whatever stage of its long history the new owners consider desirable or authentic. Whoever buys it, the house that Mr and Mrs Huddleston were able to get for a song forty years ago because nobody wanted such an old-fashioned, inconvenient property, will now be worth a small fortune.

An excited party of Norfolk school children had just taken over all but one bed at Acomb youth hostel, and the noise and bustle was so amazing after the days alone in my tent that I fled. It was quite late by this time, so I settled reluctantly for a rather grand camping site a little further on. I cycled in and found myself among serried ranks of caravans, hundreds of them it seemed, each neatly parked in its own little bay, with electricity points and water taps close to hand. It was all very regimented and not at all my sort of camping place, but I found an area reserved for tents which was on the edge of a field of heavy-headed grain, with a view across to distant blue hills. A smudge of smoke in the middle distance rose straight upwards: there was not a breath of wind. Midges were coming off the corn field in droves, with the swallows tirelessly pursuing them, swooping down almost to ground level. An evening chorus was tuning up in adjacent woods, with birds drifting homewards to join in. A throbbing chirruping sounded from all around, with the thin wailing of sheep and the bleat of lambs coming from far away.

As the light faded, all the sounds gradually shut down and peace descended, except for the dog-walkers from the caravans creeping about like felons. They were all looking for somewhere for their pets to do 'doggy dos', as one gentleman innocently phrased it, having expressed disappointment at finding my tent in a place he considered ideal for this nefarious and unlawful purpose. The dog-owners were quite without shame: in spite of notices everywhere requesting people not to let their pets 'commit nuisances' and directing them towards a little gate coyly labelled 'Doggie Path to Woods'. The parade of assorted dogs and their owners into prohibited areas continued far into the night.

CHAPTER SIXTEEN

The Kingdom in the North

Not all frontiers are immediately obvious. The continuous line of the Wall had stamped a notion of cohesion upon the terrain I had been riding through which had somewhat blinded me to the fact that I was now in quite a different country. There was an east-west divide, marked by the central spine of the Pennines, which was as real as the difference between the north and the south of England. Northumberland, I soon discovered, was not like anywhere else at all; it was a kingdom within a kingdom.

It was at Hexham that I began to see how deep the roots of this difference lay. I had gone there in order to visit the priory church of St Andrew, where the famous tombstone of the Roman standard-bearer Flavinus was kept. This unusually lively carving showed a warrior in a flamboyant headdress of tall plumes, reining in a prancing charger. It was a lovely thing and would have been well worth the detour, as would the church itself, which was a gracefully blended pot-pourri of styles, with a finely carved wooden rood screen and sedilia, and a Saxon throne. None of it however made anything like the impact of St Wilfrid's seventh-century crypt, over which the present church had been built. Sacked by the Danes in 876 AD, the simple yet strangely powerful undercroft is all that remains of the original church, which, in its day, was reckoned to be without equal anywhere north of the Alps. In this small crypt, built of dressed stones from the Wall, it was not difficult to realise the importance of the northern kingdom in keeping alight a candle of civilisation in the Dark Ages.

When the Romans withdrew from Britain at the beginning of the fifth century in order to try to secure the centre of their empire against the invading barbarian hordes, every boundary of the civilised western world was under threat. In one of those cataclysmic movements of peoples that have occurred throughout history, beginning in what Rose Macaulay called the 'hooling wilderness' of the Mongolian plains, the whole world seemed to be on the move, pushing westward. As wave after wave of tribes overran new territories, the dispossessed were forced to move on, displacing others in their turn. While Goths, Ostrogoths, Huns, Vandals and others were beating on the gates of Rome, this far-flung northern frontier was left to defend itself as best it could.

Raiding Picts from north of the Wall were one thing, but now there also came hordes of Saxons and Angles, pouring in across the North Sea and the Channel from the fringes of Europe; and they came not to raid, but to conquer territory and to settle. Native Britons who were not absorbed by the new settlers had little choice but to retreat westward to the wilder lands beyond the Pennines. The invaders, skilled in agriculture, entrenched themselves on the eastern side of Britain, forming themselves into loose alliances of tribes which eventually grew into kingdoms. At one time Northumbria stretched from the Forth to the Humber.

Christianity, which replaced Rome as the civilising influence of the West, arrived in Northumbria by a different route from the rest of England. Long before Augustine had landed in Kent, and Roman Christianity had begun to spread slowly northwards, Columba had brought his Irish monks to Iona on the west coast of Scotland, and established a monastery there to bring Christianity to the Picts.

As a boy, the pagan prince of Northumbria, Oswald, had been given asylum on Iona after his father had been slain in a tribal battle. Oswald was educated by these Celtic monks, and converted to the faith. When he eventually won back his father's kingdom at the battle of Heavenfield, in 635 AD, he invited the Iona monastery to send a mission to christianise the people of his realm. Later there would be division and grief when the Celtic and the Roman churches clashed over their respective and differing practices. Whether this separate road to Christianity which the Northumbrians followed 1,300 years ago has anything at all to do with their present marked independence of spirit was an idea which would intrigue me all the while I rode through their county.

Having seen the best of the Wall, I decided to leave it at this halfway point, and follow the North Tyne as it wound around the foothills of the Cheviots. Northumbria thrusts northwards beyond the Wall in a great triangular wedge that reaches its apex at the mouth of the Tweed, where Edward I built the walls of Berwick as another mighty bulwark against the Scots. I thought it would be a

good plan to ride up the inland side of this triangle and come back
down around the coast.

To avoid the traffic converging on Hexham, I took a small road
which ran back westwards for a little way, before swinging north to
cross the pretty South Tyne, which had been bubbling merrily along
close beside my path all the way from Haltwhistle. At the bridge,
half a mile before the South Tyne merges with the North Tyne, I
found a small unpretentious stone pub, with a Routiers sign and a
few rough tables outside it facing the water. It was so beautifully
situated and perfectly timed for lunch that it seemed like a last
friendly gesture from this pleasant river. The image of a cold beaded
glass of lager arose delightfully before me, irresistible in the midday
heat, after the long morning with Northumberland's history.

I had locked Evans to a post before I read the small notice
informing wayfarers that the pub was closed on Mondays. My map
showed that there would be no others for a good few miles, so it
seemed best to stay there and have a picnic, comforting myself with
the knowledge that lunchtime beer plays havoc with cycling
muscles.

There was a cottage close to the pub, and I went there to ask for
some water to make my coffee. The old lady who came to the door
would at a nod have had me in for lunch, for she was mortified, she
said, that her village pub should be closed for a traveller. She tried to
press gifts of eggs and lettuce upon me, and in the end I accepted the
lettuce as she said she had far too much in her garden. When she
brought it she had added a couple of spring onions. 'A lettuce is
nothing without scallions, I just love a scallion,' she said. 'Mind now
you're welcome, man, if you change your mind, it was good to meet
you.'

It was even hotter after lunch, airless too, with a summer storm
brewing; just as well the pub had been closed, for a beer would have
finished me. But Tynedale was such a pretty valley, with the
winding river and the views of the hills, their slopes clothed in mixed
woods, that I was only conscious of the discomfort where the slopes
were particularly steep. Unexpected treasures lined the way. At
Warden, a tiny hamlet in a fold of the river, there was another lovely
church that had used the Wall as a quarry, and had Roman jambs in
its Norman tower and Saxon stones in the porch. Further on,
Haughton Castle, a thirteenth-century stronghold, stood on a slight

eminence above the river. Much extended in the late-Victorian Gothic revival, it still retained a purposeful, watchful air, in keeping with its history as the stronghold of the Swinburnes. I read in a guide book I had found in Hexham that it had a grim significance for the border clan whose members kept crossing my path – the Armstrongs. One of their number had been thrown into Haughton's dungeon by Sir Thomas Swinburne, after being caught during a cattle raid. Sir Thomas subsequently, and rather absent-mindedly, forgot about him, and set off on a long journey. Only when he reached York did he recollect his prisoner, and by that time even the most hurried of returns was too late to save him. It was said that the poor wretch had gnawed the flesh from his arms before finally perishing from starvation.

Chipchase Castle, reputed to be the finest Jacobean architecture in Northumberland, was barely a stone's throw away, an elegant mansion gracing the opposite bank, and another building that had been grafted onto an earlier pele tower. Northumberland, I decided, could quite properly be described as the county of castles; not more than a two-mile stretch of Tynedale was free of them or their ruins. In medieval times, when Northumbria changed hands constantly between Scotland and England, there were only three kinds of dwellings – castles for the aristocracy, pele towers for the wealthy farmers, and variations of bastle houses for the hoi polloi. What is left of them adds immeasurably to the romance and the enjoyment of the scene.

Another old acquaintance, the Pennine Way, descended into the small market town of Bellingham, nearly at the northern limit of its two hundred-odd miles. As befits a town astride so well used a track, every other house had a B&B sign, and there was a princely teashop, the best I had come across on the whole journey; my 'pot for one' yielded five cups of tea, without the addition of hot water, and it cost just 35p.

I decided to stayed overnight in Bellingham's youth hostel in order to telephone home. Public phone boxes seem to be very few and far between in country areas, and there were certainly never any near where I was camping. Bellingham's five pubs, in which the town's phones were to be found were crammed with crowds of young men, all wearing jeans and either a white singlet or a sleeveless T-shirt, their exposed arms heavily tattooed. Rather below average height, each had a cigarette drooping from the corner of his mouth, with one eye screwed up against the smoke – all of which made for a very curious, uniform effect, like a room full of clones. They were soldiers, I discovered, having a night off from manoeuvres in the large military area to the north, and preserving their corporate identity equally effectively in civilian dress. As all these young men were also bent on telephoning, I retreated with smarting eyes from the nauseating smoke screens that filled each pub, wondering how fit and effective a fighting force they could be with all these carcinogens chasing through their blood streams.

A helpful pedestrian coming out of a fish and chip shop, which was also doing a roaring trade, told me of a street phone half a mile away, but the military had beaten me to this one too. Five fairly drunken soldiers, smoking profusely, were jammed into the booth. I decided to wait, and after some time, one of them came out to apologise for keeping me waiting. 'Me mate's 'ad a baby,' he said, swaying slightly, 'an' we bin wetting its 'ead like. He's tryin' to phone 'is mum to tell 'er.' They seemed to be having very little luck dialling, and after another long interval, the same soldier came out again to apologise. He told me they had not long come back from Northern Ireland, as though that somehow explained something of deep significance, as I'm sure it did. I offered to try the number for them, and they all trooped out, leaving me in the smoke-filled box with the proud father. He looked hardly old enough to be out of school. He was pale as death, with sweat oozing from around his hairline and trickling down his face. 'Wetting the baby's head' was clearly as serious a ritual as many primitive tribes practise to mark the mystery of birth. I supposed this young soldier-father had survived his ordeal, but I also thought he might very well throw up at any moment. Fortunately I was able to get him connected through the operator, and before I hurried out into the fresh air, I heard the answer to the question I had wanted to ask – 'Yeah Mum, Linda's all right, an 'e's a lovely little boy, Mum, eight pounds . . .'

Bellingham marked a change in the weather. The threatened storm broke during the night, making me glad that I had sacrificed my privacy and stayed in the youth hostel – only a simple little wooden hut, but with a good tight roof. I was up long before anyone else, and prepared breakfast while a bold thrush sat just outside the window, carefully polishing each side of his beak on the fencepost, like a person sharpening a carving knife. When he was satisfied with the condition of his beak, he stood very still, head on one side, as though listening for the worms brought out by the rain.

A flurry of light rain was still falling from pearl-grey skies as I left, and a massed chorus of birds was pouring out a huge volume of song into the morning. Fresh scents of damp earth and new growth rose up from all around. Every hedgerow was burgeoning with newly-washed blossom; flowers of every colour pushed up along the banks, and huge buds of towering wild angelica and hogweed looked just about ready to burst open. It was the sort of day when it seemed possible to watch things growing, like a speeded-up film.

Almost at once I was climbing out of this scene of abundance. The lush fields of grain were left behind, and soon I was above the pastures also, and was riding around the 1,000-foot contour line on high open moorland. Extensive forestry stretched away northwards and westwards, with occasional isolated plantations spreading to the east. A line of crags lay just to the right of the road, with the marks of centuries of quarrying along its flanks. As I stopped to take off my rain gear, I saw a buzzard suddenly stoop in a lovely heart-stopping fall above the ridge. He rose again, mewing in fury having missed his prey, and vanished above a small stand of old Scotch pine, which I thought must be a tiny remnant of the great Caledonian Forest.

I had heard many cyclists claim that Northumberland beats all other counties for hills, and that if you could cycle there you could manage anywhere. I decided they were right. Hill followed hill, with almost no flat bits in between, and at no point did the road take an easy way around, but always went straight over the top. The reward of the often bleak moorland that met me after each long pull up to these summits was the wealth of skylarks and curlews, giving an endless concert that sounded like pan pipes bubbling through water.

Towards the end of the day I had my first experience of being refused a camping place. I had been riding for a long while in lonely countryside, where there was a wealth of fields newly-cut and eminently suitable for camping but no door to knock upon and obtain permission. It was an area of large prosperous farms, where it was easy to see why the Angles and Saxons had been keen to settle there. The lodge of Broome Park was the first building I came to. I should have realised at once from the way the man continued to unlace his boots with his back towards me that I was going to get short shift there. 'Go on, I'm listening,' he said, his back still turned. After I had addressed my request to the back of his head, he said he had no idea where I could camp. I suggested a field close by. He said no. By this time I wouldn't have wanted to stay anywhere on his land, or to be beholden to him in any way, but I was curious to know the reason for his refusal. He said I was impertinent to expect to be given a reason, but if I must know, it was because if he let one camp, he would soon have two hundred. It was hard to imagine that such an out of the way spot would suddenly be beseiged by two hundred lone cyclists, desperate to camp there; but it was a very long time since I had been called impertinent by anyone, and never before by a man twenty years my junior: I rode on feeling quite girlish.

The villagers of nearby Bolton were very helpful, but not at all surprised by the reception I had received at Broome Park. Much as they would like to help, they thought it would not be politic to let me camp there either, as it was all Broome Park land – 'It doesn't do to go flouting the landlord, no matter what you think of him'; said one. After a general discussion someone went off to telephone, and came back to tell me they had arranged a site for me – 'Its just over the water on the Duke's land, so you'll be all right there.' There was a mild air of conspiracy about the proceedings that dispelled the sourness left by the 'gentry'.

Abberwick Mill turned out to be another idyllic campsite, so matters had turned to my advantage in the end. My small green dome was soon pitched overhanging the undershot bank of a perfect little stream. The River Alne, no more than twelve feet across at its widest spot, meandered here through water meadows, in a series of flamboyant bends and ox bows. Tremendous variety was created in the space of the one small field. In some stretches the water was transparently still, in another it flowed around a gravel bank, creating a deep pool where later I saw a large trout hanging motionless in the slight current. Where I was camped, the banks were closer together and the water flowed more swiftly, pulling out the long water-weed like drowned Ophelia's hair – hair starred all over by small white flowers. Miniature islands, no bigger than tea trays, hung in the water like tight little posies of forget-me-nots, sheep's bit, buttercups and sorrel. Stands of tall reeds and flags made cover against the other bank, while on the land behind was a rampant little thicket of large-leaved rhubarb-like plants, out of which young rabbits came and went. Slender birch trees overhung the water creating patches of delicate light and shade.

Under the blue morning skies, the little river became a busy thoroughfare, and so fascinating were all the comings and the goings that I went on sitting there by my tent, watching the play unfold. A swallow, its back a brilliant blue, patrolled tirelessly up and down, skimming the surface, snapping up insects, jinking and twisting endlessly to avoid the many obstacles, banking steeply to round the bends and the beds of reeds. A moorhen bobbed about near the bank, until bubbles from a fish that had just jumped for a fly caused her to turn her head, and seeing me watching her she swam off around the next bend, lurching from side to side with each thrust of her large feet.

In her wake the silver-bellied fish leaped again. An oyster-catcher passed overhead, giving piercing little calls, reminding me of how close the sea was. Among the tall flags I spotted a reed bunting and a willow warbler. A coot came by nodding his emblazoned head continuously as he steered a course through the flower-starred floating weed. A mallard followed, straight down the middle of the stream, her fluffy brood skittering along behind her, so minuscule that they appeared barely to touch the water. They were amazingly fast and scattered in all directions, while she tried anxiously to gather them all together. Eventually she had each tiny animated ball hauled out, directly opposite me on the bank by the rhubarb plants. All were clustered about her, comically going through the motions of beaking through their rudimentary feathers as she was doing. Having preened, the mallard settled down, and all the little ducklings crept under her wings. She turned her head over her back and appeared to sleep for the space of about five minutes, before taking to the water again, during which time I had not dared to move an inch for fear of disturbing so tender a scene.

It had turned into a day of summer heat and strong winds, the intensely blue sky ribbed with mares' tails. Silky uncut hay fields were rising and falling like the sea, while the barley and wheat were so thick and heavy that they scarcely rippled. I found a splendid unmade track that took me over the top of Westwood Moor, where there are Bronze Age cup and ring marks in the rock and the remains of ancient encampments. The blue Cheviot Hills looked close enough to touch, but before them the land dropped away steeply to

Wooler Water, with Wooler town set defensively in a tight little cluster on its western bank, protected by high ground on the other three sides, with several high places crowned with the remains of ancient forts and castles.

I asked at the newsagent's in Wooler where I would find the museum marked on my map. It was no longer there, I was told: it had not been a success and had only existed for a brief time, while the ordnance survey cartographer was updating the area map. However, there was a most marvellous and unusual museum which was not marked on the map, but which I must see! It was in a splendid position at the top of a steep hill, and was run by a farmer's wife. I was on a bicycle? Much too steep; never mind, he or his wife would take me up there. Just give him ten minutes to organise things.

After a little shopping I returned to find that the energetic and enthusiastic newsagent had rung the bank where the daughter of the museum lady – yet another Mrs Armstrong – worked, and had elicited the information that she was coming into town to pick up her son from school. She would take me up to her museum at Earle Hill, and bring me back again afterwards, while Evans would be cared for at the tobacconist until my return. This example of totally disinterested action, carried out with energy and initiative, was what I found so typical of Northumbrians, and it went a long way to countering the obstinacy and the tendency to take up entrenched positions, which were the other side of the coin. The tobacconist had gone to considerable trouble for no other reason than that he thought the museum was worth supporting, and that I might appreciate it.

He was right; it was somewhere not to be missed. The situation alone was worth a detour, though I was grateful not to have to climb steeply up to the 900-foot mark again on Evans that day. The view was immense and the wind so strong even on this June day that I could well believe Mrs Armstrong's claim that there were times when the hens needed to be tied down; but Mr Armstrong said that it was only when the carpet lifted with the cat sitting on it that they considered it a real blow.

The museum was housed in an old stone barn on the Armstrongs' farm, and resembled a vast magpie's nest of all manner of separate collections. There were items of domestic farm gadgetry going back to the turn of the century – milk-churns, milk-coolers, an automatic food-dispenser for hens: all extraordinarily antiquated-looking in these days of automation, but among the things Mrs Armstrong could remember being used during her childhood. It made one aware of how profound a revolution there has been in technology over the last few decades.

There were stacks of old programmes from livestock sales, with the prices fetched filled in – a treasure trove that kept farmers engrossed for hours, while their wives toured the other exhibits upstairs. These had a more directly domestic appeal. There were clothes and hats from all periods of the last hundred years, some seeming comical now, thirty years on, while others were exquisite – like the babies' christening gowns of lace and hand embroidery. Mr Armstrong's first clogs were there, smaller than most children could get into now, but beautifully made, and rather touching – as were the pairs of minute kid boots. Dolls, buttons, toys, tins, games, photograph albums, postcards going back to World War 1, oil lamps, face-powder boxes, costume jewellery, even a set of moustache-grooming tools, all built up a picture of recently-vanished times that was uncanny. It wasn't so much like being in a museum as finding oneself in someone else's house, and it was difficult to believe that the owners were not about to step in and take possession of their things.

It was a lovely place for visitors, but its real worth was in the preserving of local history and customs; I was pleased to learn that the collection was widely valued, and that local people often came there and were happy to donate their bits and pieces to it.

Mrs Armstrong was a native Northumbrian, and as independent as most. Some time later, when I was in the tourist office in Morpeth, enthusing about the collection, I was told that they have been trying to give Mrs Armstrong a grant for years to help with the running of the place, and that she simply puts the letters on her mantleshelf and they receive no answer. But I don't think Mrs Armstrong wants any interference with a collection she has been building ever since she found her first pretty button as a little girl. She charges a pound for admission, and all the proceeds go to charity. Sometimes when there is a party, she said, she and her friends dress up in the Thirties and Forties hats and dresses, for it pleases her to see them being used.

I was entertained to tea in the farmhouse kitchen afterwards and listened to Mr Armstrong's decided views on farming. We were in agreement over the disastrous effects of the depopulation of the Highlands and islands of Scotland, but he was ahead of me in his fear that conservationists want to bring about the same conditions in other marginal lands. He thinks the idea of land simply as a playground is inherently wrong, and considers that all land needs to be worked in some way, and to have an owner. I think he would be very fierce in defence of his acres of the Cheviot Hills, where he runs his sheep, patrolling on horseback, summer and winter, as do most hill-farmers in these parts. I was sure he would lend a corner of a field to a passing camper if approached in the right way, but I also learned from some walkers who had taken refuge in one of his barns on a winter's day without his permission that they were turned out into the snow immediately, without the chance to argue their case.

Everything about the Armstrongs impressed me, but nothing more so than their teenage children, of whom there were several still at home, including the son at school and the daughter at the bank. Not since the family whose tiny lawn had housed my tent in sodden Staffordshire had I met such biddable, pleasant and seemingly contented young people. The farm was certainly no sinecure, and each had farm or home chores to do after work or school, but this also appeared to confer a status and maturity upon them, giving them a real stake in the place, and the right to be heard in family matters. I thought they were Mr Armstrong's best argument for his way of life.

CHAPTER SEVENTEEN

Northern Castles

A great advantage of travelling in the North is that the hours of daylight are noticeably longer than in the South. With midsummer less than a week away, darkness had barely time to fall before the dawn chorus had begun. It was becoming difficult to tell the days apart; they had all begun to merge into a summer journeying – wind and sunshine, blue hills, bird song and water. Heavy-headed grain ripened daily to a richer gold, and in particularly well-favoured valleys harvesting had already begun. Sheep-shearing was in full swing, and the bleating of bewildered lambs temporarily separated from the ewes hung ceaselessly on the air. Flowers had never seemed so exuberant – charlock, forget-me-not, speedwell, yarrow, corn cockle, periwinkle, eyebright, heartsease, and a hundred more wove their thread through the journey like a remembered tune. To have had all this bounty coincide with the continuing spell of halcyon weather was the greatest of good fortune. I could remember no other such continuous span of time, since childhood, when I had felt so content to be in England.

The people I met added to the pleasure. At Abberwick Mill the farmer's son had said, 'Farming is all contract work now. You pay for extra help; the old co-operation between neighbours is dead.' But on my visit to the Earle Hill museum, above Wooler, I had eaten chocolate cake which a neighbour had made because she knew the Armstrongs were busy with their shearing and hadn't the time to bake. The sense of community and co-operation certainly did not seem dead to me in this area of Northumbria, and it was part of what kept me pottering about the foothills of the Cheviots.

Then, one day, after topping a series of low summits on the last straight stretch before the Tweed, I became aware of a new luminous quality in the air, and realised that the grey-blue, slightly darker line on the horizon was the sea. After the inevitable surprise and moment of wonder that always accompanies the first sighting of that limitless expanse, I quickly found myself in another world. The roaring A1 came up on my right and I had to make rapid mental adjustments, before I became embroiled in the traffic pouring north to converge upon Berwick.

The problems and difficulties of re-entry into twentieth-century hustle and bustle, however, was as nothing to trying to unravel the complicated status of the exciting walled town, set high on the northern bank of the wide Tweed. 'Politically it is part of Northumbria and therefore English,' said the man in the tourist office, 'but it is also a royal burgh of Scotland, a right reaffirmed by the Lord Lyon King of Arms in 1958. Indeed,' he continued, warming to a theme he had doubtless had to explain many times over, 'a Scottish regiment has its headquarters in the town, and the football team plays in the Scottish Football League, so it is no wonder people are confused as to which country they are in. We like to think that we still hold a unique position in Berwick, as we did in the days when the British Isles were described as consisting of "England, Scotland, Wales, Ireland and Berwick-on-Tweed".' And with that he sent me off with various pamphlets designed to help me appreciate the area, and with exhortations 'to walk the ramparts'.

Berwick lost what remained of its castle when the railway was brought straight through the middle of it, and the station has the rare distinction of being within what was once the Great Hall. But Berwick's glory lies in the Elizabethan walls, begun in the reign of Mary Tudor, and these remain. There is no other place, certainly not in England, that can boast the like. Approaching the town from Tweedsmouth across the water, as I did, is spectacular. The wide Tweed is spanned by three bridges (the A1 now has a bypass and crosses a mile upstream). The Royal Border bridge is the most impressive; built in 1850, it carries the railway on a viaduct supported upon twenty-eight Roman arches, soaring 120 feet above the river. Traffic crosses on a rather ugly 1926 bridge, while bicyclists are able to go over on the more romantic stone bridge, built in 1634. A sturdy structure supported on massive squat cutwaters, it makes a splendid entry into the town.

The walls begin immediately on the waterfront, and they sweep up around the residential part of the town, northwards to the Brass Bastion where they turn southwestward back to the quayside. Built along Italian lines, they are twenty feet high and originally had a 150-foot wide ditch in front. Two rows of cannon were set in between the ramparts and the bastion to provide crossfire along the face of the walls. Last put to military use during the 1745 Jacobite Rising, the wide ramparts have provided generations of citizens of Berwick with the most regal promenade, complete with panoramas of sea, river, hills and plains. Walking a dog, I decided, could never become a chore in Berwick.

I wandered all around the walls, and through the linings of the town – which, as in Venice, are the slim dark alleys and byways that make alternative secret routes to the wider thoroughfares. Up many crooked stone stairways, through courtyards, and along terraces they led, into small squares of fine Georgian houses, and finally back again to the walls. At last, tired out, I tried to get myself organised with a camp site. I had got it into my head that I had to stay within the walls for the night, which was easier said than done. I would have been quite prepared to put up in a B&B for once, but I could find no vacancy. Eventually I approached a stalwart-looking gentleman to see if he had any bright ideas about where a body might pitch a very small tent for the night. Anxious to oblige, he racked his brains visibly, knuckles to puckered forehead; then, like a latter-day Newton, his face expressed all the joy of hitting upon a solution. Fascinated by the display I waited, quite expecting him to cry 'Eureka'.

Instead, rather more prosaically, he said, 'I know a lady who would be delighted, no, very delighted, to put you up in her garden if all else fails; but alas, I cannot remember her name, or how to direct you there. Oh what a fool I am!' More knuckling of forehead resulted in further thought – 'But wait, I have another idea.' The gist of idea number two was that I could pitch my tent in his garden, an invitation he had hesitated to offer at first because his wife was away from home. However, as he was a minister of the church – I could not have known this fact as he was not wearing a clerical collar – the absence of his wife should not raise suspicions of impropriety. Problem solved.

On the way to his house he started to tell me about himself with great enthusiasm. He was a minister of the Church of Scotland, who, after thirty years, had found he was out of sympathy with his flock. He had ideas about peace, disarmament and so forth which were incompatible with theirs, so he had bought a redundant church building here in Berwick, which he was in the process of refurbishing. He had no time to elaborate upon his personal credo, because in a short while we had arrived at his house, and he was calling out jocularly to his neighbours who were gathered in a bunch on the pavement before their front door, 'I'm entertaining a lady friend, so be sure now you don't tell my wife, ha, ha' – which merry jest was greeted in stony silence, and with dark looks of disapproval.

By the time I had pitched the tent on the pocket handkerchief of a lawn at the side of his house, my benefactor was back with a long face. His neighbours, he explained, were 'less liberated' than he was, and thought it most improper that he should allow a lady to pitch a tent on his lawn while his wife – a headmistress of a Scottish girl's school – was not at home. Therefore, at their insistence, I was to use the toilet facilities in their house, so as to have no occasion to cross his threshold. I offered to go, but he begged me not to, saying that it would only make matters worse.

It is seldom that one is privileged to see the causes of a man's tragedy so patently displayed. What had brought about the breakdown of the relationship between himself and his former congregation was plainly going to occur here also. Public opinion would be sure to destroy his work in the new church, as it had done in the old. With all his enthusiasm and openness, he was incapable of not unwittingly arousing suspicion, and of not caring desperately what people thought of him in consequence. As for the attitude of his Berwick neighbours, it made me suspect that he had leapt from the frying-pan into the fire.

I met some Dutch people later in Lindisfarne who had also come across my minister on the walls of Berwick, and he had told them all about his 'church for preaching peace'. It had confirmed for them the 'delightful eccentricity' of the English. 'Buying a church,' they said, shaking their heads in admiring disbelief: 'only in England could such a thing happen.'

I saw no more of him, which was a pity, for I would like to have heard more about the ideas he wished to preach. He disappeared immediately, announcing loudly, for the benefit of the neighbours, that he was off to Tweedsmouth to spend the evening with a married couple. I walked the walls again in the evening light, and watched a vast concourse of some two hundred swans milling about in the estuary, pink as flamingoes in the setting sun. Then I rode out to Branxton Hill, that lies just before the Scottish border. It was here on

Flodden Field, on Black Friday, 9 September 1513, that the saddest battle of all between the English and the Scots was fought. It was a battle with no clear grievances or real objectives, and it cost the life of a most able king of Scotland, James IV, and the flower of his nation with him – twelve earls, fifteen lords, bishops and abbots, together with at least 10,000 Scottish soldiers, and half as many English; a slaughter still almost beyond comprehension. It was dusk when I reached the place. In a cornfield almost ready for reaping I could just make out the granite Celtic cross with the simple inscription:

Flodden 1513
To the brave of both nations.

I read in one of my pamphlets that a service takes place there each year, during which a piper plays that loveliest of all laments, 'Flowers of the Forest', which was written to commemorate the awful day:

I've heard them lilting at our ewes milking
Lasses a'lilting afore break of day;
But now they are moaning on ilka green loaning,
The flowers of the forest are a'wede away.

England's most northerly town awakened me next morning with the most raucous of dawn choruses. On every red-tiled roof, above the grey stone houses, perched rows of clamorous gulls, screeching at one another with outstretched necks and hugely gaping red-spotted beaks. With such an awakening, and the air smelling so excitingly salty and fresh, I lost no time in striking camp and getting on my way. It is one of life's pleasures to be abroad in a town that is still asleep.

By six o'clock I was pedalling fast down the empty A1, making all speed to get to the little seaside town of Seahouses before the narrow trunk road became a death trap. I was in a hurry to see the National Trust warden in charge of the Farne Islands. When I knew I would be able to make this summer journey, the one place in all England I most wanted to visit was the Farnes, not so much because of its being a famous bird sanctuary – having spent my two weeks on remote St Kilda for the Scottish National Trust, I had already seen the ultimate in British bird reserves. My reason for wanting to spend a quiet day or two alone on the Farnes was because of St Cuthbert, that most charismatic of all Celtic monks, who had spent his last years as a hermit there. He had figured largely in my studies at university, and I wanted if possible to make a closer acquaintance with him through his beloved island hermitage.

I had written some months back to the N.T. asking permission to spend at least a day on the Inner Farne, but had received no answer other than that the matter was being considered. I had been advised by someone at head office to call directly on the warden when I arrived. By dint of enquiring around the town, I eventually found a large and rather grand house on the front. My knock was answered by an unsmiling woman, who told me that Mr Hawkey, her husband, was out on the Farnes, as he was all day, every day, and that I should come back at five if I wanted to see him. After which she closed the door firmly, just as I was about to ask if she thought I might be able to catch him out there.

Seahouses, once a small fishing port, is now a bustling seaside town of amusement arcades, fish and chip shops, cafés, and a large caravan site. It was not the sort of place I would have chosen to kick my heels in for five hours. When I returned to the house, Peter Hawkey himself answered the door, and showed me into his office. There was no preamble, or even the offer of a cup of tea. He came straight to the point, like a man who has no time to waste on frivolities.

'I have no good news for you, I fear. We considered your case last week at regional office, and it was decided not to grant your request to stay out on the Farne. We decided that for the purposes of your book, you could see all you wanted on a normal day visit.' The 'normal' visit was on a crowded boat with a carefully shepherded half-hour ashore. I said I couldn't possibly get any feeling of the place under those circumstances. 'Well, you had better leave it out altogether then, hadn't you?' was his reply. Other 'important' people were always being turned down, he said, attempting to soften the blow. Well-known photographers and naturalists were applying all the time, and had I wished to stand any sort of chance of having my request granted, I should have applied at least eighteen months in advance.

It was what appeared to me as the sheer, breathtaking arrogance of it that I found most annoying, as though I had been begging a personal favour of him, the owner of the island, rather than making a request to the employee of a charitable trust, of which I was a member. There hadn't even been the courtesy of a letter to inform me of the decision. Had there been, my husband could have told me of it when I telephoned, and this unpleasant interview and a wasted day could have been avoided.

Who, I asked, made these decisions, and by what criteria? Were there not two sides to the existence of the Trust – conservation certainly, but availability to the general public also? Decisions, he said, were made by the regional office, and each region was autonomous. 'As far as the Farnes are concerned,' he said, 'the birds are everything, people don't count. People disturb birds, so we keep them off.' If this was the case, I wondered why he himself spent each day out there. On none of the group of islands was anyone but himself and N.T. employees allowed to land, except for the limited access to the Inner Farne.

This sounded to me more like a private kingdom than a national institution. 'We justify our policy by the results,' said Mr Hawkey. 'The numbers of nesting birds have doubled on the Farnes since I came here seven years ago, so our policies are working.' Doubling the numbers of any particular species is not necessarily a good thing, within the total ecology of an area, but I didn't get the chance to put this point, because at that moment a buzzer sounded on his desk, and he said that he was being summoned to his dinner, so I would have to leave. 'In any case,' he informed me 'there isn't any more to say.'

I went away sadly, not just because I wouldn't now see these long-anticipated islands, but also because I was depressed by this autocratic attitude, and by the lack of accountability. I had felt previously that the National Trust was a part of my heritage, whereas here it seemed more like an exclusive club. Peter Hawkey's arguments had not been very different to those of the private landowner who hadn't allowed me to camp on his property. Both had raised the spectre of 'setting a precedent'. Also, by a curious coincidence, my husband had been asked a few years previously to prepare a treatment for a film the N.T. wished to make in order to raise money to protect Britain's threatened coastline. He had arrived there with very little advance warning and had been taken wherever he wished to go on the Farnes by this very same warden.

Next day I backtracked northwards in order to visit Lindisfarne. I went by the coast road, following the continuous stretch of golden beach to Bamburgh. It was a blustery day, and having started without breakfast, I sought shelter among the dunes to boil a kettle, but immediately ran into problems. Everywhere suitable had already been visited by dogs, who had left copious evidence of their passing. Even as I cast about for a small unsullied spot, more and more dogs appeared on the ends of leads, dragging their owners behind them, all desperate to find a fresh patch of sand to foul. All had emerged from cars, and as soon as they had done what was expected of them, their owners hurried them back, and away they drove. It seemed by far the greatest use that this part of the marvellous Heritage Coastline was put to, and it gave a whole new slant on pollution. It also put me off my breakfast.

The splendid profile of Bamburgh Castle soaring so dramatically into view, quite restored my spirits. On a lofty whin sill outcrop rising 150 feet from the sea, it was as perfectly positioned a coastal fortress as I have ever seen. I had no wish to go in, which was just as well as it wasn't open yet. Its attraction lies in the picture it makes, with the great sandy expanse of Budle Bay beyond it, and the waves dashing against the rocks below. The great spur provides such a natural spot for a castle that I was not surprised to learn that it has been fortified since prehistoric times, and that the Romans had built there too. Today's romantic battlements rise above layers that go back to 547 AD, when Ida the Flamebearer, king of Northumbria, made it his capital, in a kingdom which stretched from the Humber to the Forth.

The village of Bamburgh nestles in the shelter of the castle, neatly clustered around a triangular green, with a broad spacious church across the way. This present peaceful spot had been the hub of northern history for more than two hundred years, until the terrible Viking raids of the ninth century brought a temporary return of the Dark Ages to the Northumbrian coast. When Oswald became king of Northumbria in 634 AD his capital was here, and with St Aidan established in his monastery on Lindisfarne, just across Budle Bay, king and monk could work together for the conversion of the realm.

The rather plain thirteenth-century church, enormous for the size of the present village, was built over the site of the original Saxon wooden church where St Aidan died – leaning, it was said, against the wall, looking out to sea. Inside the church a venerable baulk of timber is preserved, which is believed to have come from that original church – perhaps the very timber against which St Aidan had rested.

The 'saint' most revered today in Bamburgh is Grace Darling. I found an effigy of her in the church, and a large Victorian monument in the churchyard – some distance from her grave, so that it could be seen by passing ships, and not far from the grave of a pirate, which was suitably marked with a skull and crossbones. There was also a museum of memorabilia associated with her, including the actual coble in which she and her father had rowed out to the stricken ship on the Outer Farnes. The place could well be described as a Grace Darling shrine, and it struck me as rather odd, when one considers the momentous kingdom-shaking events which have happened here, that this little local incident should have aroused such waves of adulation throughout the country.

A gale had forced a coastal steamer, the *Forfarshire*, onto a huge basaltic rock, which lay some distance from the Longstone island, where William Darling was the keeper of the lighthouse. His own letter, sent to Trinity House, gives a graphic account of what followed:

> . . . On the morning of the 7th September [1838], it blowing a gale with rain from the north, my daughter and me being both alert before high water securing things out of doors, one quarter before five my daughter observed a vessel on the Harkers rock; but owing to the darkness and spray going over her, could not observe any person on the wreck although the glass was incessantly applied, until near seven o'clock, when the tide being fallen, we observed three or four men upon the rock; we agreed that if we could get to them some of them would be able to assist us back, without which we could not return; and having no idea of a boat coming from North Sunderland, we immediately launched our boat, and was enabled to gain the rock, where we found eight men and one woman, which I judged too many to take at once in the state of the weather, therefore took the woman and four men to the Longstone. Two of them returned with me, and succeeded in bringing the remainder, in all nine persons safely to the Longstone about nine o'clock. Afterwards the boat from North Sunderland arrived and found three lifeless bodies . . .

Grace Darling was twenty-three at the time of the rescue, and within four years she had died of consumption – the scourge of Victorian womanhood. In those four years she had been received by the Duke and Duchess of Northumberland, invited to appear at the Adelphi Theatre in London for the sum of £20 a week, and inundated with offers of marriage. Artists' impressions of her were sold all over the country, and some of these were in the museum. She still figured over a hundred years later in my own childhood, and those of my contemporaries, as a model of maidenly courage, so that now I felt rather guilty at questioning her position in the nation's hagiography.

I had fewer problems with the special aura that is supposed to spread out from the Holy Island of Lindisfarne into the surrounding countryside. It had even affected the weather. The day had started with a grey cast to a sky just faintly streaked with an icy tint of aquamarine. The sea, which had been a dark, dark blue, turned black, and a north-easterly wind blowing straight off the polar ice cap had the Sunday walkers hunching their shoulders up around their ears as they pressed resolutely forward against it. This scene began to change the moment I left Bamburgh and started to ride in a great sweep westward and northward around Budle Bay and Fenham Flats. By the time I had turned east again to cross the Holy Island sands, the sea was a symphony of colour, shading from jade where it flowed over the sands to a blue that grew almost purple at the horizon. The sky was even more varied, with the cloud cover dispersing rapidly in all directions, a light serene blue flooding in to fill the spaces.

The final approach to Lindisfarne is along three miles of causeway, which reaches from the Beal Sands to the island village, and is flooded in the centre for about five hours of each high tide, when the island is completely cut off. A small tower has been built at this deep point as a refuge for those who have been caught out by the returning sea.

The whin sill ridge breaks from the sea again on Lindisfarne, and here too it supports a castle, though nothing like as theatrical as Bamburgh's, which is also visible from this point across the wide expanse of sand and sea. But marvellous views though there are all around, a traveller or pilgrim standing here on the causeway has eyes for little other than the low line of the Holy Island itself, which beckons still, as it has done across the centuries. As I rode towards it the whole world seemed to be made pristine again, a world of sand, sea and sky only, with the tide still too high for the half dozen waiting cars to follow me across.

CHAPTER EIGHTEEN

Midsummer on Holy Island

All islands have intrinsic appeal, the sense of being a world apart; but Lindisfarne, an island for only part of the time, has one distinct advantage in not needing a boat to get there. It felt strange to be cycling towards it across the receding tide, with the sea bubbling over the lowest stretches of the narrow causeway, and pulling at the wheels. My shoes shipped quantities of very cold sea water in the process, but the day had by now improved to the point where wet feet hardly mattered, and in any case a little discomfort was perfectly in keeping with journeying towards so venerable a place of pilgrimage. So enchanting was the scene that it was a delight to prolong the approach, lingering in the transitory gossamer world of the shifting tideline, that was neither sea nor dry land.

Lindisfarne is barely one square mile of solid ground, with a long narrow tongue of sand dunes tacked on to it, extending back in a curving two-mile sweep towards the mainland. The great area of sand flats that the ebbing seas expose all around this spit of low dunes, and around the northern end of the island, makes it appear far more ephemeral than when it is entirely surrounded by water.

The fluctuating light, growing brighter by the moment, reflected first off one expanse and then off another, chasing across the receding shallow seas and the wet ribbed sand, as billowing armadas of cloud sailed majestically overhead. Further out, the deeper sea was now a dazzling scintillating shield, with pinpoints of light striking off the surface and dancing in the air above, so that there was no longer any clear division between sea and sky. Outlines of long-legged birds wading through the shallows wavered and broke. It was the sea that seemed the constant solid element here, and the land that was insubstantial and mysterious.

But hunger makes itself felt even among scenes like these. I had cycled a good few miles in a breakfastless state, and the strong salt smell of the sea assailing me on all sides made me realise how ravenous I was. The spell was broken. I rode on around the curve of

the protecting dunes and onto the island proper. The sense of awe I
felt at being on such hallowed ground demanded, at the very least, an
initial brief visit to the beautiful little thirteenth-century island
church. But all serious sight-seeing had to wait until my pressing
need for food had been met.

On the edge of the village I found an inn with a sunny garden,
which was serving delicious crab lunches. This seemed exotic fare to
me, used to paying high London prices for shellfish, but I was soon
to find that crab meat was a common feature of the island, and one of
the mainstays of the economy. On wooden chairs by the open front
doors of fishermen's cottages, fresh crab sandwiches were daily
offered for sale, and during my short stay on Lindisfarne I made the
most of this local enterprise.

The life of the island is concentrated in the south-east corner,
where the priory ruins stand overlooking the harbour, with the
village and the church clustered around them. The arable fields
stretch out northwards behind the village – work and worship side
by side, as they had been since the monks first came here from far
Iona. Tourism seemed now to be the main occupation of the island,
and although the whole place has a slightly down at heel look,
visitors were well catered for, with four or five modest hotels and as
many guesthouses and B & Bs. I found it refreshingly unspoilt, and
saw no hint of the chilly commercialism so often found in English
seaside resorts.

Fishing, which had once been the island's main source of income,
had declined drastically over the last decade, I learnt, as I stood
admiring the boats in the small harbour, where the fine weather had
resulted in a spate of maintenance. Two men who were painting the
hull of a small trawler spoke very bitterly about the scarcity of fish,
laying much of the blame at the door of the National Trust's policy
of protecting such a large colony of seals on the Farne Islands, which,
they said, caused havoc among the shoals of fish. Other men,
overhauling creels, claimed that the vast numbers of sea birds on the
Farnes caused just as much depredation among the young fry, and
prevented fish stocks from building up. It was interesting that no one
seemed to be blaming pollution.

In the village shops, which were also surprisingly unspoilt and
friendly, considering the numbers of tourists who pour through in
the season, I also found a lot of dissatisfaction expressed over

National Trust policies. This centred on Lindisfarne Castle, which was in the Trust's keeping, and which had opening times which were thought to be totally inadequate – only four hours a day, excluding Friday, when it was closed altogether. Moreover, although these times were printed in the Trust's handbook, most tourists were not members of the National Trust and did not have access to the information. They came to Lindisfarne after a long circuitous drive, often with delays for tides, only to find the castle closed. I met lots of disappointed visitors while I was there, including the Dutch couple who had met my church-owning minister in Berwick – to them the situation on Lindisfarne was yet another example of the incomprehensible behaviour of the English.

The lovely ruins of the Benedictine abbey, on the other hand were open all day and every day throughout the summer, because they were in the charge of English Heritage, whose policy is to put the convenience of visitors first. Tourists who did not appreciate the difference between the two organisations often vented their frustration upon the English Heritage custodian, who had, as she told me, ample opportunity to practise the Christian charity for which the island was so famous.

Nor was this all; worse was afoot. Apparently the N.T. considered that the castle was all too successful, and was attracting more visitors than they wanted, with the result that the carpets were wearing out too fast. Rather than finding adequate means of protecting the floor coverings, the regional council had decided to cut down the opening hours still further. The villagers fear that, with this important attraction made so difficult of access, the island will have far fewer visitors. Already cafés and gift shops close on Fridays, and now the owners are wondering if it will be worth opening on other days. They say the worst aspect of it all is visitors being so angry and upset, which spoils the atmosphere of the island.

It did seem a bizarre situation on the face of it, when even the most unlikely places I had visited on the journey had been trying so hard to encourage tourism. I thought I would probably hear the other side of the argument when I made my visit to Lindisfarne Castle the following day, but instead the attitude of the regional council became even more incomprehensible, for the National Trust custodians themselves were equally up in arms about the proposed new regime. It was already very difficult to run the place, they told me; large queues were always building up, as only a few visitors could be let in at a time since it was such a small castle. The administrative staff on the ground had asked if they could extend the daily visiting times, and so spread the load. Because most of the helpers come from the mainland, they too were dependent upon the tides, and wanted opening hours to be geared to this, but in spite of their requests and recommendations, the regional office of the Trust was as implacable as it had been with me. It took a positively Canute-like attitude to the sea's activity, and decreed that the new limited access would be strictly according to Greenwich Mean Time. When these new hours are brought in, it looks as though on some days the castle will be open only when the island is entirely cut off by the tide. Sad though the situation was, at least I could now begin to appreciate that the cavalier refusal of my request to visit the Inner Farne was not anything personal, but merely typical of the N.T.'s attitude to its role in Northumberland.

Personally, I would not have minded foregoing the pleasure of viewing this bone of contention; it is not a very ancient or significant fortification. Even more than with most castles, its charm lies in the focus and the drama it adds to the scene. Sited on its steep-sided little pyramid of rock, a miniature Bamburgh scaled down to island proportions, it is the very stuff of romance. It was built originally simply as a gun emplacement around the year 1540, when Henry VIII was keen to have all his harbours secured against the Scots. No shot was ever fired from it in anger, and no one languished there, nor apparently did it acquire a single ghost. It merely mouldered away quietly and unremarked.

In 1902, the ruins were bought by the founder of *Country Life*, Edward Hudson, who commissioned Edwin Lutyens to convert it into a dwelling. Lytton Strachey stayed there, and didn't like it at all – 'too dark, and nothing but stone over, under and around you,' he said. I felt this too – it does not make a satisfactory dwelling, nor does the spot enjoy the atmosphere that is so prevalent over most of the island. But from the top platform there are splendid views which extend from Berwick to Bamburgh, and from the Cheviot Hills to the Farne Islands, and I could quite understand why visitors lingered there on the leads, creating a bottleneck. It was also a very good place to take leave of an island that had given me one of the most memorable days of my journey.

It was by great good fortune that I had arrived on Lindisfarne on midsummer's day, which, after its inauspicious beginning, had turned into as perfect a summer's day as anyone could hope to experience in a lifetime. At the time, it was difficult not to believe that the weather was entirely due to the renowned hospitality of the island, attempting to make up for the churlishness of the National Trust. And yet, whatever the weather had done, I don't think it would have affected the special atmosphere of Lindisfarne. That was unmistakable; something it shared with Iona, Skellig Michael, and other remote islands where there had been a concentration of spiritual life over many centuries. Because I had not been allowed to stay on the Inner Farne, it would be here if anywhere that I might arrive at a closer idea of St Cuthbert within his setting. Camping was not allowed on Lindisfarne, but thanks to the glorious weather it would be no hardship simply to stay out all night, as the monks had frequently done. With this in mind I set about exploring the island.

I spent a long time among the lovely red ruins of the Benedictine priory, with its single remaining 'rainbow' arch soaring so movingly above the empty spaces below. The ruins were built on the site of St Aidan's simple seventh-century monastic settlement, where the inspiring story of Lindisfarne began.

Aidan and his king, Oswald, working together, had made tremendous strides in converting Northumbria to Christianity. When he died in 651, after seventeen years as Bishop of Lindisfarne, Aidan left behind him not only a reputation for great personal saintliness, but a firm foundation for the education of local-born priests and missionaries. As though the preceding barbarous centuries following the withdrawal of the Romans had built up a longing for sanctity, a great flowering of Anglo-Saxon saints emerged from this spot over the next two hundred years.

Of all these holy men associated with Lindisfarne, there was one who had that special charismatic quality – probably a superabundance of the very holiness for which the age yearned – that resulted in his becoming the most loved and most revered of all the northern saints. This was St Cuthbert, who so caught the hearts and imaginations of people that he became a legend in his own lifetime, and hundreds flocked to him for healing and spiritual counsel. From the beginning miracles were associated with Cuthbert, which had not been the case with Aidan, loved and respected though he was.

At the time of Cuthbert's death, it was customary to 'elevate' the bones of saintly men, placing them in a reliquary, the better for pilgrims to revere them. The corpse would be buried in the normal manner and a day set some eleven years later for their formal 'elevation'. To the astonishment of those assembled, when St Cuthbert's coffin was opened, instead of the expected skeleton, the body was found to be still whole and uncorrupted. From that moment on, the fame of Lindisfarne as a great pilgrim centre was assured. When the Durham monks came to build their priory here, four hundred years after his death, it was to honour St Cuthbert, whose body now lay enshrined in their great cathedral at Durham. The wheel had come full circle.

St Cuthbert had first come to Lindisfarne as prior, entrusted with the difficult task of mending the deep rift in the religious life caused by the famous Synod of Whitby. The problems of there being two distinct churches in Britain came to a head when the Northumbrian King Oswy married a Kentish queen, and the different dates for celebrating Easter, as well as the different tonsures of the monks, and other diverse practices, could no longer be ignored. There was no question at that time of there being unity in diversity. It was a far less sophisticated age than ours, where there could be only one right way of doing things. The Synod of Whitby was called in 664 to decide whose way that should be – that of Rome, operating through Canterbury, or that of Lindisfarne, with its line going back through Iona to Ireland and the influence of the Eastern Church. There was never any real doubt about the eventual decision; the Roman cause was bound to triumph eventually for political reasons, but something precious and spontaneous was lost to the church in the outcome, and a suspicion was forged between the north and the south of England that some would argue has never been forgotten.

The snub to Lindisfarne was all the greater because the case against the Celtic Church was argued by Wilfrid, whose crypt had so impressed me at Hexham. He was a very able monk who had been educated and trained at Lindisfarne before deciding to travel to Rome. Perhaps he learnt ambition there; certainly the Synod was his big opportunity, and, subsequently, he achieved great power and wealth in the church. The latter part of his life was said to have been spent defending his fortune – setting a precedent, perhaps, for later worldly churchmen.

After the Synod, Lindisfarne, like many northern monasteries, was in disarray, with some monks returning sadly to Iona, and the rest too hurt and bewildered to function as they should. Cuthbert too can have found it no easy adjustment, but he must have decided to make the most of the situation, which was doubtless why he was chosen for the post of peacemaker.

His life as prior of Lindisfarne would have been extremely busy with administrative duties and active missionary work, as well as keeping the long prescribed monastic hours of prayer and meditation. But there was also a longing in him for a more complete life of prayer and contemplation than was possible within a monastery. He began to withdraw, first to a little island in the harbour; then, as his reputation for healing grew, even this degree of privacy was no longer sufficient. He retired to the uninhabited Inner Farne island, where he built a small enclosure and lived completely as a hermit, cut off by storms for weeks at a time. Reluctantly he was persuaded to return to Lindisfarne to fill the vacancy of bishop for two years towards the close of his life. But he seems to have anticipated his end, and returned to the Inner Farne for his last winter, dying there in March 687, in the arms of his fellow monks, who had seized the opportunity of the first fine day to get to the island and administer the last sacraments. His influence was immense in the centuries after his death, and it still continues to permeate through the Christian world today, particularly in the north, where he inspires the sort of tender regard that is given elsewhere to St Francis of Assisi – they also shared the same reputation for a special relationship with birds and animals. St Cuthbert was without doubt Lindisfarne's greatest gift to the world.

Another of Lindisfarne's bequests, that the world perhaps more readily recognises today, if for no other reason than it is now a prized possession of the British Museum, is the exquisite Lindisfarne Gospels that was written 'in honour of God and St Cuthbert', and was intended to be part of the celebrations of the 'elevation' of the saint's bones on 20 March 698. I was delighted to find that a copy of this gorgeous illuminated manuscript is kept in the island's church, so near the spot where it had been made. I had gazed at the original in its glass case many times, so it was like meeting an old friend. Scholars of the period consider it the finest example of decorated manuscript in the Irish–Anglo-Saxon tradition in existence, more beautiful even than the Book of Kells, which came a little later. The vellum of the Lindisfarne Gospels was so carefully prepared, and the colours so skilfully applied, that there has been almost no deterioration, and the pages still glow today as they must have done then. Just thinking about the sources of some of the forty-five different colours used in its making gives a surprising glimpse into the age – a blue made from lapis lazuli found in the Himalayas, a red from the eggs of insects that live on oaks in the Mediterranean, a yellow from ox bile, and a green made by pouring vinegar onto copper. The lovely intricate interlacing patterns, the whorls, spirals, trumpets and, most of all, the elaborately entwined birds and slender hounds, are full of life and humour. It is a book in which there would always be something new to discover, as in the text itself. Research has established that the whole book, both calligraphy and illustrations, is the achievement of one man, a monk named Eadfrith, and that he worked on it continuously over a two-year period. Nothing else is known about him.

When the monks fled in disarray from Lindisfarne in 875 AD, after a hundred years of increasing pressure from savage Viking raids, their three most precious possessions went with them – the coffin containing the body of St Cuthbert, which was said to be still in a perfect state of preservation, the relics of St Aidan and St Oswald, and Eadfrith's glowing book. For well over another century these monks and their successors, 'St Cuthbert's folk' as they came to be known, wandered through a violently changing England, taking up temporary residence here and there, while always seeking a new permanent sanctuary for their treasures. At one time they even considered going to Ireland, but apparently a storm blew up as they got into the boat, from which the monks had surmised that their saint did not wish to leave England. Deliverance came in 995 AD, when one of the monks had a vision in which St Cuthbert told him he wished to be buried at Dunholme. No one had any idea where Dunholme was, so this didn't immediately solve anything. Then one day, when the monks were near to the River Wear, they met an old woman who told them she was following her dun cow home – home of the dun cow, Dunholme, Durham. St Cuthbert had found his final resting-place, above which the greatest Norman cathedral in England would soon rise.

After I had spent some time in the lovely island church, reading about the Lindisfarne saints and their stirring times, I was ready to wander off into the island itself. I took a little track northwards that led through the fields and out to the dunes. Looking back at the red ruins of the priory lit up by the angle of the setting sun, it was as though they were on fire. A few people were walking along the narrow field paths, and one man driving some sheep along stopped and asked me if I was looking for somewhere to camp. I replied cautiously that I thought camping wasn't allowed. 'If you get up there among the sand dunes nobody'll bother you before morning,' he said kindly.

I was in the area he had indicated within minutes, so small is the island, and yet, once there among the sandhills and craters, it was a totally different world, and one where I had to abandon Evans, for he was at once bogged down in the powder-fine sand. Waving marram grass was the main anchor of this shifting fragile island fringe, together with widely spreading beds of hop trefoil and showy purple viper's bugloss. Without these growing things to bind it, it was a habitat which a gale could destroy in an hour. It was currently being seriously undermined by vast number of rabbit burrows. They were everywhere. I could hear constant warnings being drummed underground by muscular back legs as I passed, and as I topped the crest of each sand dune, long ears twitched out of every hollow, and hundreds of fat brown agile forms skittered every which way, white bobtails disappearing down a plethora of holes.

This close intimate world of the dunes gave way abruptly to sweeping sea views from the edge of low undercut cliffs, with long rocky points stretching out northwards into the sea, enclosing horseshoe bays. Kittiwakes were nesting below me on the cliff faces, clinging to barely perceptible, downward-sloping ledges. Just off Snipe Point were rocky islets uncovered by the tide, on which hundreds of seals were hauled out, sunbathing in a great jumble of bodies, calling out in a booming cacophony of organ notes across the water. A fulmar was patrolling the cliffs showing off its superb flying techniques, while curlews and oyster-catchers passed low overhead, each giving its own fluting call. Sand pipits perched beside me on the edge of the cliffs, ready to jump off if I moved an inch towards them.

From my vantage point I overlooked a great semicircle of sea from due east right round to the west, and I must have sat there for hours as the sky went through its midsummer drama of sunset. A great golden road stretched out across the sea, while a blaze of vermilion, orange, crimson, and yellow slowly grew and spread out over an immense area of sky. At 10 pm the sun was still not below the horizon. I fetched my sleeping-bag, laid it out on the cliff top, and closed my eyes on the golden day. When I opened them again, it was to a glorious morning, as though no night at all had intervened; only the sense of completeness was gone.

I wasn't sure that I had gained any deeper sense of St Cuthbert from my night on his island, but I did feel that I had shared in some common experience of elation and wonder. There had been an additional element present that was there no longer. It was as though for a short while I had been a part of the scene, and now, once more, I was separated from what I was seeing. Lovely as the morning was, I felt a sense of loss, as though a curtain had fallen back into place.

All around everything was glowing and busy – seals calling like ghostly cattle from the far rocks, turnstones working the tideline for small crustaceans, and fulmars practising precision flying through the gaps at the cliff's edge. I went back to Evans and fetched the things to make breakfast.

It was still only six o'clock as I set out to walk around the great sandy bay east of Snipe Point. The newly-washed sand and the sparkling water looked so inviting that I threw off my clothes and waded in. The water was not as cold as I had known it sometimes around the islands of western Scotland, but I had no desire to prolong the swim. St Cuthbert, like other Celtic mystics, had stood all night up to his waist in these waters and prayed and recited Psalms, in order to concentrate his mind. I had once tried this for myself in the waters off Iona – I attempted the twenty-third Psalm, which I thought I knew backwards, and found to my surprise and annoyance, that it took tremendous effort and concentration to get beyond the first few lines. More than that I could not do; my mind simply went blank, while every part of my body was clamouring for release from remaining still in that icy water. It was an exercise that taught me more about asceticism than any amount of reading, and I would recommend it to anyone who doubts the power of these early saints.

As I dried myself in the shelter of the dunes, I saw the thrilling sight of a lithe young fox trotting along the beach. Almost before I had time to register his presence, he had changed direction, darted through the seaweed into the shallow waves and snatched a bird from amongst a small flock swimming on the edge of the sea. It must have been killed instantly, because he dropped the limp body on the sand and looked as though he would go in after another, but the birds were wary now and kept their distance from the beach. Very soon the fox picked up his prize and trotted off briskly with it along the tide line, before turning and vanishing into the waving marram grass. I had thought it was a turnstone he had taken, but when I walked down to look more closely I saw that the water was full of families of brown eider duck, St Cuthbert's chickens they call them here, and it was one of these the fox had killed.

CHAPTER NINETEEN

Making Tracks South

It was amazing how fast the weather changed as I stood on the castle leads at Lindisfarne, taking my last look at the jade and silver scene, before turning my back on it and heading south. Time was running out on me now; duties awaited me in London, and my idyll as a carefree wandering bicyclist was almost at an end. There could be no more leisurely pottering about, drifting off here and there, wherever fancy or chance led me. There were still a few places I wanted to see before the journey came to an end, and to do so I would need to put a bit more purpose into my pedalling, and point Evans in a more direct line.

As if in sympathy with this mood of regret, a mist suddenly descended, as though an enormous cold grey blanket had been dropped over the day. All in a moment the sun was gone, and the gentle breeze had become a cold wind. Equally suddenly, I felt so tired I could hardly keep my eyes open. I had been planning to get off the island on this tide and cycle a good few miles on my way before stopping for the night. Now I decided I had better camp somewhere near the end of the spit, and cross the causeway early the following morning when I had caught up on some sleep. I bought a final supply of crab sandwiches and set off to find a camping spot.

Halfway along the dunes, I noticed a building beside an ancient watch tower that stood quite alone among the dunes, and remembering that I had forgotten to fill my water bottles, I thought I would see if I could get some there. A good few people were milling about outside, and one of them went off with my container. Before he came back with it, however, I had a plate of fresh salmon in one hand and a glass of wine in the other, and was in the middle of a party to celebrate the opening of the salmon-fishing season.

It was an appropriate place for such a party, as it had once been a salmon-fishing station operating under Scottish rules – which means that fixed posts and nets are used, which is less sporting but more effective than the haaf-net fishing I had seen on the other side of

England, in the Solway Firth. The station, a long narrow building, had comprised a large store for nets and tackle, and a bothy for the fishermen, and was now in the process of being turned into a holiday home by a couple of Edinburgh publishers. Most of the guests were writers and journalists, so conversation flowed. And what with the wine, the music from an accordion, drums and pipes, and the quantities of delicious food, the time flowed too, and my desperate tiredness was entirely forgotten.

The refurbishing of the building had only just reached the stage of rendering the place waterproof, and there was no electricity, but we danced eightsome reels and strip the willow – a dance for each side of the Border – until it was too dark to see, and then continued by candlelight. When everyone was finally thinking of going home, or putting up tents – for I was not the only camper – the rain which had been threatening for hours began to fall with a vengeance, and the great outdoors suddenly seemed very uninviting.

Fortunately there was a large loft with a few mattresses spread out on the floor, so guests who were benighted by wine or weather were able to sleep there safe and dry. Goodness knows what time it was when I scrambled up the ladder into this roof space – all over-nighters had lent a hand with the mountains of washing-up. When I next surfaced in the dark windowless space, it was 8.30, at least three hours later than my normal waking time, and I had to fly to make it over the causeway in the teeth of the returning tide. My feet dipped even deeper in the sea on this crossing, but it had been such a very good party that I could not object to wet shoes.

Making time in order to see something of Alnwick on the way south, I pressed on strongly down the superb but lethal A1. Of all blessings, I had a north-easterly to speed my passage and my tyres sang on the smooth tarmac. Arrow-straight, as the Romans built it, and dangerously narrow, cars and heavy lorries hurtle along it with all the speed they can muster. Not for the first time, I thought how different a bicyclist's perceptions are on such a route, compared with my usual little lanes. Here all my attention was on survival. Not for a moment could I afford to take my eyes off the mirror, gauging the speed and position of traffic looming up behind: 'Will he slow down? Will he give me enough room? More importantly, how many cars are there behind this first one?' So often they come in convoys, nose to bumper, and if the first in line doesn't indicate that he is overtaking, the ones behind have no idea that I am there, and each one cuts me ever closer in passing. The only way to counter this is to have the courage to move out, away from the kerb, as soon as I see a car in the mirror; this will normally force the driver to signal his intentions, and also give me room to manoeuvre. If I feel the driver will still overtake me too closely, or at too great a speed, a little warning wobble is no mean inhibitor. But such ploys become very wearing, and so, very soon, I gave up the idea of speed, and took to the lanes, where peace and quiet immediately descended like a blessing, and I bumbled on to Alnwick, able once more to take in the pretty surroundings.

I had ridden barely thirty miles to this ancient Percy stronghold, but I got no further that day because as soon as I caught sight of the great column that stood some distance before the town, I knew at once that the place would prove too fascinating to be hurried through. The column seemed even taller than Nelson's, and was topped by the distinctive, arrogant Percy lion, with stiffly extended horizontal tail. Later, when I had the good fortune to get into conversation with Adrian, a man who made his living driving lorries, but whose passion was local history, I learnt that the impressive monument was known locally as the 'farmers' folly'. It had been erected by the Duke's tenantry, in grateful thanks for reduced rents. But their gesture backfired when the Duke remarked that if his tenants could afford such a column they didn't need rent reductions, and promptly put them up again. 'Mind you,' said Adrian, 'I doubt the last part is really true, but it makes a good story.'

I could have listened to Adrian for hours, if only for his strange Northumbrian accent, which had vowel sounds like no others I had heard, and very soft r's. He said Germans often commented on this too, and claimed that an Alnwick accent resembled their own. More importantly though, Adrian had the history of Alnwick and the Percys at his fingertips, and could give me the sort of thumbnail sketches, that made all the difference to a visit to such an historic town.

The house of Percy ruled the north for nearly three hundred years; years of incessant bloody border skirmishing, particularly with their arch-rivals, the Douglases. They were the trusty force holding back the tide of the Scots, until the seventh Earl foolishly became embroiled in one of the plots concerning the rescue of Mary, Queen of Scots, and was beheaded in 1572. For two hundred years after that, the Percys disappeared from the scene, and the eleventh earl died abroad in 1670 without male issue. Thanks to some judicious marriages, however, a comeback was made through the female line. The heiress to the family estates married a Yorkshire baronet in 1750. He promptly changed his name to Percy, assumed the earldom, and was created Duke of Northumberland a few years later. The family has flourished ever since.

Perhaps their two hundred years in the wilderness had made the family appreciate their seigniorial role more than most, for there was a definite medieval atmosphere in Alnwick that went beyond the ancient buildings, and even beyond the 'medieval' pageant that was in progress. Everyone I met spoke well of the present Duke, not in any deferential sense – Northumbrians were quite the most independent-minded people I had come across – but as though they were all part of the same family. There seemed to be an old-world sense of mutual dependence in the town, a *noblesse oblige* that I met nowhere else on my travels.

The medieval festival was a part of this co-operation and involvement, a week-long celebration which had ancient roots going back to the days of the great fairs. Its main function now was as a tourist attraction, but the pleasure and enthusiasm that all the townspeople seemed to bring to it saved it from any hint of cynicism. Many of the shopkeepers and stall-holders were in costume, but apart from the tourist office officials, who tried to maintain the medieval theme, the outfits were wonderfully eclectic. Nearly all periods earlier than the twentieth century were represented, and often costumes were a mixture of several different historical times, which I thought fitted in rather well with the varying styles and periods of architecture in the town. As it was such a raw day, those clad in sixteenth-century doublet and hose and ermine-lined cloaks were a lot more comfortable than girls in skimpy eighteenth-century milkmaid's outfits. All this colour and diversity flooding the grey stone streets, which had names like Bondgate Within, Bondgate Without, Narrow Gate and Pottergate, certainly added a bit of period flavour for visitors.

On a stage rigged up in the ancient market place, kilted pupils from a local dance school were entertaining the small crowd with a

selection of sword dances and Highland flings, while those waiting
their turn, bare knees blue with cold, held down the bunting to stop
it flogging about in the wind. No one, it seemed, was prepared to be
put off, and the level of determined cheerfulness in those bleak
conditions was impressive.

A different, though equally pleasant atmosphere prevailed in the
castle, which was situated right in the town and seemed very much a
part of it. Old retainers and estate workers showed visitors around in
a friendly courteous way, with no hint of talking down, but with a
quiet modest pride, as though it was their own history that was on
display, as indeed it was. When the Percys repossessed it, this castle,
the greatest of all border fortresses, was transformed into a Palladian
palace, the 'Windsor of the north'. So extensive is it and so full of
treasures and fine paintings that it could redeem several wet days for
any visitor. In addition, there is a wealth of evocative little
mementoes – the true family 'relics', souvenirs of great occasions in
the Percy fortunes – such as Edward IV's coronation gloves; the
sheet on which Cromwell died; a lock of Charles I's hair, together
with his nightcap; Elizabeth I's gloves, a letter she had written to
Lord Howard, even the knife, fork and spoon she had used on some
occasion connected with the Percy family; and, as a reminder
perhaps of their fall from grace, a net made from Mary, Queen of
Scot's hair. There was something particularly moving about all these
royal memorabilia, so carefully preserved through those two
hundred years of exile. They were certainly more entertaining than
all the yards and yards of painted earls around the walls of the
dining-room.

Outside, the palatial castle still attempts to look like a fortress,
though not altogether successfully. Lifelike stone statues of medieval
warriors, weapons in hand, command the battlemented roof, as
though raiding Scots had just been sighted. It makes for a most
uncanny effect; though by moonlight, as I later saw it, it was suitably
romantic.

I enjoyed a particularly good view of the castle from the grounds
of a primary school where I camped for the night. I was taken there
by an old lady out with her dog, who told me she walked miles and
miles every day for fear her legs would stiffen up on her. I had
doubts about her claim that the school would be pleased to have me,
but with true Northumbrian independence of spirit, the caretaker

declared that he could see no reason why not. I looked 'perfectly decent', he said and I would not be in anyone's way. There was plenty of grass to pitch the tent, and I could use the teachers' toilet facilities. It made an excellent site, especially with all those ghostly Percy warriors keeping watch over it.

The wind was still blustering out of the north in the morning, so although the day was grey and the light flat, there was charm just in the effortless progress along gently undulating lanes that ran through newly-shorn fields. I was returning parallel to the route I had taken going up through Northumbria, and was only a few miles from it as a crow flies, but the difference in terrain and conditions made it seem like another country. In the distance the sea was steely under a rosy grey sky. There was no depth at all to the scene. Everything looked two-dimensional, like a theatre backdrop, so that small incidents and individual features stood out with a sudden heightened sense of drama – like the hawk hanging on the wind, the River Coquet falling over rocky shelves, and the gaunt remains of Brainshaugh Priory beside a weir.

'English weather might be often unpleasant,' my mother-in-law once observed 'but it is never boring.' This journey had proved the truth of that. Hardly one day had been like the one before, and of the endless variety of conditions I had experienced, it was only torrential rain or strong headwinds that I hadn't enjoyed. Weather had helped to ring the changes and provide variety, so that there was always something novel to look at, particularly in the skyscapes. The problem, if there was one, was of having to choose where to look, when there was such a choice.

No sooner had I thought this, than a movement in the hedgerow caught my eye, and I drew to a halt as a family of hedgehogs emerged, moving quite fast but with that lovely distinctive waddle from side to side, like sailors ashore. There were four of them – fat round prickly bundles, one large and three smaller, moving in line ahead along the edge of the road, until, just as suddenly as they had appeared, they disappeared back beneath the hedge again.

I planned my route to pass through Morpeth so as to ensure somewhere for lunch. It seemed a dull town after Alnwick, but to fill in time until the pubs opened, I went into the tourist office, which was housed in the one really attractive building – a heavily restored thirteenth-century chantry by the bridge. Inside I found an unexpected and splendid new bagpipe museum. It was made particularly interesting because of a clever audio system which enabled the visitor to hear as well as see the exhibits. Earphones were supplied, and as I wandered between the glass cases, an infra-red beam was broken, which automatically activated a tape recording of whichever set of pipes I was looking at. I could go from one to another as I chose, and the sound changed instantly. I had never realised that there were so many different kinds of bagpipes – Irish union pipes, Scottish half-longs, Northumbrian small pipes, to name but a few. Nor had I any idea that such different sounds could be produced from them. With the interesting collection of prints, and all the background information on reed-making and materials, famous pipers, schools of piping, and the history of their development, I thought it one of the best mounted exhibitions I had seen. It was most appropriate for Northumberland too, where the Duke still employs his personal piper – to perform on the Northumberland small pipes, naturally.

Had I not been running out of time, I would probably have taken the trouble to give Newcastle a miss. I did make a half-hearted attempt to plan a route around it, but what with the paucity of bridges over the Tyne and the difficulty of map-reading in a high wind, as well as a slight hankering to see this famous town, I decided to head straight through the middle of it and spend the night at the youth hostel there.

This was a mistake on all fronts. Newcastle terrified me. Even these few weeks away from a large city had unfitted me for the rough and tumble of rush-hour traffic. In London, I survive as a cyclist because I know exactly where I am going, and can concentrate all my attention on coping with the traffic. Here I was like a fish out of water, and no one seemed able to direct me to the area I was heading for. The city is bisected by a motorway and I was on the wrong side of it. People have told me since that there is another Newcastle if you know where to look for it; there are even cycle paths in places, they tell me, and a few pleasant parks. I saw none of that. For me, Newcastle was a town entirely subjugated by motor vehicles. The whole place, as I saw it, was carved up into small islands of shops or houses without gardens, cut off from each other by the roaring tide of one-way, three-lane highways.

After a quite horrendous hour on roads no cyclist should have to negotiate, I arrived at the youth hostel only to be told by a rather hostile young Indian woman with a Geordie accent that the place was full. I would have had no choice but to enter the maelstrom again, going round and round the one-way system like some desperate Flying Dutchman, had not some young men then appeared, to whom the warden offered the use of the lounge floor. I asked why I too could not sleep on the floor, and, after some persuasion, I was grudgingly permitted the use of the dining-room. Later I discovered a cupboard on a landing, filled with camp beds for use in such contingencies, and although the discovery elicited a sour 'You shouldn't go looking in cupboards', it promised a reasonable night's sleep.

I tried to explore Newcastle on foot when the worst of the evening rush hour was over, but met with no greater success. I walked for miles and all I could find were some newish municipal buildings and shopping precincts indistinguishable from those in a hundred other towns. In the end, when I had decided that Newcastle had defeated me, and I was hopelessly lost, a woman kindly brought me back to the youth hostel in her car. I wasn't all that far away from the hostel, and she lived just around the corner from it. 'Aye,' she said with that flat 'a' of the Geordie, 'Newcastle's all changed now, even the taxis get lost.'

CHAPTER TWENTY

A Vision on a Hill Top

I delayed my start the next day, until the worst of the morning rush hour was over, but even so, Newcastle still remained impregnable. I managed to find a tourist office in one of the anonymous shopping precincts, but they knew nothing of safe routes or of cycleways through their city. A pity this, for had I been able to find a way through which allowed for a more relaxed frame of mind, I might well have gained a totally different impression of this famous northern city. Negotiating one mammoth ascending concrete spiral after another, with roaring ramping monsters breathing down one's neck was no way for a bicyclist to enjoy any place. Large blue motorway signs also caused me considerable anxiety, for they seemed to signify that I was being drawn irrevocably onto the sacred ground forbidden to mopeds, invalid carriages and other humble road-users such as Evans.

It was with feelings of profound thankfulness, therefore, that I found myself at one point on a bridge crossing the Tyne, which meant that I was heading south, out of the place. The bridge was bobbing up and down like a ship at sea, shuddering and bouncing under the weight of the heavy traffic rushing along beside me. A welcome pavement gave me the opportunity to lift Evans out of the maelstrom and take stock of the situation. It was as claustrophobic a cityscape as I had seen anywhere. The sullen black Tyne, unrecognisable now as the merry dancing river I had known earlier in the journey, was spanned by several bridges, built so close together that the shadow of each seemed to blot out its neighbour. Densely-packed buildings pressed in on every side, crowding the waterfront. Not a blade of grass was to be seen.

About seven miles downstream, before those dark waters spill out into the North Sea, is what remains of the last of the great Anglo-Saxon monasteries to be put to the torch by the Vikings. I had wanted to go to these ruins at Jarrow, to see where the Venerable Bede had written his famous book. Bede, the acknowledged father

of English history, had been a young novice of fourteen when St
Cuthbert died, and he would certainly have met and talked to people
who had known him, and St Aidan and St Oswald. Much of his
Ecclesiastical History of the English Nation was therefore a living
account of the events and people of his day, and it is because of it that
we know so much about the period, particularly about Northumbria. I had come to feel a great deal of affection and regard for the
Venerable Bede over the years, but now that I had seen something of
what I would have to ride through to get to Jarrow, I felt less than
enthusiastic about going to pay my respects to his shades. Clearly I
was not the stuff of which true pilgrims are made. Newcastle, I
decided, was no place for a bicyclist, and I was prepared to settle for
simply getting out of it in one piece, by as direct a route as possible.

Having reached this decision, it was still some considerable time
before I was able to breathe easily once more. Road junctions,
flyovers, motorway exits and entrances, and giant roundabouts
continued to loom up all around – all of them threatening to prove
my undoing. By a judicious if illegal use of pavements and slip roads,
and thanks to the basic kindness of Newcastle drivers, I was
eventually able to circumvent all these manifestations of Scylla and
Charybdis. Compass in hand, I found myself at last on a rough
narrow way, named the Old Durham Road, ascending steeply away
from the crowded valley of the Tyne.

The suburbs of Newcastle pursued me for the next ten miles along
the straight Roman road. It rained a little too, which did not help the
appearance of the nondescript blackened buildings that lined the
way. And yet, whenever a small gap appeared, I caught glimpses of
attractive open countryside stretching away to the west. Had I not
been hurrying in a straight line towards Durham, I could doubtless
have found a dozen pleasant alternative routes.

Being still in something of a state of shock from my encounters
with Newcastle's traffic, my brain was not working as efficiently as it
should, and I might well have missed the tremendous significance of
Chester-le-Street, which appeared at first glance a nondescript little
place. But making a detour down a side road to avoid the crowded
main thoroughfare, I came upon a medieval church marooned
behind the car park of a supermarket – an ancient foundation that
brought me back again on the trail of St Cuthbert's folk.

St Mary and St Cuthbert was a fine church in its own right, with a famous aisle filled with the Lumley 'warriors' laid head to foot, pretending to be tombs. Three of them are genuine medieval effigies pilfered from the cathedral ground in Durham; the rest are Elizabethan copies produced to give the Lumley family instant ancestors. An effigy of John, Lord Lumley, who was responsible for these carvings, was also there. It was all a lovely example of Elizabethan snobbery.

Tacked onto the side of the church was the cell of an anchorite, complete with a long squint made through the immensely thick wall of the church to give the occupant a glimpse of the high altar. From the year 1300, right up to the Dissolution, a series of religious recluses, both men and women, had voluntarily been walled up there, incarcerated for life, alone in that tiny space. Whereas I could understand something of the attraction of spending solitary months on the Farne Islands, approaching some sense of unity with God through His creation, the thought of this living entombment made my blood run cold.

And yet, the writings of one such anchorite, Dame Julian of Norwich, shows a freedom of spirit and experience that transcends all physical limitations, and makes her a greater traveller than many who ranged extensively through the world.

After the Reformation, the anchorite's cell had been enlarged into a three-storey almshouse, and this now makes a charming little museum, called the Anker's House, that tells the story of the greatness of Chester-le-Street's past. I had to go across the road to a council office to fetch the key, and so had the place to myself. The best had been made of the limited space, with a simple audio-visual display designed to make the long history more digestible, a few artifacts that spanned the centuries, and some wonderfully carved Anglo-Saxon stones and crosses. The system wasn't working very audibly, but it provided enough clues to jog my memory, and enable me to piece together the rest from what I already knew.

Here, to what had once been a Roman cavalry fort, St Cuthbert's folk had come with their treasures on an ox cart, and here they had settled for a hundred years, founding a church to house the saint's body. The shrine soon became the most famed centre of pilgrimage in Britain, and the devout, and those seeking healing, flocked here from all over Europe. Some of the books, chalices and vestments brought here as gifts by Saxon kings have survived the intervening thousand years, and are now part of the treasure of Durham.

Scholarship flourished too, and in the scriptorium a monk named Aeldred made a translation of the Lindisfarne Gospels into the Anglo-Saxon vernacular. This famous gloss, written in a crabbed hand above the original Latin text, is the first known translation of the Gospels into any kind of English.

Towards the end of the tenth century, a further spate of devastating Viking raids forced the community of St Cuthbert to gather together their treasures once more, and to flee. They went first to Ripon, before eventually working their way northwards again, to settle at last at Durham. From Chester-le-Street I could reach the end of their years of wandering in just half an hour.

Once or twice before, I had seen Durham Cathedral from the railway – coming down from Edinburgh by train is very like having a Cook's tour of England's east coast cathedrals; all of them magnificent, and each so different from the others. Riding on its high narrow plateau, like a great ship at anchor, Durham had looked more wonderful to me than any of them, and each time I saw it, I longed to leave my carriage to go and explore it. Having waited so long to make my visit, I was determined that I would not now arrive breathless before its walls, tossed up like a piece of human flotsam from the murderous tide of some ghastly road. I wanted to approach slowly, taking it in bit by bit, without having to give my attention to preserving life and limb. With this in mind I turned off the Roman road, which had split into two while I had been visiting Chester-le-Street – one half was now the A1M and the other the very busy A167T.

The road I took had no number, but led delightfully through the pleasant Lumley lands, and past their impressive castellated stately pile. After a while, it dropped down to a bend of the sinuous River Wear and the ruins of Finchale Priory, where once the monks of Durham had recuperated from the rigours of their duties. Idyllic as it was, this green wedge of land was also a trap. I was now boxed in by three major roads, a railway, and the river, with no obvious way out that did not involve a main road. My attempt to wriggle through ended in my becoming hopelessly entangled in a modern housing estate, which was not marked on the map, and I had to seek help.

By following the detailed instructions of a fish and chip van driver, who cycled in his spare time, I found a splendid route for the final approach – through a playing field, over a footbridge across the railway, and into a bumpy unmade country lane that ran between fields and allotments – the very allotments, I believe, that the present Bishop of Durham is proposing to sell, amid furious protests, as a site for blocks of high-rise flats. Beyond the cabbages and the ramshackle little tool sheds, with as yet no spurious modern building to mar its glory, the great cathedral rides on its hill, many-towered and majestic. The weight and mass of its golden-brown stones are tempered by the elevation, so that it has a surprisingly ethereal quality – a temporal reflection of the Holy City – in a way that not even the slender soaring spire of Salisbury quite achieves.

A plunge into a gloomy underpass took me beneath the main road, and when I emerged at the other side, I was on a sunny traffic-free bridge, with the River Wear below flowing through a deep pleasant gorge filled with leafy trees. Ahead, a cobbled street wound upwards through the medieval city towards the Cathedral. There seemed no connection at all between this lovely place and the world I had awoken to that morning. It was as though I had passed through an invisible barrier and arrived in another land – like Alice stepping through the looking-glass. This was a feeling I never quite lost while I was in Durham. Rather than proving a disappointment at closer acquaintance, as do many tourist meccas, Durham confirmed its early promise with every step I took, so that I hardly knew where to begin first.

A huge convolution of the River Wear wraps itself around a high and narrow spur of land, making it almost an island. To this natural fortress in the year 995 AD came the St Cuthbert's folk, men, women and children – for the community embraced marriage, as once did many religious traditions. Their saint had at last come to his final resting-place, and they and their order were, sadly, soon to be eclipsed. Descendants of the Vikings who had first caused them to flee were now settlers in their turn. Some of them, the Normans, who had seized a strip of coastal France, would soon be on their way to conquer England under their Duke, William. In 1071, five years after the decisive battle at Hastings, the community of St Cuthbert was expelled, and French Benedictines were installed in their place. The reign of the powerful prince bishops of Durham had begun.

In recent excavations beneath the chapter house, the remains of wattle huts and Saxon graves, including those of women and children, have emerged. These might well have belonged to the faithful little community who had guarded the body of St Cuthbert through all the years of his wanderings. There is also an ancient street named Dun Cow Lane, leading up to Palace Green from the North Bailey, and a small stone plaque high up on the wall of the cathedral itself shows an old Saxon lady, together with the legendary cow. But the true memorial of the St Cuthbert's folk are the treasures they preserved – the body of the saint himself, enshrined now in a great peaceful space behind the high altar, with the remains of the original oak coffin in the treasury; and the glorious Lindisfarne Gospels in the British Museum. From Lindisfarne to Durham had been one of the great journeys of the world; its ending marked a new period of English history.

In the closing years of the eleventh century, within defensive Norman walls, the present cathedral began to grow. In close proximity a strong keep, built by the Earl of Northumberland, was expanded into a castle which would become the bishop's palace. From the beginning of Norman rule, Durham was the seat of immense and combined military, ecclesiastical, and civil power. For the next few hundred years, the bishops of Durham would reign as mighty princes, a law unto themselves in the buffer state between Scotland and England. Although the civil powers of the bishops were whittled away after the Reformation, they remained uniquely 'prince bishops' until the death of Bishop William van Mildert in 1836.

In 1832, this same bishop and his chapter handed over both the castle and many of the ecclesiastical buildings for the founding of Durham University, the first in a spate of nineteenth-century academic centres, and unique in having so instantly medieval an aura. As it was vacation time when I arrived, all the colleges were being used as conference centres, or as bed and breakfast accommodation for tourists – an arrangement which seemed happily to echo the hostels in which medieval pilgrims had lodged. With the general absence of cars, and the wide variety of languages and accents that echoed around the ancient stones, Durham still seemed like a great shrine to which pilgrims from all of Christendom had come to marvel, and to pay homage.

I stayed in the college of St Hild and St Bede, which was the largest of them, and a little distance outside the walled city. Purpose built in the Victorian Gothic style, it had rather vocal plumbing and spartan bathrooms. It also possessed lovely green meadows running down to the river, and romantic views of the Cathedral and the castle. The half-mile hike to the dining-room through the grounds was a bracing start to the day, and one which gave the visiting American basketball teams ample opportunity to get in some of the day's training, and to arrive at the head of the long queue.

Local ladies cooked and cleaned, and ruled the visitors, as doubtless they ruled the students in term time, with firmness, humour and northern warmth. It was very good value for money and seemed like luxury after my tent; it also made me feel young and lighthearted to be in student quarters again, subject to the heavy banter of the porter every time I needed to ask for the key to unlock the bicycle shed. I stayed on there for two nights, because one brief tour of the Cathedral made me realise there could be no question of spending only an hour or two there. Yet again on this journey, I had fallen in love with a place, and time had lost all importance.

The guides make much of the fact that when Durham was a monastic cathedral, women were not allowed beyond a certain black marble line let into the floor, level with the first pier of the nave, a form of discrimination that to my mind almost justifies the Dissolution. It had also given rise to the erroneous notion that St Cuthbert was a misogynist. Nothing could have been further from the truth, or from the spirit of the place. All cathedrals are by their nature holy places that should be permeated with an aura of the numinous. This, alas, does not seem always to be the case. Perhaps it is the pressing need for money to maintain crumbling fabrics that has resulted in many of them becoming more like museums or theme parks. Durham had not so far shared this fate. It possessed an all-embracing sense of harmony that permeated every corner of it and seemed to reach out to everything and everyone. That this feeling somehow emanated from the influence of St Cuthbert himself I never had any doubt; it seemed an entirely rational view within the context of the place, and one shared by everyone else who experienced it.

The building itself I found eminently satisfying. Both inside and out, it was a great and exciting adventure in the art of organising space and mass. When it was conceived in the mind of Bishop William of Calais, few buildings anywhere in the world were roofed entirely in stone-ribbed vaulting. It worked magnificently, and was substantially completed within fifty years of its commencement. The contrast between the massive, deeply-incised Norman pillars, and the high delicate vaulting is awe-inspiring.

The Galilee Chapel was added to the west end a little later, by Bishop Hugh of Le Puiset. He or his architect must have been on the Crusades, for the aisles of slender marble columns that proliferate almost into a small forest are remarkably and beautifully reminiscent of Middle Eastern mosques. I had little enough time to enjoy this unexpected treasure, and was in fact lucky to see it at all since it was closed for extensive repair work. My guide, moved perhaps by my enthusiasm for his cathedral, let me take a quick look. This was particularly kind because also unknown to me, the tomb of the Venerable Bede was in the Galilee, with its inscription of 'Hic sunt in fossa Baedae ossa', and so I was able to pay my respects to the father of English history after all. Above the tomb in gold letters was written one of Bede's own sentences: 'Christ is the morning star who when this world is past brings to his saints the promise of the light of life and opens everlasting day.'

Cathedral and castle face each other across Palace Green, alike and so very unlike; linked by the similarity of their dog-toothed Norman entrances; and separated by the struggle between worldly ambition and the Christian virtues of selflessness and humility. They are the two faces of the growth of the English church; one mirroring the political struggles of each age, the other rising above all changes – even the present bishop's controversial thoughts about some of the central tenets of the Christian faith. This was an issue of which no one could be unaware in Durham, but I found it referred to with more humour there than is usually the case. Doubtless a place that has kept the simple steadfast faith of St Cuthbert alive through all the centuries of Norman pride and secular struggles can also cope with the occasional original bishop, without getting too hot under the collar about it.

Like the Cathedral, the castle would merit more than a visit of a few hours to appreciate all its treasures. But of everything I saw there – medieval great hall, Tudor buttery, galleries, staircases and kitchens – paled into insignificance when compared with the last item of the tour. This was a small but marvellous little Norman chapel in the undercroft, that had only recently been restored after centuries of neglect. The oldest part of the castle, and the most ancient building in the city of Durham, it had achieved, within its confined space, a most powerful sense of purpose, due largely to the fine plain stonework of the vaulting, and the six massive columns that supported it, so that it could almost have been a forerunner, a scale model of the later cathedral. Wonderfully exuberant little carvings graced the square capitals, each of which ended in a vigorous and totally idiosyncratic Ionic scroll. I particularly liked those scrolls, as much for the sudden evocation of the brilliant and creative pagan world they represented, as for the freedom of their execution. I couldn't imagine any bigoted narrow-minded fundamentalism flourishing in so eclectic an atmosphere. And judging by present-day Durham, it never has done so.

CHAPTER TWENTY-ONE

Fish and Chips and Synods

Departing from Durham, I felt that, like Christian, I was paying the price of pilgrimage – only in my case I was doing it in reverse. Difficult though the approach to my Celestial City had been, it was in leaving it that I experienced the full horror of the industrial north-east.

To the south of Durham lie the lovely Cleveland Hills and the North Yorkshire moors. In between is the broad river valley of the Tees, and one glance at the map shows this to be a solidly built-up area of the sort that no bicyclist would choose to ride through. However, as I now had only three more days before I needed to be back in London, there was no time to make a circuitous detour around it. In order to get to the coast at the start of the Cleveland Way – an area I had long wanted to visit - I had to cross that valley. So while a large party of Dutch cyclists, who had also been staying at Hild and Bede, set off to explore the Durham dales on a delightful redundant railway cycle path, the epitome of carefree journeying, I steeled myself to pass through the thick of what was left of industrial Teeside. All travellers are optimists, but even so, had there been a non-redundant train I would have taken it. In the event I found it to be far worse than I had feared.

Very soon the fields of grain and cabbages that lined the road began to take on a strange appearance, as though they were not quite real. The edges of everything were blunted, as if they were made from some worn low-grade plastic, or were masked by a clogging film of dust. Although the day was bright, a pall now seemed to be spread evenly over the sky, with a darker smudge ahead, and there was a metallic, brassy taste in the air. The smudge grew wider and denser, and as the road began to dip down to the valley I descended into ever darker layers, like an aeroplane coming down through thick cloud.

The scene I rode into would have made the perfect setting for Tolkien's ruined Land of Mordor. In fact it was difficult to believe he had not based his poisoned wasteland on this very place. Monstrous cooling towers, huge chimneys and pipes belched forth black rivers of smoke. Tangled skeins of metal tubing reared grossly upwards and outwards, erupting over acres of ground like an obscene parody of rampant tropical vines. Everything was blackened by a thick oily deposit. The ICI plastics plant was the most evident and individual feature in this metalscape, advertising itself in huge blue letters on a giant chimney as though it was proud of the part it had played in annihilating nature in this valley.

I was not unaware of the tragedy of unemployment that had devastated the lives of the people in the north east. I knew that this tortured landscape had produced a livelihood for many who now had to exist on handouts. The pall of smoke and the cloud of contaminants that I found so distressing had once been even thicker; and it was the thinning of the murk as plants closed down that had brought grief to those dependent upon the industry. Nevertheless, jobs provided at such a cost to the environment and to the workers themselves seemed a travesty of welfare; the thought of children growing up in such an atmosphere was dreadful.

Whatever economic forces had produced Teeside, riding through it now was to come face to face with the twentieth-century moral dilemma of weighing the benefits of producing cheap commodities with the wider quality of life, and of the life of generations to come. We have the technology to produce everything that is made here without the dreadful accompaniment of gross toxic emissions. It costs more, that is all.

Teeside was a much more obvious nightmare than Sellafield, though the same considerations had brought both places into existence, and have kept them going. Never had I witnessed a more graphic illustration of 'You get what you pay for' – though it would be nearer the truth to express it as 'You pay for what you get.'

After what seemed like an age in some Stygian purgatory, I crossed the lifeless, poisoned River Tees. By this time my chest was on fire with all the noxious fumes I was breathing, and the taste in my mouth was worse than ever. Another age passed before humped shapes began to loom up out of the smoky pall to the south. As I drew nearer, a certain shagginess about their outlines proclaimed them to be the outrunners of the North Yorkshire moors, and my heart lifted at the thought that nature had not been totally expunged after all.

Some miles later I was sitting in a pub in the Victorian seaside resort of Saltburn by Sea, tucking into chicken kiev and chips, while the rain lashed down outside. The bar was hung about with cheap reproductions of English painters – four Turners, a Constable or two and a few Stubbs, as though the landlord too needed a permanent reminder that nature was unquenchable.

Built on a dominating little eminence on the front at Saltburn was the wonderful Zetland Hotel, said to have been the most magnificent railway hotel in the world. It was built in 1863, at a cost of £40,000, a fortune then, and a scheme that was not happily subscribed to by all the board of the L.N.E.R., many of whom considered it a 'grandiose extravagance'. It had been designed to cater for everyone, from royalty down to the humblest commercial traveller, and had, in addition to a special entrance direct from the station, fifty bedrooms and the crowning glory of a telescope room in a circular tower. The 180-foot frontage of bow-windowed, no-expense-spared, northern opulence has worn well, but now, solid as ever, it awaits demolition. The town is altogether too near the horrors of Teeside to flourish, and the pier, over a quarter of a mile long, where promenade concerts once raised the tone, has already vanished from the front. It was a resort that had been founded upon the coming of the railway; in the age of the motor car, there are better places to go.

Remarkably, the weather pulled itself together as soon as I pedalled out of Saltburn, the hot sunshine helping to make the switchback coast road feel immensely tiring. When the sea came into view from the cliff tops, it was as blue as Alpine gentians under skies sweetly and innocently swept of everything but a dusting of the lightest white gossamer. It was as though the poisoned ground and choking clouds of noxious fumes had never existed. Only my bloodstream carried the effects of the morning's ride through Teeside, and this showed in the sluggishness I was feeling. As soon as a likely place presented itself I pulled off the road to look for an early pitch.

I enquired at a charming Georgian farmhouse with pedimented stables and stone barns built around four sides of a courtyard in a classical style that would have fitted perfectly into Bath or Cheltenham. An elderly couple, yet more Armstrongs, received me warmly, and soon I was installed in a sheltered secluded corner of their garden, with an outside loo nearby, and a shed for Evans that also had hot and cold running water; altogether a most superior pitch.

I learnt something of the history of the place when Mrs Armstrong asked me in for tea, to keep her company while Mr Armstrong was at a meeting. She and her husband had lived in the area all their lives and had bought Boulby Grange fifty years before when property was cheap. They are retired now, and their son runs the farm and lives in a modern house along the way. The lovely grange with its classical pediments and long history has recently had a preservation order put on it, a fact which worries the Armstrongs desperately, for there is no grant to cover the heavy maintenance requirements of the order. They think they will have to convert the barns into dwellings, and the house into flats in order to make ends meet.

I was glad of the opportunity to see over the place before this happened, and to enjoy the perfect proportions of the large simple rooms, and the solid staircase lit by a splendid long fan-topped Georgian window. Smuggling had been a feature of the economy of this coast too in the seventeenth and eighteenth centuries, and Boulby Grange, set on the top of cliffs honeycombed by caves and mine shafts, had its share in the trade. A tunnel had led up from a cave into the cellar, and from there a secret staircase climbed to the loft where the booty was hidden.

Even more interesting were Mrs Armstrong's memories of life on this coast in her youth. She had lived through the last of the ironstone mining boom and could remember the infamous Tin City, a line of about forty cottages that had been built nearby to house itinerant miners. Ironstone has a high enough mineral content to be used as an ore, and a thick seam of it extended along the coast south of Boulby, practically as far as Saltburn. Teeside and Tyneside were largely created by the nineteenth century's sudden need for iron, and their blast furnaces were at first fed by these coastal mines, so convenient for transportation by sea. The industry had brought an influx of workers from all over Britain, including skilled men from Wales and Cornwall – job mobility is no new concept. But, as is often the case, the newcomers found conditions and pay less favourable than for indigenous folk. By 1914 the rich seam was played out and inland mines, served by railways, took over. The miners moved away, and Tin City lingered on until it fell down from neglect.

Mrs Armstrong could remember details of domestic life that are scarcely credible now, only a few decades on – like outside privies being emptied by horse and cart, and the contents spread on the fields for a fertiliser – something I have only seen done in India and Africa. She also remembered how alien the children of Tin City had seemed, and how they had been treated as though there was a caste system operating in England at that time, with the itinerant workers and their families the untouchables.

The area was rich in other minerals too. Jet – since ancient times regarded as the traveller's stone, amulets of which were traditionally given to those about to go on a journey – had been laid down here 150 million years ago, when monkey-puzzle trees, in which the area abounded, died, floated out to sea, and became fossilised into the strata that make today's cliffs. Beads of jet had been worked here since long before Roman times; they had been traded along the Ridgeway Path in Berkshire from which my journey had started, and had been found in the Bronze Age barrows I had visited there. The industry enjoyed a renewed surge of life when Prince Albert died and Queen Victoria favoured jet as jewellery for mourning.

Alum too, invaluable in the fixing of dyes, had been mined here in the early seventeenth century, enabling the Vatican's control of the trade to be broken – not that this helped the miners, since alum immediately became a crown monopoly instead. Vast quantities of burnt seaweed and urine were needed in the processing of alum. Urine was collected locally from jars left on people's doorsteps, but large quantities were also shipped in from as far away as Hull and London; while potash, made from burnt seaweed, came from even further afield, for the best of it was made on the western shores of the Outer Hebrides.

All this to-ing and fro-ing through coastal waters led to the development of a particular type of ship – the 'Whitby cat'. Later, the locally- and humbly-born Captain James Cook would come to value this craft above all others, and would insist that, in spite of all opposition, they should be the vessels for his voyages of discovery in the Pacific Ocean.

Having touched on so many aspects of the past of this now little-known coast, and having drunk such quantities of tea in the process, it was good to wander for a little way across the tops of the bare, tunnelled cliffs that had been the background to all these memories. The contrast between the busy teeming world Mrs Armstrong had painted and this lonely backwater was uncanny. The ground carried the history of a people tattooed into it, scars which could still be read, and which would become more precious the fainter they grew. Already the ground was well on the road to recovery, and had taken on a new role as part of the Heritage Coast. A single tall chimney inland of Boulby Grange still points skyward, linking it to its busy past. Here the deepest mine in Britain stretches nearly two miles under the sea, extracting potash. Mrs Armstrong had told me that it was supposed to be a marvellous place down there, an enchanted world full of beautiful crystal formations.

As I came back to my garden site in the dusk, a fat hedgehog left his place on the porch where he had been feeding on bread and milk left there for him. He bumbled speedily across the lawn, scuttling between my fragile tent and a low stone wall. For a short time he stayed there, nibbling an offering of chocolate while I cooed over him and stroked his prickles, and then suddenly he simply vanished, as Mrs Tiggy-winkle had done on her Lakeland hillside.

The wind promised earlier by the high gossamer cloud howled all night around my tent, so that sheltered though it was, the walls shivered and I snuggled down thankfully into the downy warmth of the sleeping-bag.

In the morning the sea was a jumble of sharp white waves, with scudding clouds racing overhead, and seagulls flaunting their flying skills and making a great raucous din. I felt equally madcap flying down the one-in-four cobbled way to the tiny Dickensian fishing port of Staithes, in a deep cleft at the bottom of the cliffs. At first, I experienced a pang of regret that I had not stayed there the previous night in the fine little B&B inn on the hard, with lobster dinners, and with seas practically breaking against the windows. But if I had, I would not have met Mrs Armstrong and seen Boulby Grange, so I went in for coffee instead, and made another mental note about a good place to visit some other time.

Staithes is famous because Captain Cook was apprenticed to a grocer there – a position he didn't take to, and so was removed to serve a sea-faring apprenticeship at Whitby instead. There is no reason why Staithes needs its Captain Cook connection: it has quite enough going for it in its own right, including the narrowest street in England – Dog Loup, winding steeply up the hill, is only eighteen inches wide. Staithes is all steep winding cobbled streets, small Georgian houses and a jumble of fishermen's cottages, built tightly one above the other up the cliffs, and so unaffectedly picturesque that the visitor is amazed not to find it swarming with tourists, like similar little fishing ports on the Cornish coast. A smell of coal fires, and a lack of pretension, enhance the Victorian flavour.

Huddling from the cold wind in the newsagent's, I learnt that there had once been a thousand miners to swell the ranks of Staithes' native fishermen, and seven churches and seven pubs had catered for their needs – 'Seven for t'devil, seven for t'other'. Miners were non-conformist, Methodist mostly, but always hiving off into new sects at the drop of a hat, said the enthusiastic newsagent, an incomer totally in love with Staithes. He said he never tired of walking across the cliffs and being almost on top of the place, before seeing the amazing jumble of it down below, clustered on either side of the little creek, with its diminishing fleet of small brightly painted fishing boats sitting on the mud. I also thought it uniquely strange and satisfying, so much so that I didn't even mind the terrible push back up the cliff, though I did find the double yellow line painted on either side of the twisting narrow cobbled alleys an incongruous touch.

It is only about ten miles to Whitby from Staithes, but the road takes a great sweep inland, which is fine for preserving the coastline, but it meant that if I wanted to see anything of the sea and cliffs, I had to keep detouring back to it on any sort of path or road I could find. The Cleveland Way keeps to the cliffs, but is no good to a laden cyclist, even one used to rough tracks.

The wind had continued to rise until it was almost gale force, so one leg of my zigzags would be a wild impetuous dash, while the return was a tortured gasping snail-like progress into the teeth of the storm. The effort, though, was well worthwhile. I came upon great empty sandy bays, backed by tall striated cliffs, with the sea running in like polished pewter. Long creamy breakers began far out to sea and, getting ahead of themselves, they overturned in ruin before they could thunder onto the beach; so that for a good few hundred yards out from the land all was a confused white boiling chaos. It was clear to see why Cook had put his trust in Whitby cats – ships that were designed to live in that sea were safe in any ocean – and this was only a summer blow! When I finally turned for Whitby, the wind took me in like an express train.

Wonderful Whitby – there could have been no better place to end my journey. It came as a total surprise; a town full of delightful contrasts. A rough working port, together with a modestly elegant town ascending the cliffs in hundreds of steps, it was also a seaside resort, filled with large northern families – often three or four generations of them, all patently having a good time. I had no trouble deciding where to begin; it was lunchtime and the wind had made me ravenous. I wandered along the quaysides by the moored fishing boats to choose somewhere to eat. Never had I seen so many fish restaurants, seafood stalls, and fish and chip counters so crowded together: it was as gastronomically self-conscious as a French port, and something like it in atmosphere too, if only because of the seriousness with which everyone treated the business of eating. I chose to go up-market as it was my last day of freedom, and I had my excellent fish and chips served on china instead of newspaper. Everyone seemed to have time to be kind, from the busy waitresses to the shop girls who helped me find my way around.

In Grape Lane, one of the town's narrow Georgian streets, I found the Captain Cook Memorial Museum, which gave a good impression of what Whitby had been like in the eighteenth century, when it was one of the leading seaports and ship-building centres of Britain. The modest three-storey house had belonged to the shipowner, John Walker, to whom Captain Cook was apprenticed as a youth. The seventeen apprentices had slept in the large attic of the house when not at sea, and the superb little colliers – the Whitby cats – taking coals from the Tyne to the Thames had tied up at the quayside at the back. Much of the house has been carefully furnished to recreate the atmosphere of the Quaker household, of which Cook had become a part. The straight-backed chairs and longcase clock, the plain uncluttered rooms and soft-coloured Georgian panelling without any form of decoration or pictures, had all been recreated from a detailed inventory left by John Walker. I thought that the quiet dignity Captain Cook seemed always to have been able to exercise in the difficult circumstances of his life might well owe a great deal to the sober good taste of this pleasant house.

The 199 steps up which I pushed Evans with some difficulty, led me to a church which seemed neither peaceful nor holy, but which had one of the most delightful eighteenth-century interiors I have ever seen, totally out of keeping with its stern and weathered Norman exterior. It was extraordinarily but delightfully fussy, with dainty Georgian windows contrived out of the minimal Norman embrasures, and a wealth of tinkling chandeliers. Far too many Georgian box pews jostled for space around a fine Jacobean three-decker pulpit. White wooden staircases, squashed in between the pews, ascended to the low galleries and to the Cholmley Family's Pew, which, laden with winged cherub heads, impudently assumed the place of a rood screen across the chancel arch. It was impossible not to imagine an unruly and irreverent congregation calling out pleasantries across the crowded spaces, while the hard-of-hearing wife of Minister Andrews took down the sounding-board from its place behind the pulpit, and engaged both the ear trumpets so as not to miss a breath of the exchanges. It was an interior with more than a trace of Restoration comedy.

A little higher than St Mary's, and dominating the cliff top, is the impressive ruin of Whitby Abbey, which enjoys the unique distinction of being the only abbey ever to have been shelled by the Germans. Whether this was the site of the original Anglo-Saxon monastery that had such a decisive effect upon English history is not entirely clear, but I think it must be, if for no better reason than the magnificence of the setting. From this high point above the sea the gaze strays from weathered grey stone and empty arched sockets to the white-topped breakers below, careering shorewards beyond the tranquil close-cropped turf.

One of the world's most remarkable women first made Whitby famous. St Hild was a Northumbrian, a friend of St Aidan, who had persuaded her not to join a monastery in France, but rather to stay in England and found a community at Monkwearsmouth – where, later, the Venerable Bede received his early training. In 648 she moved to Hartlepool to be abbess of a larger community, and this in turn became so renowned, that in 657 she was asked to reform Whitby. Under Hild, Whitby's reputation soared, and it became the centre of assembly in the north. So it was that the famous Synod came to be held here in 664, and the sad decline of the Celtic church spread northwards from this spot. No one can have been more saddened by the Synod's findings than Hild herself, steeped as she was in Celtic Christianity. She had clearly delighted in the scholarship and the arts of her age, and in the last years of his life she had sheltered Caedmon – the Cowherd of Whitby, and the greatest of the Anglo-Saxon poets. The romance that he wrote here also keeps green the memory of Whitby's first flowering, and was to be the inspiration for centuries of English verse and prose. Milton is believed to have based *Paradise Lost* on Caedmon's passages relating to the Fall of the Angels.

In 867 the Vikings put the Abbey to the torch, and when it was refounded in 1073, it was in post-Conquest England, in an altogether different age. And yet, now that I thought about it, in this significant place, I wondered if it was so entirely different. Riding through England today, slowly enough to take in what is there, is to discover that the past doesn't simply disappear, nor does history lie quietly, layer on layer, like rock strata. Rather it seems to have a habit of impinging upon the present when least expected. I had stumbled haphazardly on so many separate threads along the way, which had surfaced briefly before disappearing back into a vast and constantly changing tapestry. Each thread had its roots somewhere else, and each had exercised a lasting influence on what followed. Somewhere as momentous as Whitby brought many of these threads together to give a sudden illuminating glimpse, another clue to the overall picture, before the veil came down on it again, reducing it into separate pieces.

It was much the same with the geography of England. The variety had been tremendous, and had I followed another route, even just a few miles away, I would have had very different experiences. The precious green places of England still exist, between the expanding motorway complexes, sprawling conurbations, sinister nuclear dumping-grounds, and a shrinking industrial environment. At the speed of a bicycle, an overall pattern could be discerned – a pattern that was in a perpetual state of change; nature gaining a bit here, and losing a bit somewhere else. The secret, intimate world of *The Wind in the Willows* was still there for those who had the time and could take the trouble to look for it. Apart from the tremendous beauty of what remained of the English countryside, I had been particularly heartened by the number of people I met who were actively concerned over its preservation. If I was left at the end of the journey feeling in the least optimistic about the future of England, it was because of that.

By this time I had, once again, the loveliest of weather to encourage me to sit among the grey stones, ruminating over what I had seen in the past few weeks. The wind had been dropping ever since I reached Whitby, and, as had become the pattern of the late afternoons, the sun once more shone out of a sky triumphantly blue. This was my final day as a carefree tramp; tomorrow I and the trusty Evans would be in a train heading south, to days hedged about again by daily tasks, and the necessity of earning a living. I had been going to stay in Whitby in order to make an early start, but now these last few hours seemed far too precious to spend indoors, even in as fine a town as this. I unchained Evans and pedalled off inland towards the high moors, for one last night under the stars.

Equipment for the Journey

Evans is a black 21-inch, 531 double-butted, hand-built bicycle made by F. W. Evans of The Cut, Waterloo, London. It is fitted with Suntour components, has a triple chain ring and a six-speed block, with gear ratios ranging from 26 to 82.

I used Specialised touring tyres and had no punctures the entire journey.

The Karrimor panniers were carried on Blackburn racks, with the 'low loader' front model.

The tent I used was the Goretex Phreerunner made by Phoenix.

The self-inflating mattress was made by Thermarest.

The stove was the smallest model Trangia.

I used 25 Ordnance Survey maps of the 'Landranger' series.